PENGUIN BOO

FROM BOOM TO

David Smith is economics editor of the *Sunday Times*. He has also been economics correspondent of *The Times*, economics and deputy editor of *Financial Weekly*, economics and business writer for *Now!* magazine, a forecaster with the Henley Centre and an economic report writer for Lloyds Bank.

He studied economics at the universities of Cardiff, Oxford and London, having been introduced to the subject while at West Bromwich Grammar School. David Smith is author of *The Rise and Fall of Monetarism* and *North and South*, both published by Penguin.

He was born and brought up in the West Midlands but now lives in London. He is married with four children.

FROM BOOM TO BUST

TRIAL AND ERROR
IN BRITISH ECONOMIC POLICY

DAVID SMITH

PENGUIN BOOKS

PENGUIN BOOKS

Published by the Penguin Group
Penguin Books Ltd, 27 Wrights Lane, London w8 5tz, England
Penguin Books USA Inc., 375 Hudson Street, New York, New York 10014, USA
Penguin Books Australia Ltd, Ringwood, Victoria, Australia
Penguin Books Canada Ltd, 10 Alcorn Avenue, Toronto, Ontario, Canada m4v 3b2
Penguin Books (NZ) Ltd, 182–190 Wairau Road, Auckland 10, New Zealand

Penguin Books Ltd, Registered Offices: Harmondsworth, Middlesex, England

First published 1992
Reprinted with an additional chapter 1993
1 3 5 7 9 10 8 6 4 2

Filmset in 9½/12 pt Monophoto Ehrhardt
Printed in England by Clays Ltd, St Ives plc

For Molly and Joan

CONTENTS

ACKNOWLEDGEMENTS

The beginnings of this book were in a suggestion, from the Editor of the *Sunday Times*, that I undertake a project to examine why the British economy, apparently on the verge of an economic miracle at the time of the June 1987 General Election, had succumbed to inflation, followed by a severe recession. The project, which I called 'From Boom to Bust', appeared in the *Sunday Times* as a four-page special article but even this did not allow sufficient space to do full justice to the subject. Thanks are due to Parin Janmohamed, who helped research the project, as well as the officials, politicians, economists and colleagues – too numerous to name – who provided a wide range of different perspectives on the period. Most of all, I extend my gratitude to Jane, my wife, and to Richard, Thomas and Emily, my children, for their support, patience and forbearance while this book was being written.

INTRODUCTION

From time to time, events conspire to produce a period so rich in content that its story has to be told. The years that began in 1987 with Margaret Thatcher's third term as Prime Minister were, I believe, just such a period. The British economy began it apparently on the brink of a permanent escape from the post-war shackles of slow growth, high inflation and a weak balance of payments. But within three years the prize of a low-inflation, high-productivity growth economy had been thrown away. Rapid economic growth gave way to recession, high inflation returned and Britain's overseas trade slid into record deficit.

Politically, the fall-out was spectacular. By the time of Thatcher's tenth anniversary in office in May 1989 it was clear that there was little on the economic front to celebrate. Over the next eighteen months, the political giants fell like ninepins. Nigel Lawson, after six and a half years as Chancellor of the Exchequer under Thatcher, resigned in October 1989. Sir Alan Walters, Thatcher's personal economic adviser and a particularly spiky thorn in Lawson's side, went on the same day. A year later Sir Geoffrey Howe's resignation sparked the final crisis that led to Thatcher's own departure. Europe and the poll tax were cited as the principal reasons for her downfall. In fact, without the return of inflation and the subsequent recession, a challenge for Thatcher's leadership of the Conservative Party would have been unthinkable. Responsible economic management was supposed to have been the mainstay of Thatcherism. But it was economic mismanagement, in which she was by no means an innocent bystander, that brought her down.

In the middle of all this turmoil, Thatcher was finally persuaded to take the decision to allow the pound to enter the exchange rate mechanism (ERM) of the European Monetary System. After years of delaying entry until the time was right, Thatcher agreed, in probably her last major decision as Prime Minister, to enter in conditions of high inflation and recession. The framework that its supporters hoped would prevent the return of the boom–bust cycle in the future was finally put into place. As far as the boom of the late 1980s and the recession of 1990–91 were concerned, however, the stable door was locked only after the horse had already bolted.

Five years ago, I wrote a book for Penguin called *The Rise and Fall of Monetarism*. At the heart of it was an account of Margaret Thatcher's first two terms, covering the period from 1979 to 1987. In it, I attempted to catalogue and explain the Thatcher Government's gradual abandonment of the monetarist experiment it had embarked upon enthusiastically upon taking office. At that time a pragmatic approach to economic policy appeared to be serving the Government well. The monetarist experiment may have been deemed a failure but the economy's performance was improving. Inflation was low, and unemployment, after rising sharply in the first half of the 1980s, had begun to fall. Thatcher won her third general election victory in June 1987 on a tide of economic optimism. Soon, the economic renaissance of Britain, even a Thatcher miracle, was being proclaimed.

This book is a natural sequel to the story of the abandoned monetarist experiment. If all had proceeded according to plan, Thatcher's third term would have been a time of continued low inflation, perhaps even stable prices, alongside robust economic growth and strongly rising productivity. For a time after the 1987 election, this economic nirvana appeared to be attainable. Before long, however, things began to fall apart dramatically. The Government came to believe its own publicity about the supply-side transformation of the economy. Inflation had been beaten, or so it was thought. It was time to cast caution aside and bury the memory of the sacrifices of the early 1980s. Britain, it appeared, had the most dynamic economy in Europe and was ready to press home its advantage.

Unfortunately, Britain was not quite the well-oiled machine that it had been made out to be. Pressing down hard on the accelerator resulted in an initial burst of speed, followed by the rapid onset of overheating and, finally, a damaging breakdown. Inflation, far from proceeding gently down to zero, returned to double figures. And, as it did so, the argument over who was to blame tore the Government apart. Public disagreements between Prime Minister and Chancellor of the Exchequer are rare enough. In the case of Margaret Thatcher and Nigel Lawson the spectacle was more akin to prolonged guerrilla warfare.

I have tried to set the events of the 1987–91 period in context, by reference to earlier examples in the post-war period of sharp cyclical movements in the economy. In the case of sterling's entry into the exchange rate mechanism of the European Monetary System, I have traced the debate as it developed within the Government.

Why call it *From Boom to Bust*? The first part of the title is clear enough. In the late 1980s Britain certainly experienced an economic boom, the likes of which had not been seen since the early 1970s under an earlier Conservative Chancellor, Anthony Barber. But 'bust' may be thought of as too strong a description for a recession in which the overall fall in gross domestic product, at just over 3.5 per cent, was less than the 5 per cent drop recorded in 1980–81, shortly after Thatcher came to power. What struck me most about the recent period, however, was the contrast between the optimism of 1987–8 and the gloom of two years later. The recessions of the mid-1970s and early 1980s were, in a sense, accidents waiting to happen, and were exacerbated by the external blow of a sharp rise in world oil prices. This one was different. Apart from the fact that it was very largely a home-made recession, its shock value was bigger than its predecessors, and not least to the millions of people and thousands of companies who had borrowed in the expectation that the good times would go on for ever. Bust captures the magnitude of the change in mood, and it also accurately describes the condition which too many firms and individuals found themselves in.

This is a book about economics, and the politics of economic policy. But it is, I hope, written in a way that is easily accessible to non-economists. The terminology is standard. A billion is defined as one thousand million. Where I have quoted financial or fiscal years, rather than calendar years, these run from April to April. Economists have used a number of different definitions of recession over the years. For the purposes of this book the current favourite – the American definition of at least two quarters of declining national output (gross domestic product) – has been used.

I

BOOM AND BUST, OLD AND NEW

For Karl Marx, the business cycle was part of 'the fundamental contradiction of capitalism'. John Maynard Keynes, in his *General Theory*, wrote, 'The right remedy for the trade cycle is not to be found in abolishing booms and thus keeping us permanently in a state of semi-slump; but in abolishing slumps and thus keeping us permanently in a quasi boom' (1936, p. 322). Most modern economists would accept neither Marx's gloomy diagnosis nor Keynes's deliberately overstated prescription. The business cycle, which has itself spawned a whole branch of academic literature, would be regarded by most specialists as a fact of economic life. There is, however, a world of difference between a regular but relatively muted pattern made by an economy weaving on either side of its long-run growth rate, and destabilizing shifts from boom to bust.

In the late 1980s, Britain certainly had a boom, which gave way by the early 1990s to a condition for which recession was too mild a term. The spectacular fortunes that had been made in the boom years were now replaced by equally spectacular failures. Those who had flown the highest crashed to earth in the most dramatic fashion: boom and bust. Retailers competed in a madcap battle for space, on the high streets and in out-of-town shopping centres, only to find that the demand they were relying on to sustain their expansion had, in many instances, disappeared. Klondyke conditions in the housing market, with prices rising by 50 per cent a year in some areas, were replaced by the weakest market in living memory. In stagnant conditions, those that had to sell houses, and were successful in doing so, often had to accept prices that, compared with the market peak, were drastically reduced. The hardest hit were those who had bought properties they could ill afford, on 100 per cent mortgages, in the expectation of continuing price rises. If they had to sell up, they had thought, the worst they could do was to escape with a profit. As boom turned into bust, this was no longer the case. An investment in bricks and mortar was no longer as safe as houses. Repossessions, by banks and building societies, reached record levels.

For the economy as a whole, it was like the iciest of cold showers. Growth rates of between 4 and 5 per cent in 1987 and 1988 became a distant memory as the economy stagnated in 1990, with growth of a paltry 0.5 per cent, and went into reverse in 1991, its estimated decline of more than 2 per cent exceeding even the horror year of 1980.

How did it happen? Over the previous two decades, the British economy had experienced two painful recessions, around the years 1974–5 and in 1980–81. In both cases government policy contributed to the severity of the decline. Anthony Barber, Chancellor of the Exchequer in Edward Heath's 1970–74 Conservative Government, was responsible for bringing about an inflationary boom. Margaret Thatcher's 1979 Government inherited a situation of increasing inflationary pressures, particularly in the labour market, and imposed upon it a crash programme for reducing inflation.

The recession trigger in both cases was, however, provided from abroad, and in particular by the external 'shock' of sharply rising world oil prices. The first oil crisis, following the Yom Kippur war in October 1973, resulted in a quadrupling of the price of crude oil. The second, five years later, saw prices virtually treble. We cannot know for sure what would have happened, in either period, if there had been no sharp rise in world oil prices. The boom conditions of 1972–3 would, even without the effect on the world economy of the Organization of Petroleum Exporting Countries (OPEC) oil price hike, probably have necessitated a harsh period of adjustment for Britain. Similarly, the desire of the 1979 Thatcher Government to break the country's inflationary psychology was probably not achievable without a period in which economic growth would be sacrificed. Indeed, although higher oil prices hit the world economy and helped to push sterling higher (because by this time Britain was an important oil producer), the tightness of the Government's monetary policy, together with its determination not to intervene in wage negotiations, were factors of arguably greater importance.

Even so, in both 1974–5 and 1980–81, external events provided extenuating circumstances. In neither case could the recessions be said to be entirely 'home-grown'. This was not, however, the case in 1990–91.

World oil prices, having fallen sharply in the mid 1980s, had remained subdued, their only contribution to the inflationary boom of the late 1980s being the possible negative one of persuading UK policy-makers that inflation was no longer a serious problem. The October 1987 global stock-market crash, often cited as an explanatory factor, did not, on any serious analysis, play more than a minor role in determining the course of the British economy. In explaining what went wrong, therefore, the choice is clear. Either there were very serious errors of policy, which transformed an apparently well-balanced economy into an unpredictable animal whose mood swung wildly between excessive optimism and black despair. Or, the economy had developed the sort of instability predicted by Marx for unfettered capitalist systems. Before attempting to examine this in detail, however, it is necessary to set the scene briefly with some historical background.

Different Eras, Similar Problems

Since 1945 the world has, in most respects, been turned upside down. Technological advances have occurred at an unprecedented pace, transforming the lives of millions, at work and in the home. The Cold War has come and gone. Whole industries, in Britain and other advanced industrial economies, are no more, supplanted by competitors from newly industrialized countries that were, at the end of the Second World War, economically insignificant.

Any overview of post-war British economic policy from 1945 until the present day must, however, conclude that there are a remarkable number of recurring themes in the story. Throughout the period there has been a perception that, in comparison with other countries, the British economy has performed badly, and that action was needed to raise long-term performance. Such action could be judged to be successful only if, over a sustained period, Britain's relatively poor post-war record of modest productivity growth, inadequate investment and a vulnerable balance of payments position could be said to have changed decisively for the better.

Initiatives for raising Britain's long-run economic growth potential, sometimes grandiose, at other times more modest, have been a regular feature of policy. Almost without exception, they have ended in tears. Governments have found that it is difficult, if not impossible, to lift supply without having an impact that is at least as great on demand. The all-too-familiar result has been inflation and balance of payments problems – in the caricature, periods of 'go' followed by abrupt 'stops'.

Related to this, economic policy has had to adjust to Britain's changing role in the world. Between 1939 and 1945, Britain won a war, but effectively lost an empire. Partly as a result of this, for most of the post-war period, Britain has been losing her share of world trade. The economy has been shifted, of necessity, to a position of greater integration with Europe, and away from the old empire and transatlantic alliances.

Sterling, again partly as a legacy of history, has been a constant preoccupation. The pound's role in the international financial system, disproportionately large in relation to Britain's status in the post-1945 world economy, has contributed to the frequent difficulties created by sterling. Chancellors of the Exchequer have proceeded with one eye on the domestic economic indicators and their importance for the ballot box, and the other on sterling and the state of the official reserves. Sterling, following devaluations in 1949 and, after years of agonizing, in 1967, was floated after a brief and embarrassing flirtation with the European currency 'snake' in 1972. The pound, problematical for the British authorities, also contributed to the break-up of the post-war system of fixed exchange rates, emanating from the Bretton Woods conference of 1944. Eighteen years of floating, much of it highly volatile, were ended in October 1990 when, after one of the longest engagements in history, sterling was married to the exchange rate mechanism of the European Monetary System. It remains to be seen whether that decision signalled the end of the sterling problem, or merely that it had entered a whole new phase.

There are other recurring themes. In the 1930s, Keynes had pointed out that the labour market did not behave in the competitive way expected of it by the eighteenth- and nineteenth-century 'classical' economists. In the 1980s and early 1990s, the labour market continued to be dogged by inefficiency and inflexibility. Between the two periods, governments have veered between incomes policies, either explicit or implicit, and virtually unfettered collective bargaining. There have been social contracts and there have been bitter confrontations, both legal and physical. Trades union law has been reformed. Throughout it all, however, many of the inflexibilities of the labour market, and the problems created by them, have continued.

The interplay of politics and economics, central to the story, has thrown up frequent tensions. In any democracy, politicians have to seek the approval of the electorate every few years. This may mean, for one thing, that they cannot often afford to take the long view. The discipline of the ballot box can produce an indiscipline in economic policy. A government that imposes sacrifices on the electorate for the long-term good of the economy may simply be handing on the benefits to its political opponents. Roy Jenkins, the Labour Chancellor from the 1967 devaluation to his party's 1970 election defeat, eliminated the balance of payments problem that had been the bugbear of policy in the 1960s. He also achieved a Budget surplus. But financial prudence, partly through bad luck, was not rewarded at the ballot box.

More often, incoming governments have to live with, and endeavour to correct, the pre-election imprudence of their predecessors. The political cycle – relax policy before elections and tighten up again after – may go a long way towards determining the economic cycle. If there is a pattern to the conflicts between the political and economic pressures on policy-makers it is usually that those directly responsible for the conduct of economic policy, the Treasury and the Bank of England, try to pursue a tougher line than is acceptable to non-economic ministers and, perhaps most importantly, to the Prime Minister. There are exceptions, as we shall see, even to this rule.

Golden-age Economics

Nostalgia, in economics as in most things, is a powerful emotion. Looked at through the telescope of history, the past can be seen to have been better than it ever appeared to be at the time. The 1950s and 1960s, certainly in comparison with the decades that followed, come across as something of a golden age for the British economy and, by extension, for economic management. Inflation and unemployment, both of which were later to explode with great force, were low. The economy grew at a respectable rate. The balance of payments, always thought of as the Achilles' heel of the economy, was a potential problem, but its actual performance was within acceptable bounds.

Sir Peter Middleton, Permanent Secretary to the Treasury from 1983 to 1991, described the mood there when he first joined in 1960:

It was a period of confidence and consensus in the Treasury. A post-war deflation had been avoided. The commitment in the wartime White Paper on employment policy to maintain a high and stable level of employment had been achieved to an extent greater than anyone expected – and was reiterated both in the 1956 White Paper on the economic implications of full employment and in the Radcliffe report in 1959. We had lived within the Bretton Woods arrangements – a little precariously at times but successfully.   (1988)

In the period 1953–69, the economy grew by an average of 3 per cent a year. In only one year, 1958, did recession produce a full-year decline in gross domestic product (GDP), and then by just 0.2 per cent. Inflation, on an annual average basis, ranged between 0.6 and 5.4 per cent, and averaged 3.3 per cent. Later politicians made a point of boasting whenever the growth rate of the economy was greater than its inflation rate. For much of the 1950s and 1960s the two ran so closely together that this was a common occurrence. At its lowest, unemployment was equivalent to just 1.2 per cent of the workforce. At its highest the rate was a mere 2.6 per cent. Average unemployment, at 1.9 per cent, was extraordinarily low. Although the two are not directly comparable, the unemployment rate was generally below the inflation rate. The current account of the balance of payments fluctuated between small deficit and small surplus. The biggest deficit was 1.1 per cent of GDP, the biggest surplus 1.5 per cent.

Economic historians, viewing the period from some distant age, might be tempted to conclude that they had stumbled across something very special. After the Great Depression of the inter-war years, the Second World War itself and its immediate aftermath, and before the turbulence of the 1970s and 1980s, the 1953–69 period stands out as an oasis of economic calm.

As an illustration, the 1972 edition of the *Penguin Dictionary of Economics*, under the definition of the trade cycle, said:

> In the post-war years, the trade cycle has been controlled to the point where absolute downward movements in the level of output have been largely eliminated in the Western industrial countries. The trade cycle has, in consequence, been replaced by the recession, in which temporary pauses in the advance of total output occur and are followed by a resumption in growth.   (1972, pp. 399–400)

Even golden ages tend to be a little tarnished, however, and digging a little deeper into the period, this is exactly what we find. Indeed, policy-makers were never allowed more than an occasional measure of smug self-satisfaction. Rather, throughout the period, economic policy was subject to the strongest criticisms.

Wynne Godley, who joined the Treasury a few years before Sir Peter Middleton (and left in the 1970s for Cambridge), offered a different perspective on the golden age. In a collection of essays called *Slow Growth in Britain*, edited by Wilfred Beckerman, he wrote:

> Let me cast my mind back to the mid-fifties when I first joined the Treasury. This was the period of 'you've never had it so good' when the economy could be – and was – run at full stretch for years at a time; there was in effect no unemployment at that time – it hovered around the 1.5 per cent mark for a prolonged period. But we had periodic checks to growth when the inability to export enough to pay for our imports produced a balance of payments crisis and the growth of aggregate demand had to be cut back ... The complaint about 'stop-go' was essentially a complaint that *fluctuations* were taking place – and indeed the problem of the British economy, apart from slow growth, always appeared as essentially a cyclical one. But there lies in the figures for the fifties and sixties, when looked at *ex post facto*, a clear trend for the worse. Each crisis produced a recession deeper than the previous one; each expansion-ary period came to an end with a higher level of unemployment than each previous one.   (1979, pp. 227–8)

Godley's language, replete with talk of crises and deep recessions, is colourful. But it gives a flavour of the period that is, if anything, as useful as the raw statistics of the golden age. The downside of the business cycle may have been more limited than in earlier or later periods but the overwhelming impression of policy was that, whenever the economy appeared to be building up momentum the brakes would be applied. It may not have been boom and bust, but it was certainly stop-go. The role of economic policy, to quote former Federal Reserve Board Chairman William McChesney Martin's dictum for central bank-ers, appeared to be 'to take away the punch-bowl just as the party gets going'.

Dissatisfaction with the economy's performance, and with the stop-go cycle, was one thing. Equally important was the perception that, in comparison with other countries, Britain's record, even in the golden age, was a poor one. International comparisons of productivity growth (output per man-hour) by Angus Maddison, also contained in *Slow*

Growth in Britain illustrated the problem. In the 1950s, productivity growth in Britain averaged 2.3 per cent a year. In the 1960s it was even better, at 3.3 per cent. This was a marked improvement on, for example, the 1913–50 productivity growth rate of 1.7 per cent a year, and that of 1870–1913, just 1.1 per cent a year.

The difficulty was that Britain's performance, in terms of international comparisons, was in pursuit of a moving target. In the 1870–1913 period, annual average productivity growth among the industrialized countries was 1.7 per cent, rising to 1.8 per cent for the period 1913–50, 3.9 per cent in the 1950s and 5 per cent in the 1960s. As the years progressed it became clear that Britain's performance was particularly poor in relation to the defeated Second World War powers. The German *Wirtschaftswunder*, or economic miracle, produced productivity growth rates of 6.8 per cent a year in the 1950s and 5.4 per cent in the 1960s. In Japan, 5.8 per cent annual productivity growth in the 1950s gave way to 10.1 per cent in the 1960s. These were dramatic examples. But was there any reason why France, with 4.4 per cent annual productivity growth in the 1950s, 5.3 per cent in the 1960s, and Italy, 4.3 and 6.5 per cent respectively, were also driving ahead?

These golden-age comparisons also help to explain why British businessmen, and the public, were served with such a heady brew in the 1980s. Not only, after the pain of the 1980–81 recession, was stop-go apparently no more. The talk, after fears of a recession in 1985 proved unfounded, was that the Chancellor, Nigel Lawson, had somehow managed to abolish the business cycle. In addition, for once, the British economy appeared to have laid the ghost of its past under-performance. For much of the 1980s, Britain's productivity-growth record in manufacturing outshone that of Europe and the United States. The competitiveness of British industry, on most measures, improved significantly. The sick man of Europe had, it appeared, staged a Lazarus-like recovery. And, if the price of this had been giving up the stability of the golden age, was it not worth paying?

Was the stability of the golden age due to the successful conduct of economic policy or, simply, that the world economy did not throw up too many nasty shocks? Demand management, the use of fiscal and monetary policy to regulate the amount of activity in the economy, was, of course, the watchword during the golden-age period.

According to Samuel Brittan's classic *Steering the Economy*, demand management had been the basis for budget-making since the war years:

It is when trade is relatively slack that a Chancellor may want to put spending money into people's pockets, if this can be done without jeopardizing the balance of payments. This simple principle has been a guide and beacon to most Chancellors since Sir Kingsley Wood in 1941.   (1971, p. 128)

The highly controlled conditions of Britain's wartime economy could not, however, be said to have provided a full test of demand management. Neither, in the post-war years, with continued rationing, the 1949 devaluation and a cheap money (low bank rate) policy, did it start immediately with the peace. According to Christopher Allsop and David Mayes, writing in *The Economic System in the UK* (ed. Derek Morris): 'The era of demand management really starts in the early 1950s, after the further shock of the Korean war' (1985, p. 399).

In the 1950s, and for much of the 1960s, politicians liked to view the economy as susceptible to the most precise degree of control. It was like a giant machine which, operated correctly, was capable of optimum performance. If it was running slightly too fast, and in danger of overheating, a 'touch on the brake' was needed. If, on the other hand, the machine was under-performing, then the politician's duty was to press down gently on the accelerator. The economy was rarely in a situation where the clear policy prescription was to accelerate hard or jam on the brakes. Rather, the approach to demand management had to be more delicate, finely tuned.

Fine-tuning the economy was never, however, a straightforward task. Any decision to depress or stimulate the economy was only enacted after the most intense debate within government. Economies send out confused signals. Most of the time, policy-makers were acting on economic statistics that were highly imprecise, and this continues to be the case. For this reason alone, the precision implied by fine-tuning was always somewhat misleading. In the late 1980s, a period of much coarser economic management, politicians and officials were quick to point out the difficulties created by inaccurate statistics. As Robin Leigh-Pemberton, the Governor of the Bank of England, said in 1990:

Over the past three or four years there have been significant discrepancies in the official statistics and material revisions to them, which has made interpretation difficult ... To slip into a rather hackneyed metaphor, we put the brakes on when the speedometer indicated we were doing 60 m.p.h. Some time later it said we were doing 55. When the tachograph was opened, however, it revealed that we had actually been doing 70 when the speedometer read 60.

Thus the problem was not that the brakes were ineffective but rather that the speedometer had been misleading. And more brake pressure was therefore entirely appropriate.   (1990, p. 216)

Even the most accurate of statistics, however, suffer from another difficulty. Statistics have to be gathered, collated and prepared for publication. In the case of the most complete picture of the British economy, the data for gross domestic product, the process takes several months. Full balance of payments figures, similarly, are only available after a delay of many months, and are subject to extensive revision as new information comes in. At best, individual statistical series for industrial output, retail sales, trade and the money supply become available weeks after the event. This was one reason why, in the later period of floating currencies, policy-makers placed greater emphasis on day-to-day movements in the exchange rate. Exchange rates shift by the second, and the information is instantly available.

To add to the inevitable information lag, there was, and is, another natural delay in economic policy. Before making a change, politicians and their advisers will want to be sure that it is justified. One or two months' statistics will not usually be regarded as enough to signal a trend. When it is eventually decided that a change is required, policy itself may be insufficiently flexible. Interest rates and other monetary policy instruments can be adjusted quickly. But taxation and public spending, emphasized during the fine-tuning period, takes more time. The lags may mean that a policy decision that was correct on the basis of the available information is not implemented until it is no longer appropriate.

Suspect and out-of-date data created a major headache for policy, albeit one that was not greatly emphasized during the period. Equally important, however, was the fact that policy decisions had to suit the requirements of the politicians. Tensions frequently arose, not least when the economic situation appeared to require an application of the brakes when, politically, this was highly inconvenient.

This indeed was one of the characteristics, and weaknesses, of fine-tuning. The danger, all too frequently exposed, was of an asymmetry in policy. Populist politicians, only too ready to accept the kudos of expanding the economy when the situation appeared to warrant it, were reluctant to take action in the opposite direction. The risk, therefore, to take Wynne Godley's point, was that each economic cycle would end with higher inflation and unemployment and a poorer balance of payments position than the one that had gone before it. Creeping inflation and a steady deterioration of Britain's underlying trade position were the result.

Harold Macmillan, Conservative Prime Minister from 1957 to 1963, wrote in detail of the economic policy decisions of the period. In his memoirs, he described several behind-the-scenes battles over economic policy. One concerned the 1960 Budget. This Budget, the first since the October 1959 general election victory, was planned amid growing concern at the Treasury and the Bank of England that, with unemployment falling rapidly and the balance of payments position deteriorating, the economy was overheating.

He wrote: 'A little cloud had begun to show itself on the horizon, and the combination of increased estimates of public expenditure and the undoubted investment boom which resulted from our election victory raised new fears' (1972, p. 218). The Chancellor of the Exchequer, Derick Heathcoat Amory, supported by the Governor of the Bank of England, Lord Cobbold, proposed a 'tough' Budget, one which would raise net taxation by around £100m (then 0.5 per cent of gross domestic product). But Macmillan, having led his party to its third consecutive, and his first, general election victory, with a majority of more than a hundred seats over Labour, was concerned about the potential political damage that a post-election tightening of policy could cause. 'I am worried – not so much about the boom but the loss of nerve,' he wrote in his diary (1972, p. 220).

In 1957, he had unintentionally hit on a powerful slogan: 'Let us be frank about it. Most of our people have never had it so good.' The 1959 election victory, on a platform of continued 'you've never had it so good' prosperity, would, he argued, quickly turn sour.

After the second of two meetings with the Chancellor and Governor in February 1960, he took the unusual step of setting out his objections to a tough Budget in a detailed letter to Heathcoat Amory. Macmillan made several points. A deflationary Budget, he said, would be either very foolish or dishonest. A small increase in taxation would have little or no effect on the economy, but at great political cost. Companies, seeing the brakes being applied, might cancel important investment projects – he cited the planned expansion by the motor industry on

Merseyside. Treasury forecasts of a further deterioration in the balance of payments were unreliable, he argued. The economy was not working at full capacity. Measures other than higher taxation were available, if necessary, to slow the economy; for example, special-deposits or hire-purchase restrictions.

The Prime Minister's strong preference was for a neutral, or 'stand-still' Budget. Heathcoat Amory, who had already made it known that he intended to leave politics, offered only token resistance. Macmillan, according to his own account, won the battle 'decisively', even insisting that, in delivering his Budget speech, the Chancellor should not adopt a 'lugubrious' tone. The 1960 Budget, which could have been a highly significant political event, became a low-key affair. Macmillan, not for the first time, held sway over the Treasury. In January 1958, in a sequence of events Macmillan was to describe as 'little local difficulties', Peter Thorneycroft resigned as Chancellor, taking with him Treasury ministers Enoch Powell and Nigel Birch, over the refusal of the Prime Minister, supported by most of his Cabinet, to accept a freeze on public expenditure.

Macmillan won his battle over the 1960 Budget, but the British economy was the real loser. The boom that the Prime Minister was not overly concerned about turned out to be a powerful, if short-lived one. Growth in 1960 was 5.5 per cent, one of only two years in the period when the economy expanded by more than 5 per cent (the other was 1964), and the current account of the balance of payments recorded its biggest deficit since 1951. The seeds were sown for a sterling crisis, which duly occurred in the summer of 1961. More importantly, the Government's failure to act according to the Treasury and Bank of England's advice in the Budget of 1960 played a major part in wrong-footing economic policy, the legacy of which persisted throughout much of the 1960s.

Christopher Dow, who served at both the Treasury and as economic adviser to the Governor of the Bank of England, saw episodes such as this as typical of the shortcomings of policy in the period. He wrote, in *The Management of the British Economy 1945–60*:

> The analysis suggests that the fluctuations of the growth of demand in the years 1952–60 were due in large part to fluctuations in policy. The trend over the whole period was for tax rates to be reduced; but they were reduced not

gradually but in two or three steps. Had tax reductions instead been gradual, and had alternate restrictions and relaxations of credit been avoided, the growth of demand would probably have been much smoother. Some important causes of fluctuation would still however have remained. Some of the fluctuation in the growth of demand arose from three- or four-year cycles in the growth of demand for British exports. However well demand had been managed, it would, too, have been difficult to eliminate fluctuations in investment in stocks. But so far from countering such basic causes of instability, the influence of policy seems rather to have exaggerated their effects.   (1964, pp. 391–2)

Economic policy in the golden age was subject to political interference, flawed decisions and the problems inherent in fine-tuning. Even so, and despite the justifiable criticisms of policy and economic performance in the period, the result, certainly in comparison with the inter-war years and the boom and bust cycles that followed it, was remarkably stable. Indeed, politicians of the 1990s, given a chance to return to the 1950s and 1960s mixture of steady growth, low inflation and virtually full employment, would jump at it.

The first difference between British economic policy in the golden age and later was that it was conducted in a benign world economic environment. The post-war period was one in which technical progress and a rapid expansion of world trade combined to produce unprecedented rates of economic growth. The Western industrialized countries grew at an average 5 per cent a year in the 1950s and 1960s, alongside growth in world trade of more than 8 per cent a year. As importantly, after the sharp commodity price rises that accompanied the Korean war in the early 1950s, there were no significant 'shocks' to the world economic system, either in the form of major wars or, unlike in the 1970s and early 1980s, of a sharp rise in the price of internationally traded oil.

The second difference was that, for good or evil, the need to maintain sterling's external parity acted as a constraint on policy-makers. In the absence of a significant shift in the direction of export-led growth, something which successive British governments have yearned for but failed to achieve, the balance of payments will tend to deteriorate when demand in Britain is strong, and vice versa. As described above, governments will always exhibit a tendency towards expansion. But, under the post-war Bretton Woods system of semi-fixed exchange rates, the penalty for doing so was a poor balance of payments position and, as a result, pressure on sterling.

The question that then arises is whether, in acting as a constraint on policy, the exchange rate does so in a helpful way. There is little doubt that, for much of the 1960s, economic policy was hobbled by the reluctance of first the Conservative Government and then Labour to devalue the pound. Harold Wilson's 1964–70 Labour Government was beset with sterling crises in its first three years in power. The first came at the end of 1964, the second the following summer, to be followed by a third a year later. The fourth, and decisive, crisis set in during the spring of 1967 and lasted, off and on, until the eventual decision to devalue the pound, from $2.80 to $2.40, on 18 November 1967. Labour's aim, of lifting the economy on to a higher growth plane, partly through the use of national economic planning, was thrown off course.

The 1967 devaluation was different in character to its predecessor eighteen years earlier. It marked the beginning of the end of a period in which the exchange rate and the balance of payments imposed strict limits on British policy-makers. Less than five years later Anthony Barber, Conservative Chancellor of the Exchequer under Edward Heath, said in his 1972 Budget speech: 'It is neither necessary nor desirable to distort domestic economies . . . in order to maintain unrealistic exchange rates, whether they were too high or too low.' The reality of the exchange rate constraint, certainly towards the end of the golden age, was that Britain moved from one sterling crisis to the next. The effect, however, was to prevent the economy from embarking on a sustained boom. And, because the extent to which there is a downside for the economy depends partly on the degree to which it has been allowed to expand on the way up, the period was one in which the economy rarely boomed for long, but neither did it descend into bust.

Boom and Bust, 1972–6

The Barber boom of 1972–3 differed from anything that had gone before it. Between the first quarter of 1972 and the third quarter of 1973, gross domestic product increased by 10.5 per cent. For 1973 as a whole, in spite of a fourth quarter dragged down by the Yom Kippur war and the onset of the first world oil crisis, the growth rate was nearly 7.5 per cent. This was, by any standards, a formidable boom, and it was made possible by the removal of the exchange rate constraint on policy. Barber had said in his March 1972 Budget speech that the exchange rate should not distort domestic economies. And it soon became plain that he did not intend to allow a weak currency to stand in the way of economic growth. The pound fell from \$2.60 at the time it was floated in June 1972, to \$2.38 by the fourth quarter of 1973, a fall of 8.5 per cent. Even bigger falls were recorded against other currencies. Against the Deutschmark, sterling's drop from DM8.26 to DM6.05 over the same period represented a 27 per cent fall. The pound dropped by 25 per cent against the Swiss franc, 20 per cent in relation to the French franc and 17 per cent against the Japanese yen.

The story of the Barber boom, and the recession that followed it, is a familiar one. For a fuller account, see *The Rise and Fall of Monetarism*, particularly chapters 3 and 5. For the purposes of this chapter, the interest lies in the comparisons between the earlier boom–bust period and that of the late 1980s and early 1990s. The two booms occurred in a period of a floating pound, and a deteriorating balance of payments position did not act as an immediate constraint on policy.

In both cases, as we shall see, measures to liberalize the financial system helped to produce a powerful expansion of credit. And, having been instrumental in unleashing potent monetary forces, policy-makers attempted to persuade themselves that the effects would be benign, that they were one-off adjustments to a new financial regime. In the early 1970s the fuse was lit by changes introduced by the Bank of England in the autumn of 1971, under the heading 'Competition and Credit Control'. For much of the 1960s, the banks and finance houses had been subject to lending ceilings and, as a result, lost market share to institutions which were not subject to such restrictions, notably the so-called secondary banks. The 1971 changes removed these ceilings and the effect on credit growth was dramatic. New bank lending to the private sector rose from £1.86bn in 1971 to £6.43bn in 1972 and £6.83bn in 1973. The Bank of England, later blamed by the Treasury for mismanaging the 1971 changes, attributed these sharp lending increases to the mainstream banks claiming back market share from the secondary, or 'fringe' banks. Clearly, however, in a credit explosion of such force other factors were at work.

Common to both periods was a sharp increase in property-based lending by the banks and other financial institutions. In the 1972–3 boom, the emphasis was on commercial property loans. In the late 1980s, lending on both commercial and residential properties rose sharply. The particular concern in the early 1970s was property lending by the secondary banks, who had been pushed out of other markets by the aggressive lending of the newly liberalized mainstream banks. The property boom, which appeared to many to be the safest of safe bets, was killed off by a freeze on business rents, which took effect at the end of 1972, and by the Government's belated tightening of monetary policy, which began in the middle of 1973. One fringe bank, London and County Securities, failed in November 1973. Many others were under threat. Even one of the major clearing banks, National Westminster, more heavily exposed to property lending than its competitors, had to take the unusual step of issuing a public statement to say that it was safe. The Bank of England organized a financial 'lifeboat' to prevent widespread banking collapses.

Another common factor was that both booms came after a period when the economy, while avoiding recession, appeared to be stuck in an unsatisfactory pattern of modest growth and rising unemployment. Edward Heath's Conservative Government was elected in June 1970 against a backdrop of dissatisfaction with the economy's perceived failure to benefit, in terms of economic growth, from the 1967 devaluation of sterling. But by 1971, with unemployment rising strongly, the position, far from improving, appeared to have deteriorated sharply. Achieving a faster rate of economic growth, far from being viewed as a high-risk strategy, appeared to be economically and politically desirable. The 1980s parallel was that, in spite of the fact that an economic upturn could be pinpointed as having begun early in 1981, unemployment continued to rise for another five years and business investment remained subdued. In both cases, when growth was finally admitted to be getting out of hand and monetary policy was eventually tightened, the authorities acted aggressively. Bank rate, or minimum lending rate, 7.5 per cent in June 1973, was raised to 13 per cent by November, then easily the highest on record. In the 1950s and 1960s, bank rate had never been above 8 per cent. From the early 1930s to the mid 1950s, the rate was never higher than 4 per cent.

The big difference between 1972–6 and 1988–91 was the external shock of higher world oil prices. This was the straw that broke the camel's back. During the 1960s the posted price of Saudi Arabian light crude oil had stayed at $1.80 a barrel. In 1973 the price had crept up to $2.59 a barrel. On 16 October 1973, ten days after the outbreak of the Yom Kippur war, the Organization of Petroleum Exporting Countries raised the price to $5.11 a barrel. By the following January, the price was $11.65 a barrel. Economic policy, as Denis Healey, Labour's Chancellor of the Exchequer from 1974 to 1979, noted, was never the same again. He later described, in *The Time of My Life*, the devastating impact on the framework of policy of the oil crisis:

> I was more concerned to find that the fundamental Keynesian concept of demand management had become unreliable. Keynes believed that a government could maintain full employment of a country's productive capacity without creating inflation, by increasing or reducing the demand for its output, through adjusting taxes or Government spending. But it had become impossible to discover with any accuracy how much additional demand the Government should inject into the economy so as to produce full employment. It was equally impossible to know how people would use the money you did inject by cutting taxes or increasing public spending. It might go into higher wages or profits, creating more inflation rather than more jobs. It might be used to buy foreign rather than British goods, so worsening the balance of payments and creating jobs abroad instead of in Britain. Or it might be saved instead of spent. To the great surprise of all economists, the increase in inflation led to an enormous increase in saving, rather than the reverse.
>
> (1990, p. 379)

The 1974–5 recession took the economy decisively out of the golden age. Healey's initial attempt to expand his way out of the oil crisis proved to be a failure. Gross domestic product fell by 1.5 per cent in 1974 and 0.8 per cent in 1975. Unemployment, 459,000 in the final quarter of 1973, climbed to more than a million by the first quarter of 1976. The pattern of the recession, in addition, underlined its prolonged misery. Economists think of recessions as U-shaped, a gentle downturn followed by a muted upturn; V-shaped, a sharp downturn succeeded by an equally sharp recovery, or W-shaped, in which an initial downturn is followed by a partial recovery, to be followed again by a second downturn as recessionary forces grip the economy. In the 1972–6 period, the pattern of the recession was, to be precise, an extended W. The economy went into reverse in the fourth quarter of 1973, as business and consumer confidence was hit by the sharp rise in world oil prices. It appeared to have embarked on a recovery in the spring of 1974, but by the fourth quarter it had turned down again. The eventual low point was reached in the third quarter of 1975. But the recovery from that low exhibited at least one false start, with activity turning down in the second quarter of 1976. Only by the second half of 1976 could a recession that had begun three years earlier be decisively said to be over and recovery under way. Even then, this was only clear after the event. Unemployment continued to climb until mid 1977, and the general impression was of an economy in the grip of International Monetary Fund inspired austerity until 1978.

The 1980–81 Slump

The slump of 1980–81 was different in character and causes from its mid-1970s predecessor. It was also deeper, with gross domestic product falling by 2 per cent in 1980 and 1.2 per cent in 1981. Manufacturing output fell by nearly a fifth. Unemployment, just above 1.2 million when the Thatcher Government took office in May 1979, rose to 3 million by the autumn of 1982. For the first time in the modern era, Britain had a slump that drew comparisons with the depression of the inter-war years.

Unlike in 1974–5, the slump of 1980–81 was not preceded by an unsustainable boom. From 1976 until the end of the decade, with the International Monetary Fund supervising UK economic policy closely, growth returned, but did not exceed 3 per cent a year. The current account of the balance of payments, heavily in deficit in the mid-1970s following the sharp rise in world oil prices, had returned to surplus by 1978. Healey, as Chancellor, would like to have boosted the economy more, particularly in 1978, but was effectively prevented from doing so by the watchful eyes first of the IMF and then of the City. In June 1978, for example, the financial markets forced Healey to introduce a restrictive economic package because of concern that the Government's money-supply targets were not going to be met.

The one area where Labour policy was demonstrably unsustainable was that of pay. The Labour Government's incomes policy, which initially complemented the IMF squeeze, began to break down spectacularly in the 'winter of discontent' of 1978–9. For the incoming Conservative Government a difficult situation was made worse by an election pledge to honour the recommendations of an independent pay commission, under the chairmanship of Professor Hugh Clegg.

The 1980–81 slump was not the economy's natural reaction to an earlier boom. It was, instead, brought about by the newly elected Thatcher Government's deliberate attempt to force the economy on to a path of permanently lower inflation, exacerbated by a second world oil crisis.

This time, the overthrow of the Shah of Iran was the trigger for a sharp rise in oil prices set by the Organization of Petroleum Exporting Countries. The Iranian revolution was at the end of 1978. By the middle of 1979 Saudi light crude had risen to $35.40 a barrel, three times its level the previous autumn. Some crude oils, including those produced in the North Sea, traded at more than $40 a barrel.

Much of the second rise in oil prices had occurred by the time Thatcher came to power. Even so, the new Government was determined to persist with its intended strategy. The fact that higher oil prices implied an additional boost to inflation was not regarded as sufficient excuse to postpone the anti-inflation drive. If anything, it made the task more pressing.

Had such a delay been sought, the Government would probably not have been able to prevent a recession in 1980–81, although they might have limited its severity. The new factor was sterling's strength, partly because of higher oil prices, partly due to the tightness of monetary policy. Under Labour, sterling's climb from its 1976 lows had forced a change of policy in 1977. Attempts by the Bank of England to restrain it at between $1.70 and $1.75 in the autumn of 1977 had had to be abandoned because the upward pressure was so strong. By 1979, the high interest rates that marked the early years of the Conservative monetarist experiment, in combination with the pound's 'petrocurrency' attractions in a period of sharply rising oil prices, provided an additional upward shift for sterling, eventually lifting it above the old 1967 devaluation level of $2.40.

The Barber boom of 1972–3 had been facilitated by the Government's abandonment of its fixed-exchange-rate commitments. Now the process worked in the opposite direction. The Thatcher Government had its eyes fixed firmly on domestic monetary targets. The exchange rate was certainly not subject to any target. Nor, at first, was it a subject which merited much attention, except as a misleading symbol of national economic virility. It was, however, the main factor in forcing the economy to its knees in 1980–81.

The Government was shaken by the extent of the 1980–81 slump, which was an unintentional by-product of the monetarist experiment, exacerbated by the second world oil crisis. Unlike in the 1972–6 period, the bust of 1980–81 was not preceded by a boom. Intended or not, the Government could, in later years, present the early 1980s as the medicine that was needed to bring about change in Britain's overmanned and inefficient industry. As memories of the slump faded, the explanation gathered weight, particularly among industrialists. If it was a one-off adjustment, people said, then perhaps the sacrifice was worthwhile. But as we shall see, no such excuse was available ten years later.

2

FINANCIAL LIBERALIZATION AND THE ABANDONMENT OF MONETARISM

Control without Controls

Five days after his sudden resignation as Chancellor of the Exchequer in October 1989, Nigel Lawson gave an eloquent account of his economic philosophy. In an electrifying ten-minute speech to a packed House of Commons, he set out in detail the reasons for his departure from the Government and this, of which more later in this book, understandably captured the headlines the following day. Of equal interest, however, was that, in one short passage, Lawson encapsulated both the basis for, and a central difficulty with, the economic policy approach of the Thatcher Government. He said: 'I have long been convinced that the only successful basis for the conduct of economic policy is to seek the greatest practicable degree of market freedom within an over-arching framework of financial discipline to bear down on inflation' (1989). Lawson's comments reflected the approach of the previous ten years. The Conservative Government elected in 1979 wished to combine tight control of the money supply with the liberalization of the financial system. In other words, control without controls. As Christopher Dow and Iain Saville pointed out, in their book *A Critique of Monetary Policy*:

> After the election of mid-1979, the new Conservative Government not only put monetary control at the centre of its policy, but was equally dedicated to the removal of restrictions on competition in all spheres. Exchange controls were promptly abolished in October. By opening the way to increased inter-mediation, this would have made it difficult to retain the corset* even had that been desired. When the corset was removed in June 1980, its removal was clearly permanent. In August 1981 the reserve asset ratio was removed;

* The system under which the banks were restricted from creating credit by having to lodge additional deposits at the Bank of England.

although this had not proved to be of much effect, it signalled that the banks
could expand with less risk of being caught out by future policy
changes.   (1988, p. 192)

The removal of all Britain's exchange controls, announced by Sir
Geoffrey Howe, the Chancellor, on 23 October 1979 and enacted from
midnight that day, came sooner, and in a more dramatic way than
anyone outside government had expected. Expectations had been for a
gradual lifting of the controls, carried out over a number of years.
Milton Friedman, the prominent American monetarist who had done
much to influence Thatcher, was critical of the way that Britain's experiment in monetarism was conducted. He was full of admiration, however,
for the boldness of the Government's action in lifting exchange controls
which, he said later, was the most important single act under Thatcher.

Exchange controls had enormous symbolic and practical significance
in Britain. In the 1960s British citizens travelling abroad had been
restricted to £50 of spending money, an aspect of the controls which
emphasized the vulnerability of sterling and the weakness of the UK's
balance of payments position.

More importantly, overseas investment by financial institutions was
restricted by the fact that the foreign exchange required for such
purposes had to be acquired through a separate, investment-currency
market. Thus, currency for foreign investment purposes was available
only at a premium over the official exchange rate (the dollar premium)
and this had the effect of making the acquisition of foreign financial
assets less attractive.

The likely effect of removing the controls was, therefore, a big
increase in overseas investment by British financial institutions. The
decision to opt for a 'big bang' removal of the controls was, however,
made possible by two countervailing influences on the balance of
payments. The first was that, as a direct result of North Sea oil exports
and high world oil prices, the current account of the balance of payments
was moving strongly into surplus. Secondly, the high interest rates
adopted by the new Conservative Government in pursuit of its monetary
targets had, in combination with the pound's emergence as a petrocurrency – which made it a safe haven during a time of oil-related
world economic uncertainties – meant that London was now a magnet
for short-term capital from abroad. The removal of exchange controls

was not, therefore, accompanied by sterling weakness. The pound continued to strengthen, eventually reaching more than $2.40 just over twelve months after the October 1979 decision.

Lawson, when Financial Secretary to the Treasury, addressed the Zurich Society of Economics in January 1981. He could not resist a touch of smugness about the impact of abolition, saying:

> A whole range of other restrictions and controls have been either liberalized or abolished altogether. Perhaps the most dramatic example of this has been the complete abolition, within six months of our taking office, of the very severe regime of exchange controls which had been maintained by successive British governments for over forty years without a break. At the time this decision was widely criticized as rash, if not foolhardy. In the event it has proved highly successful in every material respect – so much so, in fact, that there are more voices today calling for the imposition of inflow controls than there are those seeking the reimposition of the old outflow controls. (1981)

The rise in the exchange rate, however, while central to the squeeze on the economy that produced the 1980–81 slump, was not sustained. Much of the inflow of foreign capital into short-term sterling assets, which added froth to the surface of sterling's rise, always looked ready to depart again at short notice. The outflow of investment by pension funds and insurance companies, and the increase in overseas lending by British banks, represented permanent changes. An assessment by the Bank of England two years after the removal of the controls suggested that investment overseas by financial institutions had increased from less than £150m a quarter in the first half of 1979 to nearly £1.3bn two years later. The Bank suggested that the absence of controls implied two things:

> First, the effectiveness of the controls in the past is likely to mean that in the absence of controls domestic interest rates are now somewhat higher. Second ... it seems unlikely that the increase in overseas demand for sterling assets has been as great as the demand by UK residents for overseas assets in response to the lifting of exchange controls. Balance in the external account must, therefore, have been achieved by some downward, though unquantifiable, pressure on the exchange rate. (1981, p. 373)

In other words, after the initial excitement had died away, the October 1979 decision meant, other things being equal, higher interest rates and a lower value for sterling than would have been the case had the controls been retained. Both have occurred in the period since 1979. The average level of interest rates (bank base-rate) from May 1979 to May 1991 was, for example, just over 12 per cent, substantially higher than in any previous period of comparable length. Until sterling's entry into the exchange rate mechanism of the European Monetary System in October 1990 it showed a tendency to depreciate, and not always steadily, from one year to the next. The pound's average value fell by about 20 per cent between 1979 and 1991. How much of these interest-rate and currency effects were due to the absence of controls cannot be gauged. But the movements were in the direction predicted by the Bank of England.

The lifting of exchange controls had direct effects on domestic monetary policy, as Dow and Saville pointed out. Earlier, the 1971 Competition and Credit Control changes had allowed the mainstream banks to compete more freely with other lending institutions, as described in Chapter 1. At the end of 1973 such freedoms were reined back. The supplementary special deposits scheme, commonly known as the banking 'corset', was introduced, with the specific aim of limiting bank lending. In October 1979, after briefly being abandoned in the mid 1970s, the scheme was still in existence. But, in removing exchange controls the Government effectively abolished the corset. This was because, in the new spirit of international freedom, it was simple for any bank to bypass the corset restrictions by lending to British customers from overseas subsidiaries. Even if they chose not to do so, the system would discriminate against British banks in favour of their overseas competitors. The corset, therefore, had to go and its demise was signalled by Howe in his March 1980 Budget speech, and occurred three months later. It resulted in an immediate, and substantial, rise in bank lending.

In August 1981, nearly eighteen months after publishing a Green Paper on monetary control, the Treasury and the Bank of England took further steps to reduce direct controls on the banking system. The reserve asset ratio, introduced ten years earlier, was abolished. This had required the banks to hold the equivalent of 12.5 per cent of their sterling liabilities in reserve assets, so-called because they were either cash or easily convertible to cash. In addition, the banks, previously obliged to place 1.5 per cent of their liabilities in non-interest-bearing accounts at the Bank of England, had this proportion – the cash ratio – reduced to 0.5 per cent. Other institutions, including the National Girobank and the Trustee Savings Banks, had not previously been required to hold cash at the Bank of England. Now they too were subject to the 0.5 per cent rule. The net effect, however, was to give the banking system considerably more leeway. Finally, minimum lending rate, the successor to the old bank rate, was abolished. Both had been used to allow the Bank of England to maintain a tight rein on interest rates. Minimum lending rate was suspended, according to the Bank of England, 'to leave as large a role as possible for the influence of market forces in determining the structure of interest rates' (1981, p. 334).

The practical effect of the changes of the early 1980s was to allow the banks to expand into areas in which their activities had previously been restricted. This recalled the changes of 1971, when an aggressive expansion of lending by the banks provided the basis for Barber's runaway boom. The result then had been that the Bank of England had been blamed for underestimating the monetary consequences of the changes it had introduced. According to Denis Healey, the then Labour Chancellor, who was left to pick up the pieces:

> In 1974 its [the Bank's] reputation had been badly damaged. The previous Governor's handling of the White Paper on Competition and Credit Control, which encouraged the banks to compete more vigorously with one another for lending, had led to an explosion of uncontrolled credit like the deregulation of the eighties. This had been a major factor in bringing Barber's dash for growth to a stop; it also helped to produce the crisis of the secondary banking system which rumbled on through my period at the Treasury. (1990, p. 374)

Ten years later, with the economy in recession, no one in official circles appears to have given serious thought to the idea that the seeds were being sown for a return of that boom. The Bank, having suffered once, did not appear to be unduly concerned about making the same mistake again. Indeed, its belief in the need for changes in the banking system was stronger than its faith in the new Government's monetarist experiment. The fact that deregulation would make it even more difficult for the Government to keep its chosen measure of the money supply (the broad money measure, sterling M3) within specified targets did not merit much attention. Lawson, in his 1981 Zurich speech, reflected the prevailing official wisdom when he suggested that the effect of the removal of the banking corset would be an unwinding of previous distortions. In other words, the expectation was of a one-off adjustment by the banks to their new freedom.

Bricks and Mortar

The particular area of interest for the banks was the personal mortgage market, previously the preserve of the building societies. Until the changes of the early 1980s, mortgage lending was dominated by these often sleepy institutions. The building societies, then some three hundred in number, ranged from the very large to the tiny. They operated, through the Building Societies Association, an explicit cartel, with interest rates fixed by agreement and, therefore, virtually no price competition.

The societies, as their name suggests, were mutual organizations, committed not to achieving maximum profits but, instead, to balancing the conflicting requirements of their members, who included both savers and borrowers. The result was that building-society interest rates, both on mortgages and in savings accounts, changed far less than, for example, bank base rates. Typically, mortgage rates were kept at lower levels than would have been the case if they had followed market interest rates. The peak for mortgage rates in the 1970s, for example, was 12 per cent, compared with a base-rate peak of 15 per cent. Therefore, mortgages represented a cheap source of finance, the more so since home-buyers were entitled to tax relief on mortgage interest payments. The result, inevitably, was that demand for mortgages exceeded the supply of funds, the latter being determined by the growth of savings accounts.

To cope with this problem, the societies adopted a system of rationing. Potential home-buyers applying for a mortgage were usually told that their name would be added to a waiting-list. And those who were most likely to succeed in their application would have demonstrated that they were capable of saving over a sustained period, typically with the building society from which they hoped to obtain the mortgage. In this way, the process of channelling funds from savers to borrowers was sustained. A two-year waiting period for a mortgage was quite common. And, for first-time buyers in particular, the societies operated strict criteria governing the amount of a mortgage they could obtain. Existing home-owners wishing to trade up in the housing market were also subject to the overall scarcity of mortgage funds, and were required to demonstrate that the additional finance they required was justified. It was difficult for borrowers to take out a larger mortgage than they needed and use the balance to finance other types of expenditure. This contrasted with the situation in the 1980s, where 'equity extraction' from the housing market, to finance other types of expenditure, became commonplace.

The banks were keen to expand their mortgage lending for several reasons. They believed that, protected by their cosy cartel, the building societies were hidebound and inefficient and, because of this, vulnerable to competition. In addition, the banks had had their fingers badly burnt in lending large amounts to Latin America and other less developed regions of the world. Such lending, in which the banks essentially acted as middlemen between the cash-rich oil exporting countries and the Third World, had originally appeared to be the neatest of profitable financial tricks. Lending to sovereign governments was apparently the safest lending of all. Whether it was this, or the fact that no banker wanted to be left out of this 1970s' gold rush, many of the loans were made without due regard for the ability of Mexico, Brazil, Argentina and the other cash-hungry countries to be able to generate the export earnings needed to service their debts. By the early 1980s, the banks were looking for genuinely safe outlets for loans, not least to balance the dubious risks they were carrying in their Third World loan books. In this period too, with British industry having been through its worst recession since the 1930s, prospects were not bright for bank lending to corporate customers. Defaults on business loans at home, although on a far smaller scale than the problem of Third World debt, had increased as a direct result of the recession.

The Government, apart from favouring the deregulation of Britain's financial system on free-market grounds, had another reason for encouraging an expansion of mortgage lending. This was that, as part of its programme for increasing home-ownership and reducing the size of the public sector, local councils were to be made to sell off their housing stock. And, while the 'right to buy' legislation provided for substantial discounts on market value for tenants, there would still be a significant requirement for extra mortgage finance. The one thing that would be guaranteed to dampen the ardour of potential purchasers was the prospect of a two-year wait in a building-society mortgage queue.

The Government's policy of selling off council houses to their tenants was successful, with around one million homes being transferred in this way in the 1980s and the proportion of the housing stock owned by local authorities cut from 31 per cent to less than 25 per cent. Although the sell-off process was facilitated by greater availability of mortgage finance, there is no strong reason to believe that it could not have occurred if the old system had remained in place. In the 1950s, for example, more than two million homes were bought from private-sector landlords, and the number of owner-occupying households increased by 2.8 million.

The building societies, their traditional market under threat from the banks, did not intend to let the grass grow under their feet. Strains had begun to emerge in the building-society cartel during the late 1970s, with some of the more innovative societies starting to compete more aggressively with one another by offering new-style accounts. In September 1981, the Building Societies Association announced that, in future, it would only recommend basic borrowing and lending rates, with members free to announce variations in rates on different types of mortgages and savings accounts. In October 1983, after the Abbey National, then the second largest society, threatened to withdraw from the Association, the cartel was further weakened by the announcement that, in future, rates would no longer be fixed by agreement. Instead, the Building Societies Association would only advise on rates, with members free to take or ignore such advice. By 1986, the Association had stopped setting even advisory rates; the societies were free to compete against one another and, as importantly, compete against the banks.

The societies, it will be recalled, had been limited in the number and size of mortgages they could supply because they relied on deposits from savers. Two things happened in the 1980s to free the supply of building-society mortgage lending. The first was that, in the recession of 1980–81, personal savings rose to very high levels. Saving as a percentage of personal disposable income, the saving ratio, reached the high level of nearly 15 per cent late in 1980 and averaged more than 10 per cent in the first half of the 1980s. Much of this saving was channelled to building-society accounts. Secondly, from 1983 onwards, as a result of tax changes which allowed the payment of interest gross (rather than net of tax) the societies were able to gain access to the money markets for funds. This wholesale funding, initially limited to 20 per cent of total funding, meant that the societies were no longer as constrained in their lending activities as in the past. On 1 January 1988, the limit was increased to 40 per cent.

With increased access to funds, and with the new competition from the banks in the mortgage market, the societies were keen to expand their lending activities in other areas. This was made possible by the Building Societies Act of 1986, which took effect at the beginning of 1987. The Act, while preserving housing lending as the main purpose of the societies, allowed them to issue credit cards and lend on an unsecured basis for the purchase of cars, holidays and consumer durables. They were, in general, allowed to behave more like banks.

Finally, the mortgage market was further expanded later in the 1980s by the emergence of new lenders. Some, like The Mortgage Corporation, a subsidiary of the American investment bank Salomon Brothers, relied entirely on wholesale funding. Others offered foreign-currency mortgages to British home-buyers, providing lower interest rates but with a significant element of exchange rate risk.

Increased competition in the mortgage market had far-reaching effects. The banks quickly built up their market share to 40 per cent in the early 1980s, before falling back and then achieving this 40 per cent share again in the housing boom of the late 1980s, with the new lenders taking around 10 per cent. Interest rates, on both mortgages and savings accounts, followed market levels much more closely. The banks even had to start offering interest on current accounts.

The key point as far as mortgages were concerned was that anyone who wanted one could have it. The rationing system which had, however imperfectly, acted as a brake on borrowing, was no more. And, the more competition increased among lenders, the easier it was to borrow. It no longer became necessary for first-time buyers to scrape together a 10 or 20 per cent deposit in order to obtain a mortgage; 100 per cent mortgages were widely available. In a minority of cases, indeed, lenders were prepared to advance more than the value of the property, 105 or 110 per cent mortgages, with the surplus available for the borrower to spend on furniture and other requirements.

Under the new regime, not only was there more competition, but there was also much more lending. Net mortgage lending doubled from £7.3bn to £14.1bn between 1980 and 1982. By 1988, the peak of the housing boom, lending reached £38.5bn, an increase of more than 425 per cent on the 1980 figure. The supply of new housing increases only slowly, although the private housing sector was boosted in the 1980s by council-house sales. Even so, a sharp increase in mortgage lending would normally be associated with a similar rise in house prices. And this was indeed the case. By 1990 the average house price at mortgage completion stage was £64,657, 175 per cent above its 1980 level. There is a lot of difference, however, between a 425 per cent increase in mortgage lending, and a 175 per cent rise in house prices. The question is, where did the rest of the lending go?

Equity Extraction

Equity extraction is the process by which capital that has been locked in the value of the house can be unlocked and used for general spending. Suppose my house, bought a few years ago for £50,000 with the aid of a £40,000 mortgage, is now worth £80,000. I want to trade up to a £100,000 house and decide that I can afford the repayments on a mortgage of £80,000. I increase my mortgage from £40,000 to £80,000 but the new house has only cost me an extra £20,000. Therefore, I have extracted £20,000 of equity, which I can use to buy a new car, a boat or any number of other non-housing goods The more freely mortgages are available, the easier it is for me to do this.

According to a Bank of England paper, 'The Role and Scope of Mortgage Limits', published in 1991:

> Increased availability of mortgage finance encouraged greater investment in housing. But because of planning and other constraints, the supply of housing did not keep pace with the finance available. This clearly helped to fuel the increase in house prices, but a proportion of mortgage finance was also leaking out of the housing market in the form of equity extraction.   (1991, p. 260)

The Bank of England and the Treasury were clearly aware of this danger. Gordon Richardson, Governor of the Bank of England until 1983, said in a speech to the Finance Houses Association in January 1982, 'There is a danger that as a by-product of this competition the funds provided on favourable mortgage terms could increasingly be used to finance an expansion of cheap consumer credit. This would have undesirable consequences for monetary growth and the general level of interest rates.'

One worry among officials was that borrowers would take advantage of tax relief on mortgage interest payments in financing their non-housing spending. Since 1983, the ceiling for tax relief on mortgage interest has been £30,000. Suppose that in my example, the initial mortgage was £10,000 and I want to buy a property worth £10,000 more than my existing one. Instead of increasing my mortgage from £10,000 to £20,000, I go to £30,000, and £10,000 of tax-subsidized borrowing is available for general spending.

As a result of this, the banks and building societies were sent official guidance at the beginning of 1982, asking them to ensure that 'lending for house purchase was not significantly inflated by borrowers realizing house equity for consumer purposes unrelated to the purchase or improvement of residential property'.

Policing the banks and building societies on equity extraction was clearly very difficult. And, in an atmosphere of intense competition, few lenders wished to reject borrowers' requests for mortgages over and above their strict housing requirements. If they did so, they risked losing the custom to the bank or building society along the road, who perhaps would not be so diligent about applying the official guidance. And, as the Bank of England pointed out, a certain measure of equity extraction was unavoidable:

> Much equity extraction is the natural process by which houses that come on to the market following the death of their owners are purchased by a younger generation using mortgages. But there is also a component of equity extraction that corresponds to consumption out of the capital gain on the occupier's own home. For households that change dwelling, a measure of equity extraction is the extent to which the increase in the mortgage exceeds the difference between the purchase price of the new home and the sale price of the old home. For households who do not move, equity extraction occurs when they take out a second mortgage or home equity loan on the unencumbered value of their existing property. The scope for equity extraction clearly increases with the rate of house price inflation, but there is evidently substantial equity available to be extracted even in the absence of further house price rises. (1991, p. 261)

The official guidance issued in 1982 was ineffective and was quietly withdrawn in 1986. At the same time, an earlier piece of guidance, encouraging the banks to lend to industry in preference to property companies or consumers, first issued in 1972, was also withdrawn. The banks and building societies could lend to whoever they wanted, without prompting the disapproval of the authorities.

The scale of equity extraction has been the source of much debate among economists. Unpublished estimates by the Bank of England suggest that, over the period 1981–9, a massive £112bn of extraction occurred, peaking in 1988, when the total exceeded £20bn. By any standards, this represented a massive boost to consumer finance. The building societies have traditionally argued that such figures exaggerate the true picture, in that many of the funds were used in housing, for example in maintenance and home improvements. Even allowing for this, the problem for policy-makers was a significant one.

Equity extraction is not the only way in which a free market in mortgages, leading to rising house prices, can help create the conditions for a consumer-led economic boom. The mere fact that house prices are rising, and at a faster rate than prices generally, creates expectations of substantial capital gains among home-owners. Higher house prices add to personal wealth which, in turn, feeds consumer spending. The fact that many capital gains in the housing market are never realized is less important than the belief, among consumers, that they exist. Thus, for example, people will be more willing to run up debt if they believe there is enough wealth tied up in their property to repay it in the event of loss of job and income.

The housing market was both a blessing and a curse for the Thatcher Government in the 1980s. The encouragement of greater levels of home-ownership, the success of the right-to-buy programme for council houses, the belief that owning your own home was an important freedom, even the emergence of a vast do-it-yourself industry, all represented aspects of the decade that, to a greater or lesser extent, embodied the success of Thatcherism. The other side of the coin was that the housing market provided the springboard for a boom in consumer spending that, for a government which emphasized the control of inflation as its primary economic objective, was far less desirable. In addition, the old problem of the British economy, that it was easier and safer for people to make money in unproductive housing, rather than in productive investment elsewhere in the economy, exerted itself. Only at the end of the decade was this belief tested.

Encouraging the Consumer

Deregulation of the banking system provided consumers with ready access to finance, some of it diverted from the housing market. In 1982, Sir Geoffrey Howe, the Chancellor, provided more direct encouragement for the consumer. Post-war British Chancellors had used hire-purchase controls to influence consumer spending, particularly big outlays on cars, televisions, washing-machines, refrigerators and other consumer durables. When the balance of payments signalled the need to tighten policy, and higher inflation was threatening, the hire-purchase regulations would be made more restrictive, typically by shortening maximum payment periods and increasing the proportion of the value of the goods required from the buyer as a down-payment or deposit. When economic growth slackened, these rules were relaxed.

The Crowther Committee, which investigated consumer credit, had reported in 1971 on the use of hire-purchase controls. They were useful to governments, it concluded, because they had an immediate psychological impact and affected consumer spending without much delay. They also had the advantage, unlike tax changes, of not affecting the retail prices index. However, the committee criticized them because of their disproportionate impact on certain sectors, most notably the motor industry. Partly as a result of this, controls were lifted in July 1971, although they were reimposed at the end of 1973, in an effort to deflate the Barber boom.

When the Conservative Government took office in 1979 the controls were available as a weapon in the Treasury's economic armoury. On 26 July 1982, Howe announced their abolition. Consumers were free to finance their expenditure on the 'never never', and industries producing cars and consumer goods could act in the knowledge that they were not going to be pulled up sharply by the sudden imposition of controls.

According to Andrew Britton, director of the National Institute of Economic and Social Research, in his book *Macroeconomic Policy in Britain, 1974–87*:

> The growth of personal loans that did not involve hire-purchase agreements had largely circumvented the control, which now appeared as nothing but an unnecessary interference with the way in which finance houses and their

customers chose to do business. Thus was abandoned what had been one of
the most powerful and reliable instruments in the hands of the authorities to
manage aggregate demand. It happened that this period saw the beginning of
a sustained growth in consumer spending and borrowing which was to go on
for many years. No doubt liberalization of the financial system (including the
abolition of hire-purchase control and also the restriction on the banks),
facilitated this growth.   (1991, p. 62)

The abolition of hire-purchase restrictions was just one way in which,
after years in which controls of one sort or another had applied, Britain's
consumers were provided with easy access to finance. If the 1980s was
the decade of the home-owner, it was also a period in which the credit
card came into general use. The major clearing banks offered Access and
Barclaycard (Visa) cards to their customers in the 1960s and 1970s, but
the really rapid growth in card use came in the 1980s. Later, following
the liberalization of their activities, the building societies moved in too.
Retailers, large and small, offered their own in-store credit cards, one of
the most successful being that of Marks & Spencer.

Do credit cards encourage a higher level of spending, or merely
change the way in which that spending is carried out? The majority of
credit-card users operated their cards merely as a means of payment,
and paid off their accounts before incurring interest. As a result, the
credit-card companies introduced card charges, typically around £10 a
year, in the late 1980s and early 1990s. And, given the other factors
providing for a boost to consumer spending during the period, it is hard
to say with any certainty that the widespread use of plastic cards, in
itself, contributed to the spending boom.

Nigel Lawson, in a speech to the Finance Houses Association in 1987,
was certain that, contrary to 'popular mythology', the build-up of
credit-card debt did not constitute a problem for policy. Some 85 per
cent of personal debt was in the form of mortgage borrowing, he said,
with 15 per cent in traditional consumer credit. And, within that 15 per
cent, only a small proportion, about 5 per cent, was credit-card debt. In
so far as there could be a problem, he suggested, it was in individual
borrowers overextending themselves.

Even allowing for the importance of other types of lending, however,
particularly mortgages, it is difficult to believe that the availability and
convenience of credit cards did not play a role in the strength of
consumer spending, and the associated fall in the saving ratio, during

the 1980s. The period was one in which consumers were bombarded with credit offers, to the evident discomfort of the Government, particularly when, in many cases, such offers encouraged the young and the financially unsophisticated to run up large debts. In 1988 the credit-card companies offered their card-holders gifts, based on a bonus points system. The more the cards were used, the greater the number of bonus points gained, and the bigger and better the gifts available. Such tactics went beyond merely encouraging the consumer to change the way he or she paid for goods.

Big Bang

In July 1983 Cecil Parkinson, the then Secretary of State for Trade and Industry, concluded an agreement with Nicholas Goodison, Chairman of the Stock Exchange. The deal was that, if Stock Exchange participants voluntarily reformed and restructured existing City arrangements for dealings in equities and bonds, then the Government would drop the case it was pursuing against the Exchange in the Restrictive Practices Court.

The pressure for change had come from two quarters. The Office of Fair Trading, under the direction of Sir Gordon Borrie, saw the Stock Exchange's rule book, which included restrictions on market entry and (high) minimum commissions on trading, as anathema to the principles of free competition. Meanwhile, the Bank of England, which heavily influenced the thinking of the Treasury and of Prime Minister Margaret Thatcher on this issue, was greatly concerned that, in the absence of far-reaching reform, the City's cosy eighteenth-century club would be swamped by international competition from other centres, notably New York, Tokyo, Frankfurt and Paris, to the detriment of the British economy.

Parkinson's decision to strike a deal with the Stock Exchange caused some controversy. It looked to many as if the Government had let its City friends off the hook. But Parkinson argued that legal action through the Restrictive Practices Court would take far longer than an agreed timetable for the City to put its own house in order. The Stock Exchange was given a deadline of the end of 1986 to introduce competitive changes. And so it was just over three years later, on 27 October 1986, the day of the Big Bang, that the majority of the agreed changes came into force, in one move. Traditional practices were abandoned, and the City would never be the same again.

The changes were, in line with the Bank of England's wishes, far-reaching. Under the old system, stockbroking partnerships took orders to buy and sell equities and bonds from financial institutions and private investors. But the stockbrokers did not deal on the floor of the Stock Exchange. Instead, this was carried out by a smaller number of separate partnerships, the jobbers, whose business was to make markets in stocks and shares on the floor of the Exchange, executing orders that they received from the brokers. Under the Big Bang changes this system, known as single capacity, was replaced by a dual-capacity framework under which the distinction between stockbrokers and jobbers disappeared. From 27 October 1986 onwards, financial institutions and private investors were permitted to deal directly with market-makers. The old jobbing firms were absorbed into stockbrokers who, in turn, were mainly acquired by banks and other larger institutions.

The old jobbing system had operated on the basis of face-to-face dealing on the floor of the Stock Exchange. As with all financial markets, a trading system had developed which, while mysterious and impenetrable to the outsider, appeared to work. To accommodate the new and larger network of market-makers, the Stock Exchange had developed, prior to Big Bang, an electronic trading system, based on a network of computer terminals, called the SEAQ (Stock Exchange Automated Quotations) system. The expectation was that trading on the floor of the Stock Exchange would continue, perhaps indefinitely, in parallel with the new electronic trading method. As it was, Big Bang effectively signalled the death knell of face-to-face trading on the Stock Exchange floor. Within weeks, 95 per cent of business was being conducted off the trading floor. Within months, it had become redundant, and three centuries of City tradition had been wiped away.

The Stock Exchange's agreed framework of minimum commission levels was a clear restriction on competition, and was replaced by individually negotiated commissions on 27 October 1986. (Big Bang was first coined to describe the fact that the abandonment of minimum commissions would occur immediately, rather than over a period.) The Government had been particularly irritated by high commission rates on trading in its own stocks (gilt-edged securities). For the new, all-purpose market-makers, however, the commission they received from clients was only one way in which they could make money on a share transaction. The other was in the old jobber's 'turn' or 'touch', the difference between the price at which they took shares on to their books and the price at which they sold them. Even so, the pressure of competition, forced down both commission levels and the average touch. If there was money to be made, it had to be achieved through a higher volume of transactions, or turnover.

This, certainly, was the view that Stock Exchange outsiders took in the period leading up to and around Big Bang. Until 1982 the maximum permitted stake that non-Stock-Exchange organizations could have in a member firm was 10 per cent. This was raised to 29.9 per cent in that year, with the promise of a further relaxation later. The 1982 relaxation of the rules was followed by a period in which the profits made by member firms increased sharply, partly because, under the old restrictive system, commission levels had been raised. It also tapped into the desire of British clearing and merchant banks, and their foreign equivalents, to move into the securities market. If London was to be the third leg in an international triangle, the others being New York and Tokyo, no serious player could afford to be left out. When the deal between the Government and the Stock Exchange was announced in the summer of 1983, the floodgates were opened. A madcap race to buy into Stock Exchange member firms ensued. Barclays took stakes in De Zoete & Bevan, the broker, and Wedd Durlacher, the jobber; National Westminster, similarly, took stakes in broker Fielding Newson Smith and jobber Bisgood Bishop. Midland acquired a holding in W. Greenwell, the broker. Merchant banks such as Hill Samuel, Morgan Grenfell, Kleinwort Benson and Hambros quickly moved in, as did the big American banks and investment houses such as Citicorp, Chase Manhattan, Security Pacific, Merrill Lynch and Shearson Lehman. From Europe came the likes of Union Bank of Switzerland, Banque Paribas and Banque Bruxelles Lambert. Only the Japanese stayed out of the fray, initially at least, mainly because of a long-standing dispute between the British and Japanese governments over restrictions on foreign entry into the Tokyo stock market. The 29.9 per cent limit on outside stakes was lifted to 100 per cent on 1 March 1986, and this was followed by a period in which the banks transformed their minority stakes into outright ownership of member firms.

The Government, in pressing for an end to the Stock Exchange's restrictive practices, had, whether intentionally or not, created a bonanza for the owners of member firms, the partners. Having done well out of the old system, partners now enjoyed unheard of riches as a result of the transfer to the new. Anyone who had been a partner in a respected City firm for a number of years could count themselves unlucky not to emerge as a millionaire as a result of being bought out by the banks. They had everything in their favour. It was a sellers' market, driven by the belief, wrongly as it turned out, that Stock Exchange trading in the future would be a highly profitable activity. Hundreds of millions of pounds poured into the City as banks, British and foreign, bid against one another for the ultimate control of member firms. The Stock Exchange fat cats became even fatter. And, because the new owners were buying the contacts and expertise of the existing staff, the majority were kept on, on generous terms. 'Golden handcuffs', contracts which required former partners to remain with the business for several years, were offered, and many of these were also worth huge sums of money.

It did not end there. Even for many of those who had not made it to partner level with their firms, there were rich pickings to be gained. In 1984, rumours began to circulate that Merrill Lynch, the American investment bank, was actively recruiting top research analysts for a minimum of £100,000 a year. The streets of the City of London, it appeared, were indeed paved with gold. As Adrian Hamilton, in his book *The Financial Revolution*, described it:

> While the headhunters sought new recruits, the advantages of movement began to seep down to the 'marzipan set', the bright middle-rankers 'just below the icing and just above the cake'. Packages guaranteeing £250,000–£400,000 over two years were offered to analyst stars in certain sectors, heads of research and specialist dealers, while even quite junior salesmen and dealers were being offered £50,000–£100,000 a year compared with an average wage of £10,000 a year for professionals in Britain. For those on the gravy train the professions had never seen a chance to earn capital like this. The price of country houses on the main roads into London, particularly the M4 motorway into the West Country, went up 30 per cent in a year. Flats in the centre of London shot up at the same pace. In the City a new class of privileged was created, limited in number but large in individual gain. The public looked on in amazement. The many in the City who were not part of the deals looked on in resentment.   (1986, pp. 143–4)

Deregulation in the City, like deregulation elsewhere in the financial system, had created the conditions for a boom. A huge injection of capital into the Stock Exchange was followed by a boom in investment, particularly in computer equipment and new offices, and resulted in an enormous increase in personal wealth for the beneficiaries, the old owners. The new class of highly paid yuppies (young upwardly mobile professionals) was a source of resentment and envy. Others wished to emulate them. The City salaries boom, lavishly reported in the media, helped to pull other earnings higher. Meanwhile, share trading, particularly in the Government's regular flow of privatization issues, brought effortless capital gains within the reach of a wider public. Finally, the nature of the new Stock Exchange trading arrangements, and the City's unaccustomed high profile, meant that sensitivity to shifts in stock-market prices was heightened. As we shall see later, this meant that, when the worldwide stock-market crash of 'Black Monday' occurred less than a year after Big Bang, the Government felt obliged to respond.

Deregulation and the Monetarist Experiment

Financial deregulation, as we have seen, helped to sow the seeds for a rapid expansion of credit and, in other ways, served to stoke up the boom in the British economy in the second half of the 1980s. It also assisted in the derailing of the Thatcher Government's experiment in monetarism.

The incoming Conservative Government in 1979 inherited a situation in which, for three years following the intervention of the International Monetary Fund, Labour had operated within the constraint of money-supply targets with some success. Inflation was already falling when the IMF moved in, having reached a peak of 26.9 per cent in August 1975. The fall, however, continued, and the rate touched a low point of 7.4 per cent in June 1978, before moving back up to 10.3 per cent by the time of the May 1979 general election. Labour's monetarist period, under the Chancellorship of Denis Healey, differed from the Conservative experiment that followed it in three important respects. It was imposed from outside on a Government that, publicly at least, regarded the medicine it was being forced to take as distasteful. It came at a time when the financial system was still heavily controlled, with exchange controls, the banking corset and hire-purchase restrictions all part of the armoury of economic policy. Finally, a rapid downward adjustment in wages was brought about by an incomes policy that, initially at least, was successful. Thus, Labour's monetarism had fewer adverse effects on unemployment than its Conservative successor's.

Labour's monetarism had as its target measure of the money supply the notorious sterling M3, which consists of notes and coins plus all private-sector deposits denominated in sterling. It is, in the jargon, a *broad* measure of the money supply, as distinct from a measure such as Mo, which later came to prominence, and which, because it consists only of notes and coins, together with bankers' balances at the Bank of England, is a *narrow* money-supply measure. The Thatcher Government, having considered carefully in opposition the way in which it would frame its own monetarist policy, was happy to settle for the Labour/IMF measure as the basis for it.

For the Conservatives, the attraction of sterling M3, apart from continuity, was that its growth was directly linked to the size of the public-sector borrowing requirement. Thus, the Treasury could call in additional aid in its attempt to rein back public expenditure, by warning departmental spending ministers that any relaxation would jeopardize the central aim of policy: the achievement of a sustained reduction in inflation by means of money-supply control. The March 1980 Budget document, which launched the Government's medium-term financial strategy, set out the policy clearly:

> Control over the money supply will over a period of years reduce the rate of inflation. The speed with which inflation falls will depend crucially on expectations both within the United Kingdom and overseas. It is to provide a firm basis for those expectations that the Government has announced its firm commitment to a progressive reduction in money-supply growth. Public-expenditure plans and tax policies and interest rates will be adjusted as necessary in order to achieve that objective.

The difficulty was that sterling M3, while affected by the size of the public-sector borrowing requirement, was influenced even more by the growth in bank lending. And banking deregulation, together with other measures which liberalized the financial system, had the precise effect of boosting bank lending and making sterling M3 difficult to interpret. The first, and most dramatic, example of this was in the summer of 1980, following the removal of the banking corset. At the time, the official target for the annual growth of sterling M3 in the 1980/81 financial year, was 7–11 per cent. The Bank of England expected that the removal of the corset would lead to a one-off 3 per cent increase in sterling M3, as lending that had gone on outside the banking system was brought back within it. The result, however, was much worse than this. There was an increase of 5 per cent in July and a further 3 per cent in August. In other words, over just these two months the growth of sterling M3 had exceeded the lower end of its target range. Its final growth rate of the 1980/81 financial year was just under 18 per cent, double the mid-point of its target range.

Exacerbated by the effects of deregulation, the problems in controlling sterling M3 persisted. The March 1980 medium-term financial strategy set out target ranges for sterling M3 declining gradually from 7–11 per cent in 1980–81 to 4–8 per cent in 1983–4. None of these original targets was achieved, and the newly liberalized financial system appeared to be to blame. After all, inflation did fall sharply over the period – from a peak of 21.9 per cent in May 1980, to 3.7 per cent just three years later, in time for Thatcher's second general election victory in June 1983.

Did it matter? Control of the money supply, while central to the policy, was only a means to the end of low inflation. The removal of exchange and banking controls had apparently broken the link, such as it was, between the growth of broad money, sterling M3, and inflation. In monetarist terminology, the velocity of circulation of sterling M3 had fallen sharply.

The dilemma persisted. The Government had difficulty in hitting its money-supply targets, in spite of periodically adjusting them to take into account the faster monetary growth that was occurring. But, helped by a benign world economic environment, inflation remained generally low. By the autumn of 1985, when Nigel Lawson, the new Chancellor, temporarily suspended the sterling M3 target, it was plain that the original monetarist experiment was being prepared for a decent burial. The target was revived, surprisingly, in the March 1986 Budget, with an apparently generous 11–15 per cent target range. But by the summer, with its growth rate at 20 per cent a year, the game was up.

The conundrum was tackled by Robin Leigh-Pemberton, the Governor of the Bank of England, in a speech at Loughborough University in October 1986. He began by admitting that, in spite of the Government's success against inflation, 'it cannot be said that our experience with our chosen framework for operating monetary policy has been satisfactory'.

The difficulty in interpreting sterling M3 was clear, he continued:

> Given the recent fast pace of financial innovation and liberalization, the problems of definition have unarguably become more acute. There is now a vast array of slightly differentiated financial products available to the retail and wholesale depositor or investor, ranging from cash to long-maturity marketable securities. There is no obvious and appropriate criterion for discriminating unambiguously between those which are 'money' and those which are not.

So what was the solution? Financial liberalization appeared to have made sterling M3 a living example of Goodhart's Law – the rule of thumb devised by Charles Goodhart, a former monetary adviser to the Bank of England. This was that any money-supply measure targeted by the authorities automatically becomes subject to distortions that render it inappropriate as a target.

For the Bank of England, always a reluctant operator of the Government's money-supply targets, the sterling M3 measure had become more of a hindrance than a help. As Leigh-Pemberton put it, 'It is clear then that monetary targetry, not only in this country but in many others, has become increasingly complex in recent years as both financial structures and financial behaviour have changed. The choice of target aggregates, the setting of appropriate targets and the interpretation of the developments in the monetary aggregates have all been made more difficult.'

And, in case the message was not understood, he added, 'It is perfectly fair to ask whether in these circumstances a broad money target continues to serve a useful purpose.'

The die was cast. Broad money was no longer to be targeted by the Government. Nor has it been. The Bank of England and the Treasury pledged themselves to maintaining a close watch on its behaviour. Unkindly, critics said that such a monetary policy, based heavily on judgement, would mean that the Chancellor would be 'flying by the seat of his pants'. The great danger was that, in dispensing with the broad money target, the Government would turn a blind eye to rapid rates of credit growth, characterizing them as harmless by reference to financial liberalization. The baby, it was feared, would be thrown out with the bath-water. As we shall see, such fears were fully justified.

3

BRITAIN AND THE
EUROPEAN MONETARY SYSTEM

The EMS, 'Not for Us'

The European Monetary System came into being on 13 March 1979, 'to establish a greater measure of monetary stability in the Community'. Its start, some ten weeks behind schedule, and less than two months before Margaret Thatcher swept into Downing Street, was inauspicious. The previous ten years had been littered with failed attempts by the European Community to move towards closer monetary integration. The Werner Committee on European monetary union (EMU), under the chairmanship of Luxembourg Prime Minister Pierre Werner, was appointed in 1969 and reported in 1970. It envisaged monetary union by 1980, with Community currencies irrevocably fixed against one another, and preferably replaced by a single currency. There would be a Community central banking system, setting an agreed, common monetary policy. Most elements of national budget-making, fiscal policy, would also be agreed at Community level. In 1972, just before the United Kingdom's entry into the Community, European leaders, meeting in Paris, agreed on the Werner Committee's ambitious timetable. Two years later, meeting again in Paris in December 1974, Community leaders shelved the EMU experiment on the lines proposed by the Committee. Even without the turbulence on international financial markets created by the break-up of the Bretton Woods system of semi-fixed exchange rates, and the first Organization of Petroleum Exporting Countries (OPEC) oil crisis, the Werner timetable was highly optimistic. In the light of these events, it was impossible.

The Community had fared little better in the practical first step towards EMU, the so-called 'snake in the tunnel'. Under the Bretton Woods system, each participating country had been required to maintain

its currency within a 'tunnel', the ceiling of which was 1 per cent above
its dollar parity, and the floor 1 per cent below. Following the heavy
strains on the system in the late 1960s and early 1970s it was agreed, at
the Smithsonian conference in Washington in December 1971, to widen
the tunnel to 2.25 per cent either side of a currency's dollar parity, or
central value. The maximum fluctuation of an individual currency
against the dollar was, therefore, 4.5 per cent. For any two non-dollar
currencies, however, the range of possible fluctuation was much wider
than this. As J. H. B. Tew pointed out in *The Economic System in the
UK* (ed. Derek Morris): 'If one European currency rose from floor to
ceiling while another fell from ceiling to floor, their relative fluctuation
would be 9 per cent. Such a large fluctuation was repugnant to the EC's
aspiration to move by successive stages to eventual European monetary
union, as mapped out in the Werner report of October 1970' (1985,
p. 562).

The Community therefore established the 'snake', a system of nar-
rower currency fluctuations within the Bretton Woods tunnel. In the
snake, the amount by which the strongest currency exceeded its par
value, plus the amount of the weakest currency's divergence from its par
value, was permitted to be no more than 2.25 per cent. Both strong and
weak currency countries were required to intervene in the foreign
exchange markets to ensure that this condition was maintained. Like the
Werner Committee's programme, it was an ambitious aim. And it
quickly proved to be too ambitious. The snake began in March 1972,
with the original six EC members – Germany, France, Italy, Belgium,
the Netherlands and Luxembourg – as participants. Britain, Ireland and
Denmark joined in May 1972, seven months before becoming members
of the EC. In June 1972, however, all three left the snake, principally
because of the British Government's decision to float the pound.
Norway, not a member of the EC, also joined in May 1972, and stayed
in.

Britain's speedy exit from the snake was embarrassing, and it left a
permanent scar on the attitudes of some Conservative politicians
towards closer monetary ties with Europe. The attitude of Thatcher,
who was a member of Edward Heath's Conservative Government at the
time, was certainly coloured by this episode. The decision to float the
pound on 23 June 1972 – it immediately fell by 7 per cent – had been
both a symptom and a cause of the inflationary boom of 1972–3 under

Anthony Barber's chancellorship. It was, in all but name, a devaluation of the pound, and an ignominious one.

The snake continued in existence during the 1970s. Denmark rejoined in October 1972, while Sweden, another non-EC country, was in the snake from 1973 to 1977. France left in January 1974, rejoined in July 1975, and then left again in March 1976. Italy had left in February 1973, and stayed out. By 1979, the snake consisted of Germany, the Netherlands, Belgium, Luxembourg, Denmark and Norway, hardly a solid basis for a new thrust towards European monetary integration.

When Roy Jenkins, who was appointed the first British President of the European Commission in 1976, revived the idea of moving towards EMU in a speech in 1977, it caused considerable surprise. With the snake struggling, and memories of the failure of the Werner programme still fresh, his speech appeared to be singularly ill-timed. But political momentum was again building up in favour of closer monetary integration in Europe. Both Helmut Schmidt, the German Chancellor, and Valéry Giscard D'Estaing, the French President, were also enthusiastic about the idea. In April 1978, during a European Council meeting in Copenhagen, Giscard invited James Callaghan, the Labour Prime Minister, to breakfast at the French Embassy. As Callaghan later recalled in his autobiography, *Time and Chance*:

> The morning sun streamed into the breakfast-room and as we consumed our croissants and coffee, there evolved the idea of a European-type Bretton Woods, with a European exchange rate fixed against the dollar. Giscard's comments showed that he recognized that this would effectively mean Europe becoming a Deutschmark zone, but was nevertheless ready to go along. I was sympathetic with the general proposal, but had to make clear that as proposed, the effect of the scheme would be disadvantageous to Britain, for the strong Deutschmark would have the effect of tugging sterling upwards with deflationary consequences for our economy, unless long-term credit was absolutely unlimited. Helmut did his best to persuade us that membership of a monetary system would assist us, and I undertook to think the matter over. From the drift of Giscard's contributions there seemed little doubt that France and Germany would go ahead even if Britain did not join and their joint decision would almost certainly bring Belgium, Holland and Luxembourg into the scene.   (1988, pp. 492–3)

Denis Healey, Chancellor of the Exchequer under Callaghan, had his suspicions about the European Monetary System (EMS) aroused by conversations with Manfred Lahnstein, then Permanent Secretary at the German Finance Ministry in Bonn. Lahnstein told Healey that he expected the system to work in Germany's national interest because weak-currency countries such as France and Italy would be obliged to intervene in the foreign exchange markets to keep the strong Deutschmark down. The result, he suggested, would be a lower Deutschmark than was likely in a free market and, in consequence, a sustained competitive advantage for German industry. This, together with advice from his Treasury officials, who were against Britain's participation, convinced Healey that joining would not be to Britain's advantage. As he recalled, 'The Bank of England was mildly in favour, since they thought it would exert a useful discipline on British governments. The Foreign Office was strongly in favour; it is in favour of anything which includes the word "European". I was fairly agnostic until I realized, from long discussions with Lahnstein and others, how it was likely to work in practice; then I turned against it' (1990, p. 439).

Callaghan and Healey, recognizing the strong anti-EC element within the Labour Party, knew that to accept full membership of the embryo EMS would have been politically very dangerous. They were also guided by the belief that, after the traumas of the 1970s, sterling would struggle to keep up with the strong Deutschmark. It is one of the ironies of modern economic policy that the pound would indeed have struggled to stay within EMS limits, but in precisely the opposite way. A combination of the high interest rates imposed by the incoming Conservative Government, and Britain's possession of significant North Sea Oil reserves during a period of rising world oil prices meant that sterling rose well above what would have been its EMS entry level had Labour decided to join at the outset, in March 1979. The pound climbed from an average of DM3.74 in the first quarter of 1979 to more than DM4.80 two years later, a rise of nearly 30 per cent.

The EMS consists of two related elements. There is a European Monetary Cooperation Fund, which holds 20 per cent of the gold and foreign-currency reserves of member countries, exchanging them for European currency units (ecus), which can then be used, for example, to settle debts between member states. The far more important element, however, is the exchange rate mechanism (ERM), the successor to the snake. In the ERM, each country has a central rate, denominated in terms of the ecu. For most ERM members, the maximum permitted fluctuation either side of this central rate has been 2.25 per cent. However, Italy joined in March 1979 with a wide band (6 per cent on either side of its central rate), a precedent later followed by both Spain and Britain. The Labour Government elected to participate in the European Monetary Cooperation Fund, making Britain a partial member of the EMS. For the reasons outlined above, however, it stayed out of the ERM.

The question of ERM entry was duly reviewed by the incoming Thatcher Government in May 1979 but an early reversal of Labour's position on membership was never a serious possibility. For a government embarking on a radical economic programme, which was to include the abolition of exchange controls within six months, the last thing that was needed was the added encumbrance of having to keep sterling within tightly set limits.

What would have happened if Thatcher and her ministers had overcome their repugnance for managed exchange rates and elected for entry in 1979? A simulation conducted in 1989 by the National Institute of Economic and Social Research suggested that ERM entry would have had the effect of preventing much of sterling's rapid and unplanned rise in the 1979–81 period, and would have made the recession of the early 1980s less severe than it was. But, by the same token, the sharp fall in inflation that was the notable success of Thatcher's first, 1979–83, term, would not have been achieved to the same extent. Inflation, instead of peaking at over 20 per cent in 1980, would have done so about a year later. However, by 1983 the difference between actual inflation of 4.6 per cent and the National Institute's simulation, 5.3 per cent, would have been marginal. And membership would have delivered significantly lower inflation in the 1984–8 period, with no overall sacrifice in economic growth.

As it was, the question of ERM entry, or exchange rate policy, hardly featured on the Thatcher Government's policy agenda in its first few years. Nigel Lawson, in his Zurich speech as Financial Secretary to the Treasury in 1981, said, 'The present Government has no exchange rate policy as such – for the simple reason, as Switzerland among others has experienced, that the attempt to have such a policy greatly complicates (if it does not actually make it impossible) the difficult enough task of pursuing a sound monetary policy . . .' (1981).

In January 1982, at a Downing Street meeting chaired by Thatcher and attended by the then Chancellor, Sir Geoffrey Howe, together with other interested ministers, the Governor of the Bank of England, officials and advisers, the question of ERM entry was reconsidered. According to the account of one participant, Sir Alan Walters, then personal economic adviser to Thatcher, in his book *Sterling in Danger*: 'It was decided that 1982 was not an appropriate time to join the ERM. Of course this did not mean that there would never be a good reason to join. Circumstances may change or the ERM may change. The issue was left open; we should only join when and if it was appropriate' (1990, p. 93).

In the autumn of 1984, Lawson, by now Chancellor, had moved towards a recognition of the importance of the exchange rate in policy, but appeared to be some distance away from the acceptance of the need for a target for sterling. In his annual speech at the Mansion House to City bankers, he said:

> I need only say a brief word about the exchange rate. Of course it is important to the economy, not least as one of the most obvious transmission mechanisms of the inflationary process. And by providing information about financial pressures at home and overseas, it is of key importance to the interpretation of monetary conditions. In particular its movements can throw light on whether there have been unexpected shifts in the demand for money. But equally, the exchange rate can change for many reasons, some quite unconnected with fundamental developments both here and abroad: its signals as to the tightness of monetary policy can therefore be misleading. So while we shall continue to take the exchange rate into account in interpreting monetary conditions, there will, as before, be no target for it . . .   (1984)

Lawson's Conversion

Nigel Lawson had, by 1985, virtually abandoned the monetarist experiment that he had been instrumental in setting up. On the face of it, this left economic policy without a firm basis, or anchor. But Lawson did not intend to remain without a monetary anchor for long. His public rejection of exchange rate targets in October 1984 had turned into a private acceptance of them by March 1985. Three things had impressed upon him the importance of sterling in policy. The first was the devastating effect on industry of sterling's surge in the early 1980s, when it climbed back above the 1967 devaluation level of $2.40. The exchange rate squeeze on the economy was largely unintended and arose mainly from tight monetary policy, with North Sea oil, and the pound's new petrocurrency role, an important, but secondary factor.

Lawson maintained that, intended or not, much of this squeeze had been beneficial. As he told the Treasury and Civil Service Committee in 1988, 'The exchange rates prevailing in 1980 and 1981 were very uncomfortable for many businesses, but they did have a very beneficial effect, not only in breaking inflationary expectations but in securing a state of affairs in which industry emerged very much leaner, fitter and more efficient than it had been before' (1988, p. 32).

He and other ministers also recognized, however, that there had been adverse effects arising from the pound's excessive rise, notably the injuring, sometimes fatally, of perfectly viable sections of industry. In addition, the early 1980s was viewed very much in the nature of a one-off adjustment, which did not need to be repeated.

Secondly, Lawson was quick to see that, increasingly, economic policy, particularly for an open economy such as that of Britain, had to be conducted in an international context. Treasury research showed the importance of sterling as the 'transmission mechanism' for inflation. This mechanism operated in several ways. The most obvious was that a falling exchange rate raised the price of imported food commodities, raw materials and fuel. In the case of food, the position was complicated by the operation of the European Community's Common Agricultural Policy. For other, largely US-dollar-priced commodities, the situation was straightforward. A fall in the pound from, say, $2 to $1.50, would push up the price in Britain of a barrel of crude oil, priced at $20 a barrel, from £10 to £13.33. More subtly, a fall in the exchange rate eased the financial pressure on industry, in the same way that the 1980–81 sterling rise had greatly added to that pressure. Just as imported commodities rise in price when sterling falls, so too do imported products. The result is that businesses operating in the home market have the choice between increasing their prices to match those of imports, or undercutting the imports and claiming a bigger market share. British industrial practices, worryingly, appeared to favour the former. Therefore, a fall in the exchange rate would result in higher prices for domestically produced products, arising from a combination of more generous pay settlements and increased profit margins. A similar effect occurred in export markets, where again the choice was between taking advantage of the lower exchange rate to boost market share, or settling for an easier and, initially, more profitable life.

According to Lawson, in the same Treasury and Civil Service Committee session:

> Currency depreciation is not only a weakening in the battle against inflation, which then has to be made good in other ways through having appropriate interest rates; it also tends to lead, when it goes on year in year out, to industry believing that it is, as it were, a fact of life; industry comes to believe that it is a fact of life that sterling will decline against other currencies, and decline in particular against the Deutschmark and, therefore, makes its decisions accordingly, deciding what cost increases it can afford based on an extrapolation of that trend. (1988, p. 33)

Thirdly, and probably most importantly, Lawson had been made painfully aware of the perils facing finance ministers without an explicit exchange rate policy. Twice in six months, in July 1984 and January 1985, Lawson had had to respond to a sharply weakening pound. The January 1985 sterling crisis, the more serious of the two, was probably the death blow to the Thatcher Government's monetarist experiment. As sterling tumbled towards one-for-one parity with the dollar, bank base rates were increased from 9.5 to 14 per cent in the space of seventeen days. The difficulty, apart from fears among currency dealers that a fall in world oil prices was in prospect, was that the Thatcher Government, and Lawson as a prominent member of it, had initially laid great stress on the virtues of freely floating exchange rates. In practice, no government can ignore its currency, and well before 1984–5 there had been examples of policy actions specifically geared towards preventing, or encouraging, a movement in sterling. Such moves, largely in response to currency shifts, were different, however, from making the level of the exchange rate a main priority of policy. Sterling's fall towards $1 early in 1985 was, therefore, a fascinating test case.

On 11 January, after the first interest-rate increase in response to the pound's decline, the Downing Street Press Secretary Bernard Ingham briefed Sunday newspaper journalists to the effect that heavy currency intervention would not be used to stem the pound's decline. Ingham was careful not to preclude further interest rate increases to support the pound, but the damage was done. The Downing Street view, later encapsulated by Thatcher in the phrase 'you can't buck the market', appeared to be that, more or less, currencies found their level in the markets almost irrespective of the actions of governments. This was, at a later stage, to be one of the key points upon which Thatcher and Lawson waged war with one another. For now, the main impact was to require an even bigger interest rate response to sterling's decline, to convince dealers that the Treasury, at least, was determined to arrest the fall. According to Ingham's own unpublished account, he was summoned to the Treasury on 14 January, the Monday after his fateful press briefing; Lawson, Sir Peter Middleton, the Permanent Secretary to the Treasury, and other senior Treasury officials were gathered, apparently intent on giving the Downing Street man a dressing-down. But Ingham's opening line: 'I come to you directly from the Prime Minister' headed off the Treasury attack. He also told the Chancellor and his Treasury officials, in a comment that could have been designed as a red rag to a bull, 'One thing to come out of this is that at least we will get a policy.'

Lawson, having taken the dramatic step of reintroducing the old minimum lending rate, last used in 1981, to signal an interest rate increase from 10.5 to 12 per cent was, from that moment, determined not to be subject to such criticism again. He told the House of Commons, 'I am afraid that there was a feeling in the markets that the Government had lost their willingness and ability to control their affairs.'

His new enthusiasm was for tying sterling, and Britain's monetary policy, to the low-inflation Deutschmark by joining the ERM. Sir Geoffrey Howe, the Foreign Secretary, and Sir Leon Brittan, the Trade and Industry Secretary, were powerful allies.

Howe, Chancellor during the Thatcher Government's first term, was driven by considerations similar to those of Lawson. In addition, he had long believed in the desirability of European integration, and bemoaned Britain's role on the periphery of the European Community. Indeed, one surprise among his eight record selections on the radio programme 'Desert Island Discs' was Cliff Richard's 'Summer Holiday', which he said epitomized the emerging European spirit among young people in the 1960s. As Foreign Secretary, he was exposed to the prevailing Foreign Office view, which was that Britain's non-participation in the ERM displayed a half-hearted attitude towards the Community, and that this created unnecessary difficulties for the Government in its dealings with Europe.

Brittan, who was to resign from the Government in 1986 over his role in the Westland affair, was subsequently appointed by Thatcher as Britain's senior European Commissioner, Vice-President of the Commission. Another long-standing Euro-enthusiast, in Brussels he was to play a prominent role in persuading and cajoling the Government on the question of ERM entry, leading to complaints from those close to Thatcher that he had 'gone native'.

Robin Leigh-Pemberton, the Governor of the Bank of England from 1983, had, when chairman of the National Westminster Bank, made no secret of his belief that sterling should be taken into the ERM. And, while his public utterances on the subject were much more delphic in his position as Governor, few doubted that he was still strongly in favour. Within the Bank of England there were strong voices on either side, with some senior officials of the view that, with sterling still subject to oil-related volatility and there being serious doubts about the permanence of the reduction in inflation since the early 1980s, ERM entry could mean that policy-makers were simply making a rod for their own backs. On balance, however, Leigh-Pemberton carried the Bank with him in favouring entry.

At official level, the first senior convert in the Treasury was Sir Geoffrey Littler, the Deputy Permanent Secretary with responsibility for international finance. Littler, in his regular contacts with his counterparts in Europe, the United States and Japan, picked up worries about the sustainability of Britain's success in controlling inflation and had been encouraged in the view that staying out of the ERM would, increasingly, damage the Government's anti-inflation credibility. He did not, however, push it strongly. Sir Peter Middleton, the Treasury's top civil servant, and Sir Terence Burns, the Government's Chief Economic Adviser, became converts. All three took the view that membership, when it occurred, should be on 'hard' terms, at an exchange rate which would maintain the downward pressure on inflation. In practice, allowing for the expected impact of a falling world oil price on sterling, this meant an entry level of between DM3.50 and DM4.

The conversion of Lawson and his senior Treasury officials to the principle of ERM entry can be dated to the period between the January 1985 sterling crisis and the March Budget of that year. By tradition, the Treasury retreats into purdah in the two months or so before the Budget, with the Chancellor reducing his public engagements and officials effectively cutting off their contacts with journalists. Purdah is a time of intense activity in the Treasury, beginning with an informal meeting of ministers and senior officials, usually at the Foreign Secretary's official residence at Chevening in Kent, in early January, and continuing until the Budget itself, in mid March. During it, economic policy comes under closer internal scrutiny than at any other time of year. And it was during this period in 1985 that the top men at the Treasury became convinced that ERM entry was the right policy, with a possible announcement in the Budget speech itself. But, after discreet soundings of Thatcher by Lawson it was soon recognized that she was unwilling to be rushed into a decision of this magnitude. The senior Treasury men were, however, confident of winning the argument.

Other Treasury officials were, however, less convinced of the proposed policy change. Having undergone, sometimes painfully, the intellectual adjustment needed to work within the Government's monetarist framework, they were suspicious of the conversion of the Chancellor and his top advisers to exchange rate management. Many agreed with Professor Charles Goodhart, former monetary adviser at the Bank of England, later at the London School of Economics, who said to me that the new emphasis on the exchange rate, and the decision to play down continued strong credit growth, represented 'a staggering intellectual somersault'.

Notwithstanding such doubts, the views of the senior officials and ministers, in particular the triumvirate of Middleton, Burns and Lawson, co-designers of the Government's 1980 medium-term financial strategy, prevailed. Middleton, who regarded the Bretton Woods semi-fixed currency arrangements as having exerted a 'powerful financial discipline', saw, like Lawson, that it was necessary to set UK economic policy in a wider context. He said later:

> The international developments ... have since increased in pace. Direct investment has grown at twice the speed of world trade. The value of foreign-exchange transactions is forty times greater than visible trade. Turnover in the Euromarkets is twice the value of world exports. And financial markets trade around the world twenty-four hours a day. Closing the markets – something I was instructed to arrange on a number of occasions in my early days at the Treasury – would now be a completely futile gesture. The international context of macroeconomic policy is important. Policy here is inevitably affected by actual policy in other countries and, as I have said, the behaviour of financial markets and other economies. This means that governments need to agree and support rules for international trade and monetary systems so as

to provide a framework within which the private sector can trade and invest
with confidence.   (1988)

Burns, at the Treasury since the beginning of 1980, had, in his previous
role as Professor and Director of the Centre for Economic Forecasting at
the London Business School, been associated with the 'international
monetarist' view of the way modern, open economies worked. In simple
terms, a government which allowed its money supply to grow at a faster
rate than that of other important economies would, sooner or later,
suffer a falling exchange rate. This was because, in the long-term,
currency values reflect relative inflation rates – under the familiar theory
of purchasing-power parity, exchange rates adjust so that a basket of
goods costs roughly the same wherever it is purchased. For monetarists,
relative money-supply growth rates were a lead indicator of future
relative inflation rates. High monetary growth now meant high inflation
later. The transmission mechanism from the money supply to high
inflation was, in the international monetarist view, principally the exchange rate. A government which failed to control its money supply was
effectively signalling to the foreign exchange markets that its currency
had to fall. When the currency did fall, then, through the route of
higher import prices and an easing of the financial pressure on industry,
described above, the result was higher inflation.

At the London Business School, and in his early years at the Treasury,
Burns saw the key to low inflation as, in essence, ensuring that Britain's
money supply did not grow at a faster rate than that of other countries.
By achieving this, sterling would be prevented from falling, and the
route to higher inflation would effectively be blocked. Now he saw that
it was possible to approach the same problem from the other direction.
If the Government was committed to maintaining the value of sterling
within the ERM, this would mean, in practice, that monetary policy,
and growth in the money supply, would have to be brought into line
with that commitment. In other words, the removal of the option of
allowing sterling to depreciate means that policy-makers are subject to
an important new discipline. The discipline could never be an absolute
one because the ERM, in its first few years in particular, was subject to
frequent currency realignments. The Deutschmark, for example, was
revalued (given a higher parity) on six occasions between 1979 and
1987. The French franc, Italian lira, Danish krone, Irish pound and

Currency Changes in the Exchange Rate Mechanism, 1979–87

23 September 1979	Deutschmark revalued by 2 per cent; Danish krone devalued by 3 per cent
19 November 1979	Danish krone devalued by 5 per cent
22 March 1981	Italian lira devalued by 6 per cent
4 October 1981	Deutschmark and Dutch guilder revalued by 5.5 per cent; Italian lira and French franc devalued by 3 per cent
21 February 1982	Belgian and Luxembourg franc devalued by 8.5 per cent, Danish krone by 3 per cent
12 June 1982	Deutschmark and Dutch guilder revalued by 4.25 per cent; French franc devalued by 5.75 per cent, Italian lira by 2.75 per cent
21 March 1983	Deutschmark revalued by 5.5 per cent, Dutch guilder by 3.35 per cent, Danish krone by 2.5 per cent, Belgian and Luxembourg franc by 1.5 per cent; Italian lira devalued by 2.5 per cent, Irish pound by 3.5 per cent
20 July 1985	Italian lira devalued by 6 per cent; all other currencies revalued by 2 per cent
6 April 1986	Deutschmark and Dutch guilder revalued by 3 per cent, Belgian and Luxembourg franc and Danish krone by 1 per cent; French franc devalued by 3 per cent
2 August 1986	Irish pound devalued by 8 per cent
11 January 1987	Deutschmark and Dutch guilder revalued by 3 per cent, Belgian and Luxembourg franc by 2 per cent

Source: Dennis Swann, *The Economics of the Common Market*, 6th edn, Penguin Books 1988, p.199.

Belgian and Luxembourg franc were all devalued on several occasions, either as part of the general realignments that included revaluations of the Deutschmark (and Dutch guilder), or individually, as the table shows.

Even allowing for the fact that the ERM was not a system of permanently fixed parities (although there have been no general realignments since January 1987), the discipline was still important. Currency changes between ERM members in the first half of the 1980s had been smaller than between other, freely floating currencies. In addition, British governments had traditionally viewed devaluation as a defeat for policy, and not as a flexible policy instrument. It was reasonable to assert, therefore, that faced with the 'embarrassment factor' of negotiating a sterling devaluation, a British government would favour adjusting its policies to suit the existing exchange rate, and not vice versa.

Lawson, Middleton and Burns, as architects of the medium-term financial strategy, had moved from a position where, publicly, the exchange rate occupied only a minor role in economic-policy formulation, to one where it was central. Sterling's entry into the ERM, they reasoned, was the missing piece in the policy jigsaw. They had powerful allies in government, in the City and in industry. The task now – and they were under no misapprehension about its difficulty – was to convince Margaret Thatcher.

The Thatcher Veto

Lawson, in spite of finding himself on the wrong side of two sharp shifts in the value of the pound in the space of six months, still enjoyed a high reputation, not least with the Prime Minister. Thatcher, on appointing him, had observed that 'Nigel' knew everything there was to know about money. Later she was to say, repeatedly, that her Chancellor was 'brilliant'. Middleton, appointed Permanent Secretary to the Treasury in 1983 over the heads of more senior men, was a Thatcher favourite. Burns, having been instrumental in shaping Conservative economic thinking through the London Business School before 1979 had, in his period as Chief Economic Adviser, helped achieve the low inflation that the Prime Minister regarded as paramount. Now, all three were advising that the Government should set a timetable for taking sterling into the ERM.

ERM entry was discussed by the Cabinet in July 1985 and, over the following weeks an impressive dossier of Treasury evidence was assembled, putting the case for entry. It had been right to focus policy on control of the money supply in the Government's early years, the Treasury argued. The rise in the exchange rate in the early 1980s had been a necessary adjunct to the monetary squeeze needed to exorcize the high inflation of the 1970s. Now, however, things were different. The task was not mainly that of getting inflation down, even though the official aim was to achieve zero inflation. Rather, the task was to lock in the Government's success against inflation, which had fallen below 4 per cent in 1983, was 5 per cent at the beginning of 1985 but, partly as a consequence of sterling's July 1984 and January 1985 falls, was rising to 7 per cent by the middle of 1985. Policy had undergone a gradual shift. The exchange rate, virtually ignored in 1979–80, had come to assume a vital role in interest rate decisions. The time had come, therefore, to formalize this change, by the adoption of an explicit exchange rate target in the context of the ERM.

Lawson began to drop broad hints, often in briefings to journalists, indicating his own change of stance. Thatcher was brought along gradually, and subtly. Treasury officials who were known to get on with the Prime Minister were sent to Downing Street to brief her. Within Cabinet, those in favour of ERM entry outnumbered and outranked those, like Thatcher, who were temperamentally opposed to what they regarded as artificial interference in the currency markets. There were ministers who were forthrightly opposed to entry, notably Nicholas Ridley, then the Transport Secretary. But he was not part of the Cabinet's inner circle of economic decision-makers.

Other Prime Ministers, faced with such a barrage of official and ministerial advice, might have bowed under the pressure. Thatcher was different, for several reasons. Her economic thinking, while rarely sophisticated, was powerfully instinctive. She had read, and been heavily influenced by, free-market thinkers such as Friedrich von Hayek and Milton Friedman. The whole philosophy of her Government, embodied in the decision to remove all exchange controls in October 1979, five months after her first election victory, was based upon the free market. Would it not be a huge irony for a government that was espousing the free market in all its actions to accept that, in the important area of exchange rates, the market would be subject to a high degree of governmental interference? Would it not also be, and this struck a nerve, a U-turn of the most blatant kind, of the sort that her critics were always waiting for her to commit?

A second difficulty was presented by Thatcher's attitude to Europe. She was suspicious of the motives of her fellow Community leaders and, to an even greater extent, of the European Commission. Her dealings with Europe, at a succession of European Council meetings (six-monthly summits of heads of government and foreign ministers), had been characterized by battles, often bitter ones, over aspects of the Community which she considered to be operating against British interests, and most

notably Britain's contributions to the Community budget. In this antagon-
istic atmosphere, which still existed in 1985, the idea of ERM entry
was a difficult one for her to accept. The ERM, she believed, was held
together with exactly the type of exchange controls that Britain had
abandoned six years earlier. Even had she been more in favour of the
notion of managed exchange rates, Lawson would have had a better
chance persuading her to accept a link with the dollar. Suggestions that
sterling's ERM entry was inevitable did not cut much ice either. If it
was inevitable, and the rest of the Community wanted it, then Thatcher
took the view that it could be kept in reserve, for use as a bargaining
counter in future European negotiations.

Lawson, in trying to carry the argument in favour of entry, also faced
another important obstacle. Sir Alan Walters, one of pioneers of the
revival in British monetarism, later to be described as the Rasputin in
the Prime Minister's court, was her full-time personal economic adviser
in 10 Downing Street from January 1981 to October 1983. Thatcher
thought of most economists as jargon-ridden and rarely able to devise a
clear policy prescription. Walters, who met Thatcher through the Institute of Economic Affairs, had impressed her with his plain speaking and
incisiveness. Their roots were similar, she the daughter of a Lincolnshire
shopkeeper, he the son of a Leicester shop worker. And he had succumbed to the brain drain under the 1974-9 Labour Government,
moving from the London School of Economics to Johns Hopkins University in Baltimore.

By 1985 Walters was back in the United States, with posts at the
World Bank in Washington and at Johns Hopkins. He was, however, in
frequent contact with Thatcher, by telephone and on his visits to
London. Perhaps even more than Thatcher, he considered the ERM,
and UK membership of it, to be a thoroughly bad idea. Walters had
advised Thatcher in the early 1980s that the strength of the pound,
when it climbed above $2.40, indicated that monetary policy in Britain
was excessively tight. He was not, however, in favour of exchange rate
targets. As he was to write in his book *Britain's Economic Renaissance*:

> Exchange rate movements must generally be considered as rather dubious
> indicators of monetary conditions. There are exceptional circumstances where
> very large exchange rate movements, combined with other evidence, may be
> used as a clinching argument. (I shall argue that this was the case in the

winter of 1980–81.) But one should not look to exchange rates for any subtle interpretation of monetary conditions. (1986, p. 134)

Sterling, he argued, was subject to a wide range of influences, some of them reflecting the stance of monetary policy in Britain, but others due to political or economic developments abroad, well outside the control of the British authorities. The foreign exchange markets, in addition, were liable to favour or reject specific currencies for ill-defined reasons to do with 'confidence', rumour or fashion.

Entry into the exchange rate mechanism of the EMS, which would make the management of the exchange rate the central aim of policy, would institutionalize such difficulties. He wrote:

> The conclusion is that it is difficult to see what the United Kingdom would gain from joining the EMS. Certainly under the Thatcher Government, and conceivably under alternative governments, there has been no need to bolster the anti-inflationary policies with pseudo-fixed parities of the kind practised in the EMS. At most the EMS might reduce the very short-term (weekly or monthly) variations in the exchange rate against the EMS currencies. But research suggests that because of thick and almost perfect forward markets such short-term movements have little if any effect in inhibiting trade. On the other hand, those who seek eventual monetary union of Europe had best pursue it through quantitative convergence rather than exchange rate fixity. Britain will best serve monetary union in Europe by urging the right policies rather than embracing the wrong ones. (1986, p. 130)

In his 1986 book, which was completed in October 1985, at the height of the debate over sterling's entry into the ERM, Walters advanced what came to be known as the 'Walters critique' of the mechanism. The principal argument in favour of membership, it will be recalled, was that it would exert a low-inflation discipline on the British economy, by effectively latching on to German monetary policy. The advice Thatcher was receiving from Walters suggested, however, that things would work in a very different way. In a situation in which no currency realignments were expected, he argued, the foreign exchange markets would favour those currencies which offered the highest interest rates, typically high-inflation economies such as Italy. Low-inflation economies like Germany would then, paradoxically, suffer weak currencies. The result was that Italy would be under pressure to reduce interest rates to make the lira less attractive, while for Germany the pressure would work in the opposite direction. Left to work through, the level of interest rates in high-inflation Italy and low-inflation Germany would converge, meaning, according to Walters, 'there will be great pressure to expand money and credit in Italy, whereas in Germany there will be a substantial financial squeeze' (1986, pp. 126–7).

Thus, far from bringing about similar inflation performances among the ERM member countries, the mechanism could drive them further apart. Walters recognized that there were frequent realignments of currencies within the system but this, he said, merely added to its inherent instability, resulting in large flows between currencies on expectations of realignments, and correspondingly large flows in the opposite direction once the realignment had occurred.

Apart from his economic arguments against entry, Walters also advised Thatcher that, with the general election perhaps only eighteen months away, entry could be politically very dangerous. His argument was that, with Labour then opposed to membership, the currency markets would sell the pound in the run-up to the election, for fear of an Opposition victory. A similar event had occurred before Thatcher's June 1983 election victory, when the Labour shadow chancellor Peter Shore said that his party, if elected, would seek a 30 per cent devaluation of sterling. Shore's comments then had undermined sterling, and forced a temporary rise in interest rates. Inside the ERM the situation was much more explosive. The Government could be faced with a choice between the embarrassment of negotiating a devaluation of the pound (it is the Conservative Party's proud boast that they have never devalued sterling) or raising interest rates to politically unacceptable levels. Either course, suggested Walters, would work to the Government's disadvantage and could lose the election.

Thatcher, bolstered by the anti-ERM arguments of Walters, by the minority of Cabinet ministers who supported her view and, perhaps most importantly, by her own instincts, rejected the Treasury arguments in favour of entry. Treasury officials decided that the technical arguments advanced against entry by Walters and others were the least of their problems. 'She had her prejudices, and she would use others' arguments if they supported them,' said one. 'But we were left in no doubt that her opposition went very deep.' Not for the first time, she had ruled against the advice of one of her ministers and his department, in this case the Chancellor and the Treasury, Whitehall's most important power base. The only change to come out of the episode was that it was agreed that the issue would be re-examined, although probably not until after the general election, and that entry would take place at some point in the future when 'the time is ripe'.

A crucial meeting on entry took place before the Treasury's November 1985 Autumn Statement. As William Keegan described it, in his book *Mr Lawson's Gamble*:

> Those present at the key autumn 1985 meeting about the EMS included Mrs Thatcher, Willie Whitelaw (the Deputy Prime Minister), Sir Geoffrey Howe, Foreign Secretary, and Leon Brittan, then Secretary of State for Trade and Industry, as well as the Chancellor and senior Treasury and Bank officials. All favoured joining the exchange rate mechanism. She turned to Whitelaw last. He said: 'All seven of your advisers have voted "aye".' 'Yes,' she said, echoing Abraham Lincoln, 'Ayes seven, noes one, the noes have it.'   (1989, p. 181)

By November 1985, Lawson's bid to take the pound into the ERM had been put on to the back burner. Entry, having been actively canvassed by the Treasury, was now said to be 'in a box' and not to be opened for some time. Thatcher's concession, that entry was a question of 'not if, but when', was small comfort to him. Lawson was angry and frustrated. 'Nigel told us that she wouldn't take it and we would have to go along as best as we could,' said a senior official. Friends said that this was one of two occasions before his last stormy period in 1989 when he 'flashed the amber light' over his political future, having made it clear that he had no political ambitions beyond the Chancellorship. The other occasion was when, against his advice, the Cabinet decided to press ahead with a new system of local authority finance, the Community Charge, commonly known as the poll tax.

Lawson and Howe, who were both prominent in the 1985 attempt to persuade Thatcher on ERM entry, were later to blame her refusal for Britain's subsequent resurgence of inflation and its recessionary aftermath.

Howe, in his devastating resignation speech on 13 November 1990, said, 'It is now, alas, impossible to resist the conclusion that today's higher rates of inflation could well have been avoided had the question of ERM membership been properly considered and resolved at a much earlier stage' (1990).

Lawson took a similar view. He said in the House of Commons on

23 October 1990. 'The real tragedy is that we did not join the exchange
rate mechanism of the EMS at least five years ago. It was not for want
of trying, as a number of my then colleagues can testify.'

The full extent of the conflict within the Government on the ERM
issue was to become clear later. For now, Lawson had the task of
managing the economy, having dismantled most of the Government's
monetarist framework, and without a new discipline to put in its place.

4

THE PRE-ELECTION BOOM

An Unemployment Black Mark

Baulked on the ERM, and with monetarism effectively no more, Lawson was left to run economic policy according to his own judgement. Even in the Treasury there was concern about how what was known as 'Nanny knows best' policy, would proceed. In the City, where Lawson was said to be flying by the seat of his pants, the worries were greater. The Chancellor had displayed his cleverness far more than Sir Geoffrey Howe, his trustworthy predecessor, who had acquired a reputation for dullness. Occasionally, however, financial-market pundits found themselves arguing that, where Chancellors were concerned, dullness could be a virtue. But, on Lawson's side was the fact that, whether by accident or design, the economy had consistently performed better, with faster growth and lower inflation, than the pessimists had expected.

Lawson, in his October 1985 Mansion House speech in the City, in which he suspended the target for the sterling M3 measure of broad money, was confident enough to take the pundits to task for their pessimism. Later he was to describe some of them as 'teenage City scribblers'. For now, he could afford to be slightly more charitable: 'At this time of year it has become customary for the pundits to revise upwards their expectations of growth for the current year. At the same time they invariably conclude that the next year will see a marked slowdown. They have been promising this for the past three years. I suppose if they go on for long enough, they are bound to be right. But I see no sign of it yet' (1985).

In an address which had been devoted to junking many of the principles on which the Government's monetarist experiment had been based, Lawson was also sure enough of himself to predict that the success of the anti-inflation policy would continue. In doing so he used a phrase that was to return to haunt him. He said, 'The acid test of monetary policy is its record in reducing inflation. Those who wish to join in the debate about the intricacies of different measures of money and the implications they may have for the future are welcome to do so. But at the end of the day the position is clear and unambiguous. *The inflation rate is judge and jury*' (1985). The italics are mine, but the inference was obvious. Policy had succeeded in its aims, and would continue to do so. The one black mark was unemployment, which was above 3 million, and which did not peak until the middle of the following year. In 1985, indeed, when the gentle upswing that had begun in 1981 appeared to have run out of steam, the worry was that it might not peak at all. Sir Alan Walters, in his 1986 book *Britain's Economic Renaissance*, suggested that this blemish on an otherwise generally successful picture was due to high real wages, themselves brought about by the fact that wage negotiators had consistently under-estimated the Government's success in containing inflation. Other expla-nations included the rapid growth in the labour force, both because of the number of young people reaching working age, and because of a sharp rise in the employment, and availability for work, of married women. Between 1979 and 1985, the workforce increased from 26.6 million to 27.7 million, alongside an increase in unemployment from 1.3 million to 3.3 million. One of the Government's difficulties was that those jobs that were being created, many of them part-time service-sector posts, were occupied by women entering or re-entering the workforce, and failed to make a dent in the rising unemployment total.

Ministerial speeches during this period stressed the remarkable resili-ence of the British economy. It had recovered from the worst recession of the post-war period, against the predictions of many experts. The favourite Aunt Sally was the letter of March 1981, instituted by Profes-sors Frank Hahn and Robert Neild of Cambridge and signed by 364 economists, including four former government Chief Economic Advisers. The letter warned that 'present policies will deepen the depression, erode the industrial base of our economy and threaten its social and political stability'. Unfortunately, its drafters had failed to pick up that, while pursuing a tight budgetary policy and with some limited success in controlling public expenditure, the Government was also relaxing monetary policy, through lower interest rates and a lower exchange rate, and this provided the basis for recovery. More recently, the economy had been troubled by the uncertainties of the Falklands war, which lasted from April to June 1982. And, most impressively of all, a national, although not unanimous, strike by the National Union of Mineworkers in 1984–5 had been defeated without significant economic dislocation.

But, resilient or not, there were still the considerable problems of high and rising unemployment. The Government had introduced a plethora of job creation and training schemes, initially for young workers but eventually covering all groups. A March 1985 Department of Employment White Paper, 'Employment: The Challenge for the Nation', called for a more flexible response from the labour force, including pay restraint, improvements in the industrial-relations climate, job-sharing and earlier retirement. The inference was that the Government saw little scope for reducing unemployment through faster economic growth alone. The unemployment total had been redefined on a number of occasions in order to exclude certain groups. The independent Unemployment Unit logged eighteen changes in the calculation of the official statistics, the overwhelming majority of which had had the effect of reducing the total. But the number of jobless kept on rising, tarnishing official claims of economic success and raising serious doubts about the Government's re-election prospects. In 1983, Thatcher had swept to victory on the back of the Falklands victory, a weak and divided Labour party, sharply improving prospects for those who had remained in work and the promise that, after the sacrifice of the early 1980s, better times were ahead for all. The Government was re-elected in spite of high unemployment and the severity of the 1980–81 recession. But in 1985–6 there was no guarantee that, with the rising unemployment total standing in open contradiction to at least one of those promises, the same would happen again.

Opinion polls showed unemployment to be a major public concern, often *the* major public concern. In April 1985, backed by three former Prime Ministers, Lord Callaghan, Lord Wilson and Edward Heath, the Employment Institute, and its sister organization, the Charter for Jobs, were founded. The Employment Institute, headed by ex-Treasury economist Jon Shields, was a think-tank which, in a series of academic and political papers, ensured that the debate on unemployment was high on the Government's agenda. The Charter for Jobs, a campaigning organization, enlisted the help of show-business figures to increase the publicity value of its campaign. One of its ideas, which proved too ambitious, was that the unemployed should join hands along a line stretching from Liverpool to London, called Hands Across Britain. It was attempted, in May 1987, but there were enough gaps in the line to persuade ministers that it had failed. That, however, was later.

Lord Young of Graffham, variously the Vice-Chairman of the Conservative Party, and Secretary of State in the Departments of Employment and Trade and Industry under Thatcher, recalls one meeting with the Prime Minister in the summer of 1985: 'Parliament rose for the vacation and I had my last meeting with the Prime Minister. I found her tired and worried about unemployment. She thought that we were losing the battle for people's hearts and minds on the issue. We were halfway through the term and she knew that the changes she would have to make this time would take us through to the election' (1990, p. 149).

The Government, therefore, needed to turn around the rising unemployment total before the general election and, preferably, far enough before it so that any reduction was firmly fixed in the public mind. The first requirement was for faster economic growth. The 1980–81 recession had been the worst in the post-war period and the recovery from it was slow. In 1982 the economy grew by less than 2 per cent. Over the 1982–5 period its growth rate was 2.75 per cent, below the average performance in the 1950s and 1960s, and in no sense an accelerated catching-up process after the recession of the early 1980s. The economy was not generating enough growth to absorb the rise in the labour force and the shake-out of workers from manufacturing, mining and other sectors which continued to shed labour long after the recession was over.

The second need was for further action to manipulate the official unemployment total. Lord Young was appointed by Thatcher to succeed Tom King as Employment Secretary at the beginning of September 1985. A businessman by background, he was subject to the regular criticism from Opposition politicians and, more discreetly from his colleagues, that he had risen to the Cabinet without having had to seek the approval of the electorate. Perhaps because of this he was less nervous than other ministers about the political sensitivities he risked exposing with his actions. In the autumn of 1985 he called a meeting of senior officials in the Department of Employment. He later described this meeting:

'Why don't we invite all the long-term unemployed in for an interview,' I suggested. 'Let us put every scheme we have together. We would have something to offer to all. Besides,' I could not help adding, 'it will stop them working on the black economy.' At this point some of my officials began to look uncomfortable and shortly afterwards the meeting broke up so officials could work on the details. (1990, p. 159)

The scheme that emerged, initially as a pilot programme in January 1986, was called Jobstart and later rechristened Restart. Under the scheme, first tried in Crawley and Horsham, Ealing, Plymouth, Stoke-on-Trent, Preston, Billingham, Huddersfield, Dundee and Neath, the long-term unemployed were invited to their local Jobcentre and offered either a job, or a place on one of the many government job-creation or job-assistance programmes, including the Community Programme, Job Clubs or help under the Enterprise Allowance Scheme. The aim was twofold. It would bring the long-term unemployed, many of whom had given up the search for work, back into the labour market. More controversially, it would weed out those who were continuing to claim state benefits but were working, and, with the connivance of employers who could use them as a cheap source of labour, not declaring their income.

The pilot programme was judged by its success in removing the long-term jobless from the unemployment register and, as soon became clear, it had the desired effect. A significant proportion of those invited for interview voluntarily left the register rather than attend. Overall in the pilot areas the number of long-term unemployed leaving the register was more than 10 per cent higher than in other, similar areas, where Restart was not operating. Department of Employment officials calculated that, if this experience was repeated on a national basis then 20,000–25,000 extra people would leave the unemployment register each month. Young negotiated with the Treasury for extra funds for the various employment creation schemes and, on 1 July 1986, the Restart scheme went national. Although it was not immediately clear, the introduction of the national scheme coincided with a downturn in unemployment which came, conveniently, a year before the June 1987 general election. The fall was to persist until March 1990.

Restart, despite the importance of its effects, was not quite enough to achieve the political aim of reducing public concern over unemployment. The monthly unemployment figures were subject to detailed scrutiny.

Changes in the method of calculation of the figures meant that optimistic government claims over the future course of unemployment were viewed with scepticism. On one occasion, Young took over the regular monthly briefing on the unemployment figures, normally handled by his officials, and urged journalists to put more faith in the Government's claims about falling unemployment. The assembled industrial and economics correspondents were unconvinced, and it showed in the coverage of the figures. The Conservative Party needed to demonstrate that the decline in the jobless total was genuine and sustainable, and not merely due to the one-off effects of the introduction of Restart.

Going for Growth

Economic growth was, therefore, vital. The question was: how could Lawson put the economy on to a faster growth track? The answer came in three parts. The abandonment of the Government's monetarist experiment, clearly signalled in the autumn of 1985 and hammered home over the following twelve months, had the effect of giving the Chancellor much more room for manoeuvre, although few people realized it at the time. In general, the message from the Treasury and the Bank of England, that the sterling M3 money-supply measure had become so distorted that its abandonment as a target was of no significance, was accepted.

An exception was Tim Congdon, a former economics correspondent on *The Times* and, in the mid 1980s, economist with the City firm of L. Messel & Co. Congdon argued that, after making realistic allowances for banking deregulation and changes in the coverage of the banking statistics, the underlying growth of sterling M3 had until that point been held close to the official target ranges. Thus, the Government's performance in restraining money-supply growth in line with its targets had been more successful than it appeared, or than it was prepared to give itself credit for.

The abandonment of the sterling M3 target was another matter. This, he argued, would allow the Government to expand the economy more rapidly than had hitherto been the case. But it would also lead to a resurgence of inflation. Congdon's warnings on this score began in 1985 and continued, usually as a lonely voice in the wilderness, even as most economists were prepared to put their trust in Lawson.

On the morning of the October 1985 Mansion House speech, writing as a guest contributor to *The Times*, Congdon warned of the uncomfortable parallels between the strong growth in the money supply then and in the early stages of the Barber boom in 1972–3. Four months later, also in *The Times*, he wrote that Treasury ministers and officials, 'must decide whether, having sinned, they should enjoy it or repent'. He wrote, 'Every day more evidence becomes available that the rapid growth of sterling M3 is not misleading but is having standard and predictable effects on economic behaviour' (1986).

That evidence was, firstly, that house prices had begun the boom that was to last until the summer of 1988 and, secondly, that on the back of a strong rise in bank borrowing, companies had embarked on a rash of takeover activity.

In October 1986, by which time the annual rate of growth of sterling M3 had leapt to 18.5 per cent, Congdon and his colleague Peter Warburton produced a forecast of astonishing accuracy. Writing in Messel's quarterly UK macroeconomic forecast, they said:

> Unless excessive credit growth is checked by an early rise in interest rates, or the authorities are prepared to resume overfunding, we can see no solution to the problem. If corrective action is postponed for another six months to a year, it is very likely that Britain will record sharply higher inflation than today ... That will be bad news for the financial markets. However, it is important to emphasize the positive aspects of the forecast. The cost of Mr Lawson's monetary boomlet may be 10 per cent inflation in two or three years' time, but the benefit will be rather vigorous growth – of 4 per cent in 1987 and 3 per cent in 1988 – of gross domestic product. This may be sufficient to cause a significant decline in unemployment and so ensure that the Conservatives are elected for a third term of government. (1986a)

Overfunding, the systematic process by which the Bank of England would sell more government securities (gilts) to the financial markets than was needed to meet the public-sector borrowing requirement, had been used extensively in the first half of the 1980s. But its use as a means of restraining money-supply growth was dropped along with the sterling M3 target. The only shortcoming of the Congdon–Warburton forecast was that it did not go far enough in predicting the length and exuberance of the Lawson boom. As the expansionary policy continued beyond the 1987 election, growth, rather than slowing in 1988, accelerated.

Congdon is bitter about the episode. 'Nobody was listening to me,' he said later. Officials say now that such warnings were taken seriously in the Treasury and the Bank of England. According to one senior Treasury adviser, 'There was definitely a feeling that we risked being somewhat naked and vulnerable to a resurgence in inflation. We would sit around, poring over the figures, trying to make sure that nothing was going wrong.'

The period was one in which, however, with the Government having abandoned the sterling M3 target upon which the medium-term financial strategy was based, officials were encouraged to find reasons for ignoring the message of the money-supply figures. These were not hard to find. Financial liberalization, it was argued, had changed the meaning of the monetary data, to the point where strong money-supply growth no longer constituted an inflationary danger. The Treasury and Bank of England, initially embarrassed at the failure to hit the official money-supply targets in the first half of the 1980s, now saw virtue in this failure. It had not, they said, prevented a decisive fall in inflation then, so why worry about strong growth in the money supply now?

Lawson had set the tone in his October 1985 Mansion House speech. He said, 'I am satisfied that the growth of M3 in recent years reflects a genuine desire on the part of the private sector to increase its liquidity on a lasting basis. So it does not presage higher inflation' (1985).

The result was one of those shifts in the parameters of economic policy that, all too often, have damaged the British economy. Before Thatcher, governments had paid close attention to the growth of credit, using direct controls to restrict it. The Thatcher Government, when elected, elevated the importance of money and credit in the formulation of economic policy. But, once the broad money targets had served their purpose, the Government switched to a position in which, ironically, it took a less responsible attitude to credit growth than its predecessors. The baby was thrown out with the bath-water, and only a small number of people spotted it.

Lawson did take advice from outside the Treasury. The group of outside economists known informally as the Gooeys included Professor Alan Budd of the London Business School, Professor Patrick Minford of Liverpool University, Professor Harold Rose, economic adviser to Barclays Bank, and Professor Geoffrey Maynard of Reading, as well as the journalist Samuel Brittan of the *Financial Times*. They saw few risks in what Lawson was doing.

Budd, who was appointed government Chief Economic Adviser in August 1991, succeeding his former London Business School colleague Sir Terence Burns (who had been promoted to Permanent Secretary to the Treasury), said of the 1985–6 period: 'There is an enormous amount of after-the-event wisdom around. At the time I cannot remember any strong lobbying for a change in policy. Perhaps we lowered our guard.'

Depreciating the Pound

Lawson, as described in Chapter 3, had tried to persuade Thatcher in 1985 that it was time to fix sterling's level against European currencies by joining the exchange rate mechanism of the European Monetary System. In 1986, however, he put into practice an entirely different policy, that of securing a deliberate fall in the pound in order to boost the economy. The January 1985 sterling crisis had been triggered by fears of a plunge in world oil prices. A year later, such fears proved to have been justified. Disarray within the Organization of Petroleum Exporting Countries (OPEC) in 1985–6 had the effect of producing a glut of oil on world markets, and prices responded accordingly. North Sea oil, trading at $30 a barrel in the autumn of 1985, lost more than a third of its value by January 1986 and, by the spring, had plummeted to less than $10 a barrel.

In his March 1986 Budget speech, Lawson was sanguine about the effects on Britain of such a sharp fall in oil prices. He said, 'If we can survive unscathed the loss of half our North Sea revenues in less than twenty-five weeks, then the prospective loss of the other half over the remainder of the next twenty-five years should not cause us undue concern' (1986).

Two years earlier, in a speech in Cambridge, Lawson had offered the view that a sustained fall in world oil prices would require a decline in the real exchange rate of sterling. As oil prices fell, therefore, Treasury policy was to allow the pound to decline in parallel. The arguments for doing so were twofold. Lower oil prices would reduce the balance of payments support that the North Sea had provided for the British economy in the 1980s. Thus, non-oil exports had to take on a bigger role, and one way of encouraging this was by giving exporters a competitive boost by means of a lower exchange rate. In addition, a sharp fall in oil prices would have a powerful beneficial effect on

Britain's inflation – the rate dropped to just 2.4 per cent in the summer of 1986. The Government could, therefore, afford to risk a fall in the pound, knowing that inflationary pressures in the economy were extremely subdued.

And so the pound was allowed to fall. The sterling index, the pound's average value against a basket of currencies, based on 1985 = 100, was 101.4 in the final quarter of 1985. A year later it was down to 85.1, a drop of 16 per cent. This was bigger, and achieved with far less fuss, than the Wilson Government's 14 per cent devaluation of November 1967, over which so much political blood had been spilt. This time, the pound did not fall much against the dollar. Lawson, along with fellow finance ministers and central bankers of the Group of Five (the United States, Britain, Germany, Japan and France), had forged an agreement at the Plaza Hotel, New York, on 21 September 1985, which had as its aim the achievement of a sharply lower dollar. As it was, sterling stayed in a narrow range, roughly $1.40–1.50, against the weakening dollar, but fell sharply against other currencies. The rate against the Deutschmark, which could have been fixed at DM3.75 as a result of ERM entry in the autumn of 1985, fell to DM2.87 by the final quarter of 1986, a plunge of nearly 25 per cent.

Treasury and Bank of England officials became concerned about the speed of the pound's fall as 1986 progressed. These worries came to a head at the annual meetings of the International Monetary Fund and World Bank at the end of September 1986. Sterling was falling fast and, while the official reserves had been increased when the Government had issued a $4bn floating-rate note at the beginning of the month, more support was needed. After requests in Washington by Lawson and Robin Leigh-Pemberton, the Governor of the Bank of England, the German Bundesbank agreed to help support sterling, but the episode illustrated the tightrope Lawson was walking in seeking a controlled depreciation of the pound.

The drop in oil prices had given way to market worries about the Thatcher Government's re-election prospects. But, with unemployment having started to fall after rising almost continuously since Thatcher had come to power in 1979, there was a reluctance to take draconian action to halt sterling's slide.

As one official said, 'We definitely let the pound fall too far but what else could we do. For most of that period the criticism of the Treasury was that interest rates were too high and growth in the economy too low.'

Lawson too, interviewed in 1990 for *Annual Meeting News*, a newspaper produced for the Washington meetings of the International Monetary Fund and World Bank, conceded that he had allowed the pound 'to fall further than it should have done'.

At the time, however, freed from the constraints of his money-supply target, Lawson reduced interest rates as fast as the policy of securing an orderly decline in sterling would allow. By the end of 1985 base rates had been cut to 11.5 per cent, from their crisis level of 14 per cent in January of that year. By the spring of 1986 they were down to 10 per cent.

In the autumn of 1986, however, Lawson faced a problem. Although the rate of inflation, helped by a slump in world oil prices, had dropped to 2.4 per cent in the summer of 1986, there were clear indications that it was heading higher. A further fall in sterling, through the mechanism of higher import prices and an easing of the competitive pressure on the company sector, would guarantee that rise. Not for the last time, Lawson faced an uncomfortable Conservative Party conference, rising to make his speech in response to the economic debate on 9 October with the markets waiting to hear something that would provide help for the beleaguered pound. The Chancellor, however, made a straightforward political speech, which did little to reassure the financial markets. His only reference was in a section in which he attacked the Labour Party's economic programme. 'No wonder the financial markets have been nervous,' he said.

Lawson, with the help of the Bundesbank, got through the party conference. But less than a week later, on 14 October, he had to bow to the inevitable and raise interest rates from 10 to 11 per cent. The setback was, however, only a temporary one. Although base rates remained at 11 per cent throughout the winter, the Chancellor was able to cut them well in time for the June 1987 election. Four half-point base-rate cuts, the first on 10 March and the final one on 11 May, brought rates down to a vote-winning 9 per cent level. The strategy had worked, with only one serious hiccup. Indeed, by June 1987, with talk among City dealers that a third Thatcher election victory would bring a 'wall of money' from Japan to invest in Britain, the problem was not that the pound was too weak but that it was beginning to rise strongly. The wall

of money, much discussed and predicted, never actually arrived. Amid
the market euphoria which greeted Thatcher's return to office, however,
this was not a major consideration.

Priming the Pump

Throughout the post-war period, economists had recognized that, wherever possible, governments sought to boost the economy by using fiscal
policy – higher public spending and lower taxation – to influence the
outcomes of general elections. Priming the pump to provide a pre-
election boom had become standard post-war practice.

According to one account, in *British Economic Policy, 1960–74*, edited
by Frank Blackaby:

> Excessive reflation has been explained by reference to the electoral cycle – the
> expansions of 1953–4, 1958–9 and 1963–4 closely preceded elections, though
> that of 1972–3 did not. Moreover, 'neutral' budgeting at the height of the
> boom might be partly attributable to reluctance to be seen altering course
> once an election has taken place, particularly if it might appear in breach of a
> pre-election declaration; the 1960 dispute between Macmillan and his Chancel-
> lor comes into this category, as does the budget of 1966. But interventions for
> immediate economic and political ends can come to be represented as strategic
> changes.   (1978, pp. 212–13)

The Conservative Government elected in 1979 was, apparently, immune
to such temptations. Economic policy was to be set in a medium-term
framework, based on control of the money supply and public-sector
borrowing, and not subject to the grubby influence of short-term
political expediency. In opposition, the party's grandly titled Economic
Reconstruction Group, chaired by Sir Geoffrey Howe, had set out the
aim in a pamphlet, *The Right Approach to the Economy*, published in
1977. It said:

> Monetary targets, openly proclaimed and explained, can have a crucial effect
> in reducing inflationary expectations. The extent of that influence will depend
> on increasing public awareness. The monetary authorities will often be subject,
> directly or indirectly, to political and industrial pressure to modify and relax
> their policies, frequently for reasons of short-term expediency. The danger of
> their yielding to such pressures will be reduced if monetary policy is the
> subject of regular and open public discussion, and if the authorities are
> expected as a matter of course to give an account of their conduct of policy
> and of their objectives for the future.   (1977)

Interestingly, as Christopher Johnson points out in his book, *The Economy under Mrs Thatcher*, the pamphlet also advocated an independent Bank of England. This recommendation was to be echoed twelve years later when, in his resignation speech, Lawson revealed that he had presented such a proposal, in a fully worked plan, to Thatcher, only to have it rejected.

The driving force of economic policy in the period was the great inflation of the 1970s and early 1980s, which had changed the nature of economic policy. No longer, it appeared, did governments have the luxury of nudging economic growth higher or lower for electoral purposes by fine-tuning fiscal policy. Instead, the overriding preoccupation was that of trying to get on top of inflation.

Lawson, in his 1984 Mais Lecture at the City University in London, set out the argument: 'It is the conquest of inflation, and not the pursuit of growth and employment, which is or should be the objective of macroeconomic policy. And it is the creation of conditions conducive to growth and employment, and not the suppression of price rises, which is or should be the objective of microeconomic policy' (1984a).

Sir Geoffrey Howe, in teeing up the economy for Thatcher's second election victory in June 1983, had bent his own rules slightly. In July 1982, hire-purchase controls were abolished, providing the basis for a pre-election increase in consumer spending. The abolition, convenient as it was in its timing, was presented as part of the Government's strategy of freeing the economy of controls. In November 1982, in his Autumn Statement, Howe took the unusual step of encouraging Whitehall departments and local authorities to meet their capital-expenditure targets. A government that had, with some difficulty, endeavoured to control public spending was now suddenly keen that there should be no underspending by central and local government. In particular, the Chancellor told local authorities to release home-improvement grants, which provided up to 90 per cent of the costs of renovating and modernizing older properties. The middle classes, keen to buy up properties for such purposes, were delighted. So too were the builders.

Howe, in his March 1983 Budget, provided yet more direct asistance for what politicians and opinion pollsters call the 'feel-good' factor. Income tax was cut in the Budget, although via the subtle route of raising personal tax allowances by more than was needed to compensate for inflation. Under the Rooker–Wise amendment to the 1977 Finance

Bill governments were required to raise personal tax allowances annually in line with inflation, except when specific exceptions are set out in the Finance Act. In 1981, when he froze allowances, Howe had overruled the Rooker–Wise amendment. In his 1983 Budget, the requirement was that allowances be lifted by 5.5 per cent, but the Chancellor went much further than this, increasing them by 14 per cent. In addition, against the advice of Treasury officials, but after considerable urging by Thatcher, Howe raised the ceiling for tax relief on mortgage interest from £25,000 to £30,000. There were two motives for this move. The first was that Tory supporters, notably those in the prosperous south with large mortgages, would benefit directly from such a move. The second was that for the mass of the home-owning electorate, including the many who had come to owner-occupation by buying their council house under the 'right-to-buy' legislation, Conservative policy was clearly distinguished from that of the Labour Party, which at that time was pledged to abolish mortgage tax relief.

The extent to which this was an openly political move, which went against the grain of Treasury thinking, was demonstrated years later. In 1988, when Lawson was Chancellor, and in 1991 under Norman Lamont, measures were introduced to restrict the coverage and revenue cost of the relief.

The Conservative Government, with Howe as Chancellor, had acted in the traditional pre-election manner, in spite of ministers' determined disavowal of such actions. Although the election result was a landslide victory for Thatcher, with a post-war record 144-seat majority over all other parties, convincing the electorate that the economy was improving was a closer-run thing. In the monthly opinion polls conducted by Market & Opinion Research International (MORI) for the *Sunday Times*, economic optimism did not revive decisively until April, two months before the election. Asked whether the economy would get better or worse over the next twelve months, the response of MORI's sample did not turn from negative to positive (a net expectation of an improving economy) until then.

In 1983, the contrast between the Government's pre-election generosity and its post-election policies was stark. Lawson, on succeeding Howe as Chancellor after the June 1983 election victory, introduced, in one of his first acts, an emergency package of spending cuts and additional privatization, with the aim of reining back a burgeoning public-sector borrowing requirement.

Tax Cuts Come Back in Favour

As the 1987 election approached, the question was not whether the Government would attempt to provide a pre-election boost for the economy but, rather, what form it would take. In early 1986, as described earlier, the major economic event was the collapse in world oil prices. For Britain, the concern was about the loss, both of tax revenues from North Sea oil and the crucial support that oil exports had provided for the balance of payments. Lawson's policy of making room for the non-oil manufacturing and services sectors to grow into the balance of payments gap left by falling oil prices had centred on the deliberate depreciation of the pound. Until this occurred, however, there was a risk, both of an elimination of the large current-account surpluses of the first half of the 1980s, and of a rise in public-sector borrowing as a result of the loss of oil revenues.

Lawson was, therefore, apparently restricted in his room for man-oeuvre on fiscal policy. Until the oil market settled down after the collapse from $30 to under $10 a barrel in the price of internationally traded oil, the future course of oil revenues could not be predicted with any certainty. The consensus outside the Treasury, was, therefore, that much as the Government would like to do so, there was precious little room for stimulative fiscal action ahead of the election. Not for the first time, Lawson was to prove the consensus wrong.

The March 1986 Budget, which had been expected to be neutral, contained one important surprise. The basic rate of income tax, which had been reduced from 33 to 30 per cent in Howe's bold Budget of June 1979 (and paid for by an increase in value added tax from 8 and 12.5 per cent to 15 per cent) had not been reduced further. Indeed, ministers and officials stressed that it was preferable to raise income-tax allowances and thresholds, because this helped those on lower earnings, rather than cut tax rates. In his March 1986 Budget, however, Lawson reverted to a strategy of cutting the basic rate of income tax, which he reduced from 30 to 29 per cent.

There were three reasons for this. The first was that cuts in tax rates, which had the virtue of being highly visible, were more likely to engender the recovery in consumer confidence necessary for a pre-election recovery in spending. Similarly, cutting tax rates again allowed the Conservative Government to distinguish clearly its policies from those of the Labour Opposition. Thirdly, the Government was stung by unfavourable comparisons between its tax-cutting record and that of the Reagan Administration in the United States, which had succeeded in reducing tax rates decisively, albeit at the expense of an enormous budget deficit.

The decision to cut the basic rate of tax, effectively eschewing the earlier principle that tax reductions should benefit those on lower incomes as much as possible, marked a shift towards a bolder tax philosophy within the Government. No longer was it necessary to justify each tax change on egalitarian grounds. Rather, tax cuts that benefited the wealth creators would generate the economic expansion that would, eventually, percolate through to those on lower incomes. As Lawson was to say later, 'You don't make the poor rich by making the rich poor.' He added, with reference to the higher rates of income tax, 'I think we may very well, particularly if you look at what's happened in America, need to bring our top rate down further' (1987a).

The March 1986 tax cut was significant as much for what it signalled about future policy as for its direct impact. Even so, in combination with the favourable effects on inflation of lower oil prices, with the rate touching a low of 2.4 per cent in the summer of 1986, the result was a substantial boost in spending power. Average earnings growth failed to respond to the oil-induced fall in inflation, and underlying earnings growth never fell below 7.5 per cent a year during this period. Thus, real personal disposable incomes rose by 4.2 per cent in 1986, the biggest annual increase since Thatcher had come to power in 1979. The surprise was not that the electorate felt better about their economic circumstances, but that it took so long for them to do so: a sharp recovery in consumer confidence did not take place until the early months of 1987.

Politically, the potential drawback of tax cuts was the accusation, levelled at ministers by the Labour Party, that the reductions were achieved only through the neglect of public spending. By the following autumn, following the annual public spending round between the Treasury and departmental ministers, Lawson had the means to tackle this charge. The Treasury's Autumn Statement, on 6 November, had been framed during a period of some difficulty for the Chancellor. As described above, his speech to the Conservative Party conference in October had been followed by the decision to raise base rates in defence of the pound. The general belief was that Lawson would attempt to secure the confidence of the financial markets by announcing a year of tight control of public spending.

On the day before the statement, the *Daily Telegraph* reported that Lawson would announce a £4bn boost to public spending. Embarrassingly, because the details of the statement had been restricted to a few senior officials, the Treasury press office dismissed the report as an invention, pointing out that such a spending boost ran counter to government policy. As it turned out, the only criticism that could be made of the *Telegraph* story was that it did not go far enough. The Chancellor's announcement was of a £4.7bn boost to public spending for the financial year beginning the following April, 1987–8, with an even larger increase, of £5.5bn, for the subsequent year, 1988–9. The *Financial Times*, commenting upon the Autumn Statement, said:

> St Augustine, who prayed 'Make me virtuous – but not yet', would have sympathized. After the ostentatious hair shirt of the last White Paper on public spending, we now have a more candid admission from the Chancellor: it will continue to grow, fast enough at least to meet some of the publicly provided services . . . Indeed, the Autumn Statement as a whole will certainly strengthen the expectation that a general election may now be a matter of months away. The spending increases seem to be tactical rather than strategic – a combination of improvements in the more visible services and pay improvements which will soften spending disciplines just where their effects are potentially most embarrassing, in hospital queues, obvious disrepair or disruptive disputes. If this means that the Government has chosen to ease spending disciplines rather than cut taxes, it may well have made a shrewd political choice and also one which we would favour on economic grounds. At a time when regional disparities are rising faster than at any time since the Second World War, and when personal incomes are rising rapidly, this is the rational course. However, it is still possible that the Government is hoping to combine some relaxation of spending discipline with tax cuts.   (1986)

The suspicions of the *Financial Times* were justified. Over the winter months, Lawson attempted, without much success, to play down expectations of tax cuts in his spring Budget. The Treasury's argument, which was to surface again later, was that the same pound could not be used twice, to finance both public spending and tax cuts.

Treasury officials, including Sir Terence Burns, the then Chief Economic Adviser, argued for a cautious 1987 Budget. They were aware of the strong growth in incomes that had resulted from the 1986 oil-price fall, and were concerned that this would spill over into too rapid a rise in spending, with adverse consequences for inflation and the balance of payments. The annual Budget planning meeting in early January, at the Foreign Secretary's official residence of Chevening in Kent, brought out differences between the officials, who thought that tax cuts could be risky, and Lawson and his political advisers, who saw them as part of an election-winning strategy. For Lawson, under strong pressure from his party and Prime Minister to present an eye-catching, vote-gathering Budget, there was little option but to regard the advice of his officials as little more than the natural caution of non-political civil servants. The one rearguard action he successfully fought against prime-ministerial pressure, to the approval of his officials, was in resisting demands for an increase in the £30,000 ceiling for tax relief on mortgage interest. Thatcher wanted Lawson to repeat Howe's 1983 act of raising the ceiling in the Budget immediately before the election, and sought an increase of £5,000–£10,000. He refused, but on the under-standing that there would be plenty of other popular measures in the Budget.

The Chancellor was, in spite of the caution of his officials, discovering that in the complex relationships that determine the shape of the Government's finances it was, more or less, possible to use the same pound twice. Since taking office, the Conservative Government had faced the additional public-spending burden of rising unemployment. The downturn in unemployment that began in the summer of 1986 eased this burden. In addition, as strong growth in real incomes began to feed through into faster economic growth, tax revenues received a significant boost. The public-sector borrowing requirement, far from expanding under the burden of declining oil revenues and higher public spending, was in decline. It peaked at £11.4bn in the 1984–5 financial year, when it was boosted by the effects of the miners' strike. By 1986–7 the borrowing requirement, effectively the budget deficit, was down to £4.3bn. The 1987–8 financial year, although this was not clear at the time, marked the changeover from a long period of budget deficits, to a time of surpluses, a phenomenon last seen in 1969–70, and then only temporarily. As it turned out, there was a public-sector debt repayment, or budget surplus, of £4.2bn in 1987–8.

Lawson was free, therefore, to announce a Budget in March 1987 that had all the necessary pre-election ingredients. The basic rate of income tax, as expected, was cut further, this time from 29 to 27 per cent; double the reduction of a year earlier. The Chancellor also managed to avoid the normal run of adverse post-Budget headlines in the tabloid newspapers, which traditionally focus on the Budget changes in excise duty on alcohol, tobacco and petrol. As with tax allowances and thresholds, it had become normal practice for such duties to be increased in line with inflation. Indeed, in the case of alcohol and tobacco, the various health lobbies urged far larger increases. Lawson ignored both tradition and the health arguments, instead opting for a freezing of excise duties, a cut in real terms in the price of cigarettes, beer, whisky, wine and petrol. It was a populist move in a populist Budget.

Home and Dry

The Thatcher Government sailed to victory on 11 June 1987 on a tide of growing economic optimism, for which Lawson was widely credited. Again, the decisive switch in the public mood on the economy came in the spring. MORI's economic optimism measure switched from negative to strongly positive in March, in direct response to the 1987 Budget. The Conservatives won 376 seats in the House of Commons, a majority of 146 over Labour and of 100 over all other parties. BBC/Gallup opinion poll data, quoted in *A Nation Dividing?* by Johnston, Pattie and Allsopp, showed that, in the twelve months leading up to the election, 29 per cent of voters thought their personal economic situation had improved, against 28 per cent who thought it had deteriorated. This compared with figures of 25 per cent and 37 per cent respectively in 1983. More significantly, the proportion of people who thought their economic situation would improve over the following twelve months outnumbered those who expected a deterioration by a ratio of more than 3:1. This was better than the ratio of just over 2:1 in 1983.

People also believed that the Government's policies had been and would continue to be good for the national economy. Using the same survey data, 42 per cent of respondents thought the national economic situation had improved over the previous twelve months, compared with 30 per cent who believed it had deteriorted. Over the following twelve months, 38 per cent expected the national economy to improve, and only 13 per cent looked for a decline. In all cases, the balance of respondents either expected or had experienced no change, or did not declare a view.

Unemployment, after peaking in the summer of 1986, had fallen by around 200,000 although, at just above 3 million in May 1987 (on the published figures of the time), it was still depressingly high. Real incomes, helped by the 1987 Budget, continued to rise strongly. Inflation, at 4.1 per cent, appeared to be comfortably under control. Roy Hattersley, Labour's shadow chancellor, warned of a time bomb ticking away in the economy, in the form of emerging serious balance of payments problems. He was right, but he was ignored.

There was a new mood of confidence in the economy, seen briefly during the Barber boom of 1972–3, but not on a sustained basis since the Macmillan years of the late 1950s. Lawson suggested that the economy was in its best shape for forty years. 'The British economy as a result of successive Budgets since 1979 is sounder than it has ever been for any time since the war,' he told delighted Conservative MPs at the end of March 1987. Britain, for so long the laughing-stock of the world economy could, it appeared, hold her head up high. Productivity and company profits were soaring, new businesses were being created at a record rate, the state's role in the economy had been pared back, the industrial relations climate was transformed and inflation had been brought to heel. The Conservative vision of establishing an enterprise culture in Britain was fast becoming a reality.

The most visible demonstration of this new-found prosperity was in the City of London's 'yuppy' boom. Yuppies found their natural expression in the City. Newspapers and television honed in on young men, with obligatory striped shirts and braces, who effortlessly made money, drank champagne and drove Porsches. The Prime Minister voiced her disapproval of excessive salaries and conspicuous consumption in the City, but there seemed to be little on the horizon to hold the yuppies back. During the election campaign, Lawson enlarged on his previous hints about cutting the higher rates of income tax and moving to a basic rate of income tax of 25 per cent. Such policies, he said, would be an early priority for a re-elected Conservative Government.

In the summer of 1987, Thatcher had only one criticism of Lawson. His hair was long and unkempt and threatened to deter the voters. She asked Lord Young, the Employment Secretary, to tell him to get it cut. He declined, advising her that she must do so. She did and, duly shorn, the Chancellor reappeared, to play a central role in the election campaign. Apart from presenting the Conservative Party with an economy in election-winning shape, Lawson successfully demolished the tax plans proposed by shadow chancellor Hattersley.

Lawson may have been headstrong and arrogant, but he had also been highly successful when it mattered. 'For four years Nigel ignored everybody and was the best Chancellor we have ever had,' said Lord Young.

The Chancellor, who had never courted personal popularity and had said publicly that he had no ambitions to be Prime Minister, became the favourite, both of his own MPs and of pro-Conservative tabloid newspapers. This period of favour, which lasted beyond the election, occasionally threatened to get out of hand.

The *Daily Mail*, which was later to turn savagely against him, wrote on 18 September 1987:

> Cool and confident, Chancellor Nigel Lawson declared yesterday: The economy is doing well. He was elated by another week of golden economic indicators, including another drop in the jobless figures ... Next week, the Chancellor sets off for talks with world financial leaders and he can hold his head high as the representative of a booming Britain.

The *Sun* was even more impressed, writing on 31 October 1987:

> Nigel Lawson is the most brilliant and innovative Chancellor since the war ... At Westminster, the view until now is that Nigel hasn't a hope of succeeding Mrs Thatcher. But his calm and resolute approach ... has shown the Tories that when at last Mrs Thatcher does step down they need look no further than Mr Lawson to find a leader of equal calibre.

Friends and enemies say that Lawson would have done well to quit while he was ahead, as a hero, soon after the June 1987 election victory. Sir Alan Walters, who was to play a central role in Lawson's downfall, said, 'I thought it politic not to have Lawson as Chancellor after the 1987 general election. The problem was, where could you move him? My preferred candidate would have been Nicholas Ridley. He had everything going for him – Treasury experience and intellectual honesty.'

Indeed, later, when Thatcher and Lawson fell out, she was to turn to Ridley for guidance. According to one source, 'Dear Nick would drop in to Downing Street for a whisky late at night. She would kick off her shoes and say: What is that bloody man doing to our economy?'

Friends say that it was Lawson's intention to move on soon after the election victory. He had a young family and very little personal wealth to fall back on, unlike many of his Cabinet colleagues. Lawson, whose background was in financial journalism had, ironically, seen the wealth he had inherited from his tea-merchant father, and that of his first wife, virtually wiped out in the property and stock-market crash that followed the Barber boom. 'He wanted to hang up his boots but he also wanted a job that was worth going to,' said a former colleague.

Former Chancellors, particularly those that leave office on a high note, are highly bankable commodities. And this was a time of rapid expansion in the financial-services industry. The talk was that Lawson was on the point of landing a plum job, on an astronomical salary, in the City or on Wall Street. But the right offer did not come along. Conservative Party loyalists in the City may have held back because they thought he could serve his country, and the financial markets, better if he continued as Chancellor. And, part of the demand in the private sector for former ministers is due to their impressive range of contacts. Lawson's talent, however, always greatly exceeded his tact, and the fear may have been that he had bruised too many reputations when in office to be able to slip easily into the role of opening doors and smoothing the path for valuable commercial deals.

So Lawson stayed at the Treasury, and confined his restlessness to occasional private musings about the attractions of the job of Foreign Secretary, occupied by Sir Geoffrey Howe, his predecessor as Chancellor. And by staying, while making clear his intention not to remain as Chancellor for the full Parliament, Lawson was to embark on a period in which the key policy errors were made. Less than twelve months after the June 1987 election victory, and his own major contribution to that victory, the mistakes had been made that were to guarantee that the Lawson boom turned to bust.

5

LIVING IN SIN WITH EUROPE

Had Lawson left office in June 1987, he would not have been able to complete the programme of personal tax cuts that he had begun in 1986. The target of a 25 per cent basic rate of income tax, and of big reductions in the higher rates of tax, would have been left to his successor. Both, however, were official Conservative policy and, it could be argued, did not depend greatly upon the individual administering them.

This was not the case for another aspect of economic policy, which remains the most controversial of Lawson's chancellorship. This was the strategy, embarked upon in early 1987, at first surreptitiously, of 'shadowing' the Deutschmark. The policy, later described by Lawson as 'living in sin' with the exchange rate mechanism (ERM) of the European Monetary System (1990), had its roots in his 1985 attempt to persuade Thatcher to accept sterling's formal entry into the ERM. But it was also heavily influenced by a shift in fashion among international policymakers, a shift which brought exchange rate management back into play.

Managing International Exchange Rates

The Bretton Woods system of pegged exchange rates came into being as a result of the international monetary conference of July 1944, held in a grand, sprawling hotel in the New Hampshire village of that name. The conference, with Lord Keynes leading Britain's team, established the post-war institutions of the International Monetary Fund (IMF) and the International Bank for Reconstruction and Development (the World Bank). Under the system, the dollar was pegged to gold, at a fixed rate of $35 an ounce, and most other currencies were pegged to the dollar.

The sterling area, under which the majority of Commonwealth currencies were pegged to sterling, operated as an additional layer. Currencies were not immutably fixed; permitted variations were 1 per cent either side of the central parity. Periodic devaluations or revaluations were also allowed, although discouraged, examples being the sterling devaluations of 1949 and 1967, the French franc devaluations of the 1950s and early 1960s, the revaluation of the Deutschmark and Dutch guilder in 1961 and the decision to allow the Canadian dollar to float from 1950 to 1962.

For long periods, however, and for most currencies, the Bretton Woods system was a framework of fixed exchange rates, in which domestic economic policies had to be adjusted to maintain the value of the currency within its agreed limits. Policy-makers accepted that their actions had to be conducted within a fixed-exchange-rate framework, as did the majority of economists. But the argument in favour of flexible, or floating rates, did not go away, even as the Bretton Woods system delivered the international monetary stability that helped turn the 1950s and most of the 1960s into something of a golden age for the world economy.

Milton Friedman, the Chicago monetarist professor of economics who was later to be a prime influence in the development of the economic thinking of Margaret Thatcher and her colleagues, set out the counter-argument in a paper, 'The Case for Flexible Exchange Rates', published as early as 1953. Two years later, writing under a similar title, 'The Case for Variable Exchange Rates', Professor James Meade of Cambridge also argued against the status quo. Meade, who like Friedman was later to be awarded the Nobel prize in economics, had accompanied Keynes to the Bretton Woods conference.

Friedman argued that, in a situation where the price structures of two countries have moved out of line, it is far easier to change one price, the exchange rate, than to alter thousands of prices in the errant economy. He advocated a policy of clean floating, or benign neglect of exchange rates, in which economic policy was based on achieving stable growth of the money supply, and currencies were allowed to find their own level. A devout believer in the efficiency of free markets, he suggested that currency speculation, far from being damaging, would help achieve equilibrium within the international monetary system. Meade suggested that economic policy was handicapped by the fact that there were too many policy objectives and not enough available instruments to achieve them. If one of these objectives, external balance, could be achieved by the simple device of exchange rate flexibility, then the achievement of the others, notably economic growth and stable prices, would become much more straightforward.

Their arguments, and those of others, did not gain acceptance among policy-makers at the time. There was concern about the political damage that could be done by a falling exchange rate, by raising the prices of imported goods including, in Britain's case, many basic foods and commodities. Politicians were also subject to the baser motive of regarding the exchange rate as a national virility symbol, and feared that a weak currency would be regarded as evidence of weak government. Even politicians in those countries whose currencies could be expected to rise in a flexible-exchange-rate regime had to be aware of the danger of an angry backlash from industry, if given the task of competing internationally at an uncompetitive exchange rate. There was also deep suspicion about the likely conduct of the markets and the risk that the speculators, the famous gnomes of Zurich, would wreak havoc.

Flexible, or floating, exchange rates did, however, have their day, if not by the choice of policy-makers. Strains in the Bretton Woods system increased during the 1960s. Sterling was devalued, against American opposition, in November 1967. But the principal difficulty was that, with the US economy weakened by the Vietnam war, the dollar could no longer sustain the burden of acting as anchor to the system. Financial innovation, and the development of the Eurodollar market in the 1960s, helped hasten the downfall of Bretton Woods. The Canadian dollar was unpegged from the US dollar in June 1970. The US dollar's convertibility into gold, a central plank in the currency framework, was suspended in August 1971. In December, meeting at the Smithsonian Institution in Washington, the major countries revalued their currencies against the dollar, in an attempt to patch up the pegged-rate system. But it was of little use. Sterling was floated in June 1972, after an unsuccessful attempt at membership of the European currency snake. In March 1973, after a final failed attempt to settle on a new set of dollar exchange rates, the other leading industrial countries decided to float their currencies against the dollar.

Such action was taken reluctantly. The International Monetary Fund was working towards a major reform of the system, based on 1971 proposals, the so-called grand design, by Anthony Barber, the British

Chancellor. Under these plans, the dollar would have been replaced as the reserve currency and basis of the pegged-rate system by the IMF's own special drawing right (SDR), whose composition and value was that of a basket, or weighted average, of major currencies. A special committee of twenty, of ministers and deputies of the members of the IMF's executive board, was set to work on the details of such a plan. But events, and in particular the first OPEC oil crisis of 1973–4, meant that the grand design made little progress.

Pegged exchange rates were replaced, not by Friedman's clean floating, but by managed, or dirty, floating. In other words, governments, while accepting that they could not control their currencies as tightly as before, were reluctant to leave exchange rate policy entirely to the markets. There were, however, limits to the extent that, in the absence of the disciplines of the Bretton Woods framework, foreign exchange market intervention and policy changes (notably interest rate policy) could prevent sharp currency shifts. The quadrupling of oil prices by OPEC in 1973–4 resulted in a substantial increase in the worldwide demand for dollars. And, ironically, the dollar weakness that had led to the break-up of the Bretton Woods system gave way to a period of dollar strength. It did not last, however, and by 1977 the US Administration, under President Carter, was forging an agreement with the German Bundesbank to support the dollar on the markets.

In Britain, the period from 1974 to 1976 was one in which the Treasury, under Labour Chancellor Denis Healey, was forced to authorize large-scale intervention in support of sterling, the need for which eventually resulted in the decision to apply for an IMF loan, and impose an IMF adjustment programme on the economy. By 1977, however, sterling was back in demand, partly because it had fallen so low during the IMF crisis. The decision was taken to limit its rise to around $1.75, from a 1976 low point of close to $1.50. Interest rates were reduced sharply, minimum lending rate falling from 15 per cent in October 1976 to 5 per cent twelve months later. And the Bank of England intervened heavily to hold down sterling, pushing up the reserves from $4.1bn to over $20bn during 1977. The policy was abandoned in October 1977, partly on the advice of the London Business School, because it was jeopardizing the Government's new commitment, insisted on by the IMF, of controlling the money supply. The attempt at exchange rate policy during a period in which currencies were floating had run into the very problems foreseen by both Friedman and Meade more than twenty years before. The Government moved, reluctantly, to something closer to the benign neglect advocated by Friedman.

By the late 1970s, the world was split between those countries, such as the United States and Britain, which favoured exchange rate management but had been generally unsuccessful in putting it into practice and others, notably the European members of the snake, which had attempted to supplant the Bretton Woods system with their own, more limited, framework of semi-fixed exchange rates. Japan was somewhere between the two, not belonging to any formal system, but more successful than Britain or the United States in managing her currency. There was, too, a widespread feeling of dissatisfaction with the floating rate turbulence of the 1970s. Lord Richardson, the Governor of the Bank of England, said in June 1979: 'Recent experience has indeed suggested that there are more serious limitations to the role flexible exchange rates can play in promoting adjustment than was earlier believed' (1979).

Of particular concern was the fact that a falling exchange rate resulted, fairly quickly, in rising prices. This could, in turn, lead to a vicious spiral in which the higher inflation that resulted from an initial exchange rate decline could have the effect of knocking market confidence sufficiently to produce further selling of the currency. In theory, the process was unlimited. Related to this, the activities of foreign exchange speculators appeared to result in regular currency 'overshooting', whereby exchange rates were pushed well beyond the point that was necessary to produce, for example, a required balance of payments adjustment. Thus, rather than Friedman's vision of speculators assisting the process of moving smoothly towards a new currency equilibrium, experience suggested something more akin to a zigzagging process, or a yacht tacking towards its destination. The new equilibrium, if it was ever reached at all, was rarely approached in a smooth and direct way.

Thus, there was a substantial body of official and academic opinion which favoured moving back towards a more structured form of exchange rate management, perhaps not as formal, at least initially, as the Bretton Woods framework, but some way from the volatility that had replaced it. The European Monetary System, as described in Chapter 3, was intended to be a zone of stability in a turbulent world. Outside Europe, its progress was monitored closely, in order to assess whether it could be applied on a wider scale.

Two events, however, conspired to bury the prospect of a Bretton Woods Mark II emerging at that time. The first was the second OPEC oil crisis, triggered by the overthrow of the Shah of Iran in December 1978. This led to a trebling of world oil prices between the autumn of 1978 and June 1979, and another period of exchange-market turbulence in which sterling, in its new role as a petrocurrency, was a major beneficiary. The second event was the election in June 1979 of the Thatcher Government in Britain and in November 1980 of Ronald Reagan as President of the United States. On both sides of the Atlantic, free-market governments were elected who, unlike their predecessors, had no qualms about floating exchange rates. The driving force of their argument, in both cases, was the standard Friedmanite criticism of fixed exchange rates. Economic policy had to be geared to achieving low and stable monetary growth, and exchange rate management was at best an inconvenience, at worst an actual threat to such a policy. In addition, for a US administration even more than a British government, benign neglect of the exchange rate was an easy way of demonstrating free-market credentials.

Benign Neglect?

One of the interesting, 'What if . . .?', questions of history is to speculate on what might have happened if James Callaghan's Labour Government had opted to put sterling into the European exchange rate mechanism (ERM), when the European Monetary System came into being in March 1979. Margaret Thatcher's Conservative Government, elected two months later, would have faced the choice between living with ERM membership, anathema as it was to its free-market principles, or, as in 1972, pulling sterling out of the European system within weeks of entry. The difference in 1979–80, of course, was that a decision to remove sterling from the ERM could have been justified on the basis of the pound's great strength rather than the earlier embarrassing episode when sterling weakness prompted the departure from the snake.

It is difficult, indeed, to find evidence from that time that, either publicly or privately, ministers had any interest, either in ERM membership for sterling, or in a return to exchange rate targeting after the currency turbulence of the Thatcher Government's initial period in office. Nigel Lawson's Zurich speech of 1981, in which he stated explicitly that the Government had no exchange rate target and did not intend to establish one, was referred to in Chapter 3. In the same section he said:

> The continuing strength of the pound, despite the abolition of exchange controls, is a phenomenon which has surprised many if not most observers. No doubt it has a lot to do with the UK's new-found self-sufficiency in oil; but whatever the precise mix of reasons – which in any event can never be objectively determined – the one thing that is clear is that it is the product of *the free play of market forces* [my italics].   (1981)

At this time, sterling's rise – it climbed above $2.40 against the dollar and intensified the recessionary squeeze on British industry – was meriting close attention. Industrialists such as Sir Michael Edwardes, then the chairman of the state-owned motor manufacturer British Leyland (later to be sold, as Rover, to British Aerospace) said at the Confederation of British Industry's 1980 conference that if oil was responsible for the pound's strength then it would be better to 'leave the bloody stuff in the ground'. Sir Alan Walters, newly appointed as Thatcher's personal economic adviser, argued that sterling's strength indicated that monetary policy was unnecessarily tight, even for the inflation-beating task at hand. And so, from March 1981 until the following autumn, interest rates were reduced, with the side-effect of pushing the pound lower. As so often, however, the foreign exchanges could not be persuaded to stop at the point where the Government wanted them to, and sterling's weakness resulted in a decision to raise interest rates sharply in the autumn (base rates were lifted from 12 to 16 per cent). Thus, while the period from June 1979 to March 1981 was something close to Friedman's benign neglect, the exchange rate was an important component of policy for the remainder of 1981. There is a world of difference, however, between using the level of, and changes in, the exchange rate as an occasional source of information about monetary policy, and an explicit policy of setting targets for it.

Walters, in his book *Sterling in Danger*, describes the role of the exchange rate during the period 1980–82:

> The exact role of the exchange rate in economic policy is subject to many subtle interpretations. During this period, however, there was a general attitude, albeit with different degrees of emphasis, to the exchange rate which

was broadly shared by the civil servants and ministers. First, the exchange
rate was not a target for policy. This applied to the whole range of instruments
– interest rates, funding operations and fiscal measures. All instruments were
concentrated primarily on domestic targets and indicators. The exchange rate
was left very largely to market forces. This did not mean that there was no
intervention at all, or even that it was restricted merely to smoothing operations. The Bank of England did, on occasion, intervene in markets quite
heavily, but this intervention was virtually always sterilized through the
money markets. The prime purpose was to prevent what was usually called a
'free-fall' in the exchange rate having an effect on the market for gilts
(government securities). But there was no target rate. Indeed, from the
Budget on 10 March 1981 over the next nine months (to 11 December) the
effective exchange rate fell by about 10 per cent. Although the exchange
rate was not a target it would have been foolish simply to ignore it. The
exchange rate may tell us something about the severity or laxity of monetary
policy.   (1990, p. 90)

And so it went on. The Government never ignored the exchange rate.
To do so in an open, trade-dependent economy such as Britain's would
have been foolish in the extreme. The floating-rate regime, in combination with domestic monetary targets, may have been imperfect, but
there was no obviously better alternative. Membership of the ERM,
partly because of frequent currency realignments in the early years of
the system, did not stand out as a successful discipline against inflation.
In 1980, inflation in Britain, measured by the consumer-spending
deflator, was 16.3 per cent, compared with 13.3 per cent in France and
20.5 per cent in Italy. By 1982 Britain's rate was down to 8.7 per cent,
against 11.5 per cent in France and 16.9 per cent in Italy. The following
year, 1983, the comparison looked even more favourable to Britain, with
a 4.8 per cent inflation rate set against 9.7 per cent in France and 15.2
per cent in Italy. Britain's relative success with inflation had, of course,
to be set against the severity of the recession in 1980–81, which was on a
scale unmatched in the rest of Europe. By 1982–3, however, ministers
could argue that this was now water under the bridge and that the
important thing was that Britain had come out of the recession with
sustainably low inflation. Throughout the period Germany, the anchor
of the ERM, had inflation rates decisively below those of Britain,
France and Italy, typically 3–6 per cent. The important point, however,
was that those countries whose currencies were in the ERM appeared to
be markedly less successful in achieving convergence with German

inflation than Britain, which was outside the system. Later the position was to change and ERM members, and in particular France, achieved sustained low inflation in the second half of the 1980s. In the early 1980s, however, there was little hint that this would occur. The EMS was less of a zone of monetary stability than its founders had hoped, and its economic achievements were limited.

In the Treasury and the Bank of England, and even more so in the City, there was also the widespread view that, with sterling's fortunes partly linked to volatile world oil prices, any attempt to target the exchange rate was doomed to failure. A target, whether publicly stated or privately monitored, could easily have been destroyed by the next decision on oil prices by the OPEC oil producers. In this respect, it was suggested, Britain was doing Europe a favour by keeping sterling out of the ERM. The pound, a big internationally traded currency, would have complicated the task of holding a fragile ERM together. No longer would it have been mainly a task of preserving a reasonably stable exchange rate between the French franc and the Deutschmark as the pivotal relationship in the system. This was already a difficult enough task, given the uncertain commitment of the Mitterrand Government to the ERM in the early 1980s. But sterling's entry would turn a difficult two-way relationship into a potentially unmanageable three-way link between the Deutschmark, the French franc and sterling, the more so if because of the pound's petrocurrency status it responded in exactly the opposite way to the other two currencies to changes in international oil prices.

The absence of a target for sterling did not mean, as Walters explained, that the exchange rate was ignored. Indeed, apart from during the period of the brave new world of Thatcherism in 1979 and 1980, ministers and officials had, for the most part, a strong preference for exchange rate stability. There were good reasons for this. Movements in exchange rates, as we have seen, can start as a gentle trend but turn into crises. The foreign exchange markets, in responding rapidly to news or changes in sentiment, can bring about changes that policy-makers consider inappropriate. Above all, it is difficult to maintain an image of quiet competence in economic policy if the headlines are dominated by a falling pound.

In the United States under the Reagan Administration, things were rather different. With an economy less dependent on foreign trade than Europe or Japan, American policy-makers could always afford to pay less attention to the dollar than was the case for their counterparts overseas, and their currencies. During Reagan's first term, benign neglect of the exchange rate was pursued.

In most respects, the omens for the dollar in this period were not good. The current-account deficit of the United States was increasing sharply, from a position of small surplus in 1981 to a $100bn deficit in 1984. At the same time, the budget deficit was emerging as a $200bn a year problem, brought on by a combination of tax cuts and increases in Federal spending, particularly on defence. Against the minus points of the twin deficits, however, there was an important plus, in the form of Federal Reserve Board Chairman Paul Volcker's determination to run a tough, anti-inflationary monetary policy. The combination of the tight monetary policy exemplified in generally high interest rates and the loose fiscal policy of the massive budget deficit resulted in a strong rise for the dollar. At the same time, US economic growth was powerful in comparison with a generally subdued world economy, allowing Reagan to claim, as he did in 1984, that the dollar's rise reflected the strength of the American economy, which, 'like a greyhound', was leaving the rest of the world behind.

The dollar's climb was both remarkable and, in the main, unchecked. By early 1985, the dollar index, measuring its average value against other major currencies, was 70 per cent up on its 1980 level. Sterling was a spectacular casualty of the dollar's strength, falling from a peak of more than $2.40 during the 1980-81 squeeze to just $1.0370 in February 1985. Against the Deutschmark, the dollar climbed from DM1.81 in 1980 to DM3.47 at its peak in 1985, a rise of more than 90 per cent. And, while the official attitude in the White House was one of approval, concern about the dollar's rise was growing, both in America and in the wider world. For American companies, the dollar's rise and the emergence of a large current-account deficit were two parts of the same story; the more that the dollar rose, the greater the difficulties they faced in exporting, and the easier it was for importers to make inroads into their domestic market.

Outside the United States, any advantage accruing to exporters from the dollar's climb to uncompetitive levels was more than outweighed by the disadvantages. Japan, in particular, was concerned about a surge in protectionist pressure emerging in America and beginning to find its voice in Congress. In Europe, and in Britain in particular, the main worry was the inflationary impact of a strongly rising dollar, which had the effect of pushing up the local-currency cost of dollar-priced oil and commodities. More generally, the fear was that the higher the dollar rose, the less its rise was sustainable. The risk was that a dollar bubble was building up which, if burst, would have devastating consequences throughout the international financial system.

Even Margaret Thatcher, stung by the pound's fall to virtual parity with the dollar, appeared to have shifted in her view that the markets were always right. On 20 February 1985 she headed for Washington for meetings with Reagan – the first since his successful return to the White House for a second term in office – and with Paul Volcker, the Federal Reserve Board Chairman. Advance Downing Street briefing suggested that her priority was to lecture the President on the damage that was being wrought by the dollar's unbridled rise. But, to the extent that she did so, her words appeared to have fallen on deaf ears.

Reagan, in a televised press conference within hours of Thatcher's departure from Washington, restated his view that the dollar's strength was a consequence of US economic success, and was not a matter which governments could, or should, attempt to do anything about. He said:

> I think if you start toying around with trying to reduce the value of the dollar without curbing the other side of the issue, cheap imports which are holding down inflation, we put ourselves back in the inflationary spiral and that we don't want. The problem of the dollar today is that our trading partners have not caught up with us in economic recovery. I think they have a long way to go in changing some rigidities in their customs and their methods of doing business. What we really need is their recovery to bring their money up in value comparable to ours. (1985)

Five Go to Work on the Dollar

The dollar's rise had caused many outside America to modify their faith in unfettered markets, at least as far as currencies were concerned. More significantly, the appointment of James Baker as US Treasury Secretary produced a significant shift in American exchange rate policy. Donald Regan, Baker's predecessor in Reagan's first term, was a tough investment banker best known for his highly publicized disagreements with Nancy Reagan, the President's wife, including one celebrated occasion when he committed the unforgivable White House sin of slamming the phone down on her when she was in full flow. Regan had provided intellectual backing for Reagan's first-term view of the dollar, and the reasons for its strength. Baker, a Texan lawyer by background, was more of a pragmatist. He could see the problems that the dollar's strength were creating for American industry. And in a Washington meeting of the Group of Five – the finance ministers and central bankers of the United States, Britain, Germany, Japan and France – on 17 January 1985, the concern of the outside world was brought home to him. The meeting was unusual in that both Regan and Baker attended on behalf of the US Treasury, the former introducing the latter to his new overseas colleagues and effectively handing over the reins. Lawson, together with Robin Leigh-Pemberton, the Governor of the Bank of England, attended on Britain's behalf.

The Group of Five, or G5, later to draw in Italy and Canada and become the Group of Seven (G7), was a shadowy grouping which, until its burst of headline-grabbing activity in the second half of the 1980s was only known within a highly specialized circle of international economic diplomats and experts. Most textbook accounts of the break-up of Bretton Woods and the subsequent period of volatile floating exchange rates make no mention of its inception in 1975. And yet, for the rest of the 1970s and early 1980s, this inner core of decision-makers met in an attempt to hammer out their differences in private.

The 17 January meeting of the G5 did not appear to signal any shift in the Reagan Administration's attitude towards the dollar, perhaps because of Regan's presence. The participants did have an agreed policy position to fall back on, which was fixed two years earlier at the world economic summit in Williamsburg, Virginia. This position, partly based on the 1983 report of the Working Group on Exchange Market Information, commissioned by an earlier summit and completed under the chairmanship of Philippe Surgensen, was that joint intervention by the leading central banks was permitted in order to counter 'disorderly markets'. However, currency intervention could not, in itself, bring about big shifts in exchange rates. US officials said there was no question of using coordinated intervention as part of a deliberate programme to bring down the dollar.

This position was to change very rapidly. At the end of February 1985, just a week after Thatcher's meeting with Reagan, the G5 moved into action. A programme of large-scale dollar sales was instituted by the major central banks. On one day, 27 February, the dollar was knocked back nearly 20 pfennigs from its peak of DM3.47. Sterling rose by six cents in the space of two hours, from below $1.05 to almost $1.11. For foreign exchange dealers the near-panic conditions that resulted had two effects. It destroyed their belief that the dollar was a one-way bet, which could only go higher. It also gave them a new fear, and respect, for the G5. Reagan's comments after his meeting with Thatcher, in which he ruled out such action, were interpreted by some as a deliberate act to lull the markets into a false sense of security. The explanation was, however, more mundane. Reagan was still operating on the basis of the dollar policy of his first term. With Baker at the US Treasury, the policy had changed. Interventionism was the order of the day and the G5 was a powerful force in the international economy.

The initial wave of central-bank selling in February and March pushed the dollar lower, but failed to push it down to what finance ministers and central bankers considered to be realistic levels. Lawson, visiting Washington for a meeting of the IMF interim committee in April, launched a fierce attack on American economic policy. US budgetary policy, he said, was 'grievously mistaken', the dollar was too high and 'nobody would be at all upset if it were to go down further' (1985a). Such attacks were made, if not with the connivance, at least without objections from Baker and Paul Volcker, the Federal Reserve Board Chairman. In trying to persuade both the President and Congress of the need for tough action on the budget deficit, they needed all the support they could get.

The G5's most explicit and most important action against the dollar came a few months later. Baker summoned the other G5 participants to a meeting at the Plaza Hotel, New York, on 22 September 1985. This time there was no beating about the bush. In a communiqué, the meeting called for a 'further orderly appreciation of the main non-dollar currencies against the dollar' – in other words, a dollar fall – and the central banks showed that they meant business by selling the dollar heavily. By the end of October, more than $10bn had been expended in forcing through the G5's new dollar policy. On the day after the Plaza meeting, the dollar tumbled by 5 per cent. Lawson, mindful of Thatcher's Friedmanite attitude towards large-scale intervention, was more cautious about committing the Bank of England to large dollar sales than were the other participants. However, he could give his whole-

hearted backing to a programme of interest rate cuts instituted by the
US authorities, and to the Reagan Administration's stated intention of
achieving drastic cuts in the budget deficit. The Plaza meeting was a
critical event in the economic history of the 1980s and in ushering in a
new spirit of international economic cooperation.

As Anthony Loehnis, a former executive director of the Bank of
England with responsibility for international finance put it:

> The Plaza agreement was ... a turning-point in the evolution of the inter-
> national monetary system in three important respects: the US authorities
> accepted that the international dimension mattered and that virtue might
> consist of more than just putting one's own house in order and regarding the
> level of the exchange rate as a sort of international score-card measuring
> success in doing so; the G5 countries together openly acknowledged that the
> international market-place's judgement on exchange rates could be wrong; and
> they also asserted that something could be done about it and committed
> themselves to doing it. It is unlikely that the fall of the effective rate of the
> dollar by 30 per cent from its peak of February 1985 to its level two years later
> when the Louvre agreement was signed could have been achieved without the
> Plaza declaration. Indeed, without the Plaza agreement it is inconceivable
> that such a decline in the dollar could have been accomplished without the
> 'hard landing' for the world economy that had looked so likely a prospect.
>
> (1990, pp. 130–31)

The G5 met regularly during 1986, expanding to become the G7 along
the way, as Italy and Canada, which had participated at world economic
summits since 1976, successfully pressed for inclusion. The original five
insisted on maintaining a degree of superiority, however, meeting for
dinner on the eve of G7 meetings. It was this that caused the Italian
delegation to storm back to Rome from Paris in protest, without
participating in the crucial meeting at the Louvre of 22 February 1987.
The G5/7's success in bringing down the dollar had surpassed the
expectations of even the optimists among the group. By February 1987,
of which more below, the new aim was to stabilize the dollar at its lower
level, to prevent it from overshooting on the way down.

International economic cooperation, in the newly powerful G5/7
forum, had a profound impact on the way that Lawson and his Treasury
and Bank of England colleagues thought about the role of the exchange
rate. No longer was currency management, and the loose targeting of
exchange rates, viewed with a repugnance driven by the belief, either

that such management did not work, or that it interfered with domestic monetary policy. The Plaza agreement had shown that, with sufficient currency intervention and with appropriate policy changes, the foreign exchange markets could be steered in the direction that policy-makers wanted.

As importantly, the participants in these group meetings acquired a status, in the financial markets, of something close to that of international film stars. When a G5 or G7 meeting was taking place journalists, photographers and TV reporters and cameramen followed their every move. Ferried around in large limousines, they became the hottest story in whichever town the G5 circus happened to be performing in. Their throwaway remarks, in the lobby of the IMF building in Washington or on their way into the French Finance Ministry's former Louvre head-quarters, were flashed around the world by the financial wire services. Lawson, in particular, was a star turn. As probably the most articulate, informative and controversial of the participants, his post-meeting briefings were eagerly awaited, and he rarely disappointed. Set against the mundane and often trivial day-to-day business of domestic politics, the international atmosphere was a heady one. These men were the new movers and shakers of the world economic scene, even if this was not always recognized at home.

Managing the Pound

Chancellors of the Exchequer and their officials have an instinctive preference for exchange rate stability, as described above. For politicians, it may be more accurate to say that their preference is for a gently rising currency, which confers the appropriate degree of international approval of their policies. Thus, one exchange rate ambition that Lawson and Thatcher could agree on was that they preferred a firm exchange rate. But by definition, not all countries can have gently rising currencies. It was possible when the aim of international economic cooperation was to bring the dollar down from the stratosphere. But, in the more normal circumstances that prevailed in the run-up to the February 1987 Louvre agreement on stabilizing the dollar, active policies to achieve exchange rate stability were emerging as the international policy consensus. Some of the subsequent criticism of Lawson and the 1987–8 episode of 'living in sin' with the European exchange rate mechanism by targeting sterling against the Deutschmark has taken as its basis the idea that this was a madcap scheme hatched up by the Chancellor and his advisers, which went against the grain of policy. In fact, as it started, the targeting of sterling was a natural adjunct to the wider policy cooperation in which Lawson had been a leading player.

Apart from his G5/7 experiences, Lawson came to the policy of a specific, but secret, Deutschmark target for sterling from two other routes. The first was Thatcher's rejection in 1985 of his proposal to take sterling into the ERM. Lawson, as probably the strongest personality in the Cabinet apart from the Prime Minister, did not take such a snub easily. Having been appointed Chancellor for his financial and economic expertise, he saw Thatcher's gut reaction against ERM entry as both galling and frustrating. It would be going too far to say that he decided on a secret sterling target in order to say 'I told you so' to the Prime Minister, by proving that such a target could be operated successfully without compromising the Government's main economic objectives. There was little doubt, however, that Lawson saw informal exchange rate targeting as a preparatory exercise for formal entry into the ERM, to take place soon after the June 1987 general election.

The other prime consideration, as with the initial bid to take sterling into the ERM in 1985, was that sterling remained subject to bouts of selling pressure, the most recent having been in October 1986. As the only major currency outside the ERM, the pound was peculiarly subject to volatility resulting, for example, from sudden shifts in dollar sentiment. The October 1986 episode, while eventually requiring an unwelcome 1 per cent increase in base rates, had also proved that cooperation between the Bank of England and the German Bundesbank could effectively limit movements in sterling. The trick was to convince the markets that the pound was no longer fair game, and that attacks on it would be repulsed, and to do so without actually naming a target for the pound.

The official Treasury view is that the policy of targeting sterling against the Deutschmark was merely a side-effect of the Louvre agreement to stabilize the dollar against both the German currency and the Japanese yen. These three, the dollar, the yen and the Deutschmark, were the key currencies. The French franc and the Italian lira were already linked to the Deutschmark by their membership of the ERM. In theory, sterling could have been left to find its own value, but it was natural to bunch it together with the other European currencies by linking it to the Deutschmark. The explanation is neat and, for the Treasury, it has the advantage of spreading the blame for the subsequent problems that emerged as the targeting policy was pursued. Britain, it could be said in defence, was just pulling her weight in a joint task. It is, however, too neat.

For one thing, Lawson was not an idle observer in what was now the G7 process of international policy cooperation. He had clear ideas and he was not afraid to say so. It is inconceivable that he had not already made up his own mind about the desirability of a target for sterling well before setting off for the Paris meeting. The manner of these meetings, indeed, which in the case of the Louvre agreement began with a Saturday night dinner for the G5, hosted by the French Finance Minister Édouard Balladur, and continued on the following day (22 February), was that broad agreements were hammered out by officials well before finance ministers and central bank heads came together. Lawson's enthusiasm for the agreement was, in addition, plain to see. He took the unusual step of instructing the Treasury press office to summon economics correspondents to 11 Downing Street in the early evening of his return on the Sunday from Paris. The agreement, he said, was a historic one which would be remembered long after Italy's fit of pique in departing early from the meeting had been forgotten. He was right.

It is also inconceivable that Lawson would have stuck so doggedly to the policy, which in the end degenerated into a full-blown battle between the Treasury and the Bank of England mainly on one side, and the markets on the other, had the Deutschmark target for sterling merely been a residual matter arising out of the wider Louvre agreement.

The conclusive point, however, is that the Chancellor and his senior officials, Sir Terence Burns, the Chief Economic Adviser, Sir Peter Middleton, Permanent Secretary to the Treasury, and Sir Geoffrey Littler, Deputy Permanent Secretary with responsibility for international finance, had come to the view the previous autumn that sterling's oil-related depreciation had gone far enough, and that a further fall would threaten the authorities' ability to maintain low inflation. Burns and Middleton, along with Lawson, had been architects of the Government's monetarist medium-term financial strategy in 1980. But now the three, along with Littler, were the architects of a significant shift in policy, albeit one that retained as its central aim the achievement of sustained low inflation. Burns, a cheerful northerner with a passion for golf and soccer, had long believed in the importance of the exchange rate in economic policy. In the international monetarist approach he had developed at the London Business School, the exchange rate was the main transmission mechanism from monetary policy to inflation. Middleton, a wiry balding figure known to be a Thatcher favourite, had shared Lawson's conversion to full membership of the European Monetary System two years earlier.

The basic purpose of the 1986 sterling depreciation policy remained relevant. It was to allow the non-oil economy – manufacturing and the service industries – to grow into the gap left by an oil sector whose value, in monetary terms, had been drastically reduced. Thus, the Treasury did not want what had come to be regarded as the normal roller-coaster of floating currencies to operate. Ministers and officials did not want to see the pound, having fallen quite sharply, bounce back up again in a way that would have been detrimental to growth prospects. In the winter of 1986–7, however, the chief concern was to prevent a further fall in sterling (against the European currencies; it was strong against the dollar). In November 1986, following his expansionary Autumn Statement, the Chancellor told the House of Commons Treasury and Civil Service Committee that he did not want to see sterling fall further. The pound was then just above DM2.80, which was effectively the lower limit for the target range. But officials could also look forward to a time when sterling would be back in demand, perhaps because of rising market confidence over a third Thatcher election victory. The logic of policy, which fitted in with the Chancellor's ambition of preparing the ground for ERM entry, was therefore to lock in most of sterling's 1986 depreciation by holding it at roughly the level against the European currencies to which it had fallen. It was important, therefore, to have in mind an upper limit for sterling, and as was to become clear over the following few months, this ceiling was DM3. The significance of the Louvre agreement was that it rubber-stamped such an ambition.

According to one Treasury official, involved in the formulation of policy at the time:

The policy evolved from our concern that the exchange rate was falling too far and too fast in 1986, and this evolution ran through to the time when we locked in to the Deutschmark. Once we had got to a situation where sterling was stable, we were concerned to demonstrate to the European Community that, even if we were not in the ERM, at least give us credit for achieving stability outside the system.

Unusually, although Robin Leigh-Pemberton was present at the Louvre meeting, the Bank of England was not closely involved in designing the new sterling strategy. For a policy that was to eventually involve massive currency intervention and carefully timed interest-rate changes, both of which were carried out by the Bank, this seems a strange omission.

The background to this was that in 1987 relations between the Treasury and the Bank of England were at a low ebb. Three years earlier, the collapse and government rescue of Johnson Matthey Bankers (JMB) had caused Lawson acute embarrassment. The details of the Bank's rescue, and of the scale of the problems involved, were not transmitted to Lawson, and he unintentionally misled the House of Commons over a £100m injection of funds into JMB, organized by the Bank, and about the extent of the fraud discovered within JMB. Lawson said later that the Bank 'fell down on the job' over JMB. Two years later, at the time of the 1986 Budget, the Treasury failed to involve the Bank in discussions over a proposed 5 per cent turnover tax on so-called American Depositary Receipts (ADRs), UK company paper traded on Wall Street. The tax proposal enraged the American financial establishment and Bank of England officials gleefully pointed out that, had they been consulted, they would never have condoned the introduction of the tax at such a high level.

Leigh-Pemberton, an old-style Conservative Party grandee, was a former leader of Kent County Council who, when he was appointed to the job of Bank of England Governor in 1982 (he took over in the middle of 1983), was chairman of the National Westminster Bank. His appointment bore the personal stamp of Thatcher, who had not got on well with Lord Richardson, his predecessor as Governor. Lawson, as a new-style Conservative Party meritocrat, had little in common with Leigh-Pemberton and, in embarking on a strategy for sterling that Thatcher would instinctively disapprove of, wanted to guard against the risk that, via the Governor, his embryo policy would be brought to Downing Street's attention. Lawson, who could turn rudeness into an art form, once told the House of Commons Treasury and Civil Service Committee, with reference to the Bank, 'we take the decisions but they do the work', adding quickly that of course he took the Bank's advice into account. Within the Treasury, the Bank became known, disparagingly, as the Treasury's East End branch. The Bank in turn, according to Treasury officials at the time, nurtured a 'corporate resentment' of the Treasury.

It did not, of course, take the Bank of England long to realize what was going on. Officials quickly saw, from the day-to-day instructions they received and discussions they took part in, that the Deutschmark target for sterling dominated policy decisions. But throughout the period, which lasted well into 1988, the Bank received no formal explanation of the policy. Bank of England officials, resentful at their exclusion from the formulation of the strategy, maintain that some of the subsequent problems could have been avoided if the policy had been subject to closer examination. 'The policy did not undergo the sort of detailed examination within the policy-making family that it should have done,' said one Bank official. The Treasury, however, dismisses this suggestion. 'I do not believe there was any stage where the Bank developed a significantly different view from ours,' said one senior official. 'If they did, they certainly did not say so at the time.' It would, however, have been difficult to do so with any effect. Lawson, in his enthusiasm for the policy, took on a dominant role. 'He virtually ran the whole show,' said one adviser. 'He was very sure of what he was doing and took the lead on everything. He told people what to do.' One of the group of outside economists, the Gooeys, who periodically advised Lawson on policy, ventured to suggest at this time that currency intervention did not work. Lawson's reply, dismissing such a suggestion as nonsense, was blunt and rude.

By keeping the policy within a tight Treasury circle, Lawson was also able to avoid the awkwardness of explaining to Thatcher that the Government was operating an exchange rate target. This was surprisingly easy. Thatcher did not pore over the newspapers each morning. She relied on a summary of the day's press prepared by Bernard Ingham, her press secretary. Ingham, who had a blind spot when it came to economic and financial policy, would not have troubled the Prime Minister with the minutiae of foreign exchange market reports or the speculation of City editors and economics correspondents about Deutschmark targets for sterling. The Prime Minister's own economic intelligence network, consisting of Lord Griffiths, the head of her policy unit, and Sir Alan Walters, later to return as her personal economic adviser but at that time in Washington, was sceptical about the international move back to exchange rate management but did not, initially, warn of any dangers specific to Britain.

The secrecy was maintained, even as most people in the City guessed what was going on. Lawson came close to revealing his hand publicly, telling the Treasury and Civil Service Committee at the end of March 1987 that, while it was not sensible to reveal operational details, exchange rate stability had obvious attractions. 'No doubt some light will be shed by the passage of time,' he added. And he nearly let the cat out of the bag completely on 1 April, telling industrialists and union leaders in a meeting of the National Economic Development Council that the pound's rate of DM2.90 was 'about right' and that industry should expect it to stay there. But, when the following morning's newspapers reported this as the Chancellor's admission that the Government was operating an exchange rate target, Lawson swiftly denied it, both publicly and to Thatcher. All he was doing, he said, was to illustrate a general point about the desirability of exchange rate stability with a reference to sterling's current exchange rate. Not for the first time, he accused journalists of misinterpreting his remarks.

For the first few months, the policy of targeting sterling against the Deutschmark was highly successful. Lawson had succeeded during the winter of 1986–7 in establishing a floor for sterling. Apart from a few wrinkles, the lower limit of DM2.80 held. Several factors contributed to this. The Chancellor stated on a number of occasions that he did not want the pound to fall further. Oil prices recovered from their low levels of the summer of 1986, and while the pound's sensitivity to oil price changes had diminished – it was no longer regarded by dealers as mainly a petrocurrency – this provided some modest support. Perhaps most important of all, the foreign exchange markets, largely as a result of the Louvre agreement, had acquired a new respect for the central banks and their ability to control markets by bringing the forces of coordinated intervention into play. Anyone who took on the central banks, even to attack a traditionally easy victim such as sterling, risked having their fingers badly burnt.

With a solid floor for sterling in place, the next question was whether the pound could be prevented from forcing its way through the ceiling. For the moment, however, this was not a serious problem. Lawson had embarked on the policy of shadowing the Deutschmark at a time when Britain's interest rates were relatively high, and probably too high for electoral comfort. In early 1987 base rates still stood at the 11 per cent level to which they had been raised in the wake of the previous autumn's run on sterling. As the pound began to rise from its floor, the natural response of the authorities was to cut interest rates. Base rates were reduced to 10.5 per cent on 10 March, 10 per cent on 19 March, 9.5 per cent on 29 April and 9 per cent on 11 May, a month before the general election. Had he set out the policy of targeting the Deutschmark more plainly at this time, the Chancellor would have had few objections from Thatcher, the Cabinet or the mass of Conservative MPs. The electoral benefits were clear. Indeed, Lawson had good cause for much of the bitterness he felt after his departure from office. Many in the Conservative Party were fair-weather friends, applauding the brilliance of his policies when they generated electoral benefits, but quick to stick the knife in when things went wrong.

The interest rate cuts came against the background of a strongly rising pound, again very useful in a pre-election period. As the pound moved up towards the DM3 level – but never reached it – the Bank of England also intervened, at times heavily, to restrain it. Largely as a result of such intervention, Britain's official reserves rose from $21.9bn at the end of 1986 to $34.4bn by the middle of 1987. Such intervention had potentially serious consequences for the money supply. Unless 'sterilized' by offsetting sales of government stock (gilts) a rise in the reserves of this magnitude threatened to produce what, before the 1985–6 abandonment of broad money (M3) targets, would have been regarded as an inflationary increase in the money supply.

Apart from the fact that the intention was to sterilize intervention, if not immediately, together with the reduced emphasis on broad money in policy, there was also a widespread feeling that the pound's rise was temporary. The foreign exchange markets, Treasury and Bank of England officials believed, had experienced a collective rush of blood to the head, in their expectation of a third Thatcher election victory. Intervention, to take the froth off the pound, was therefore justified. And, when post-election realities set in, sterling would settle down comfortably below its DM3 ceiling. As we shall see, policy would have been a lot easier, and much less prone to error, if the foreign exchange markets had behaved in this way.

6

LAWSON LETS RIP

Playing the Electoral Game

The rules of the game of electoral economics are straightforward. Policy is relaxed before elections, partly to put money into the pockets of the voters but also, just as importantly, to make them feel confident about future prospects. The lags between economic policy actions and their effects are long. Bank of England research suggests that it is two years before most of the effects of an interest rate change have worked through into the economy. The lags in fiscal policy – tax and public expenditure changes – are even longer. The base-rate cuts of March to May 1987 could not, therefore, be expected to have had much impact on the economy before the 11 June general election. What was important was the effect of their announcement on people's perceptions of their future well-being; the electoral 'feel-good' factor. Similarly, the cut in the basic rate of income tax from 29 to 27 per cent in the 17 March Budget, together with the promise of more to come, was mainly about influencing voters' assessments of the future.

The rules of the game, as followed by Lawson himself as well as by his predecessors, required that if tough action was required to bring the economy back into line, then the best time to do this was as soon as possible in the lifetime of a Parliament. It was one thing for people to feel good enough about the future to vote the government back into power. It was quite another for overconfidence among consumers, or too lax a policy stance, to knock the economy dangerously off balance, with all the attendant dangers of rising inflation and balance of payments difficulties.

Sir Geoffrey Howe, in his first Budget on 12 June 1979, six weeks after Thatcher's first election victory, raised interest rates (then controlled by the Bank of England's minimum lending rate) from 12 to 14 per cent. Lawson, a month after the June 1983 election, announced an emergency package to cut public borrowing by £1bn. The difficulties of the Macmillan Government in the early 1960s, which failed to tighten policy after the 1959 general election victory, were an object lesson to politicians too worried about being seen to renege on pre-election promises. Any rational voter should operate on the basis that, however cloudless the economic sky appears on polling day, it will have darkened within a month or so.

So it was in 1987. The period immediately after the Conservatives' 11 June election victory, coming as it did after a badly handled campaign, was one of relief within the party and, as described in Chapter 4, considerable gratitude for Lawson's efforts. With his political stock riding so high, as never before or since, the Chancellor was free to prescribe any post-election medicine he deemed necessary.

In the run-up to the election, the Treasury and the Bank of England surmised that much of sterling's strength derived from short-term capital inflows driven by political considerations. The pound's performance in the weeks immediately after the election justified this assessment. Talk in the financial markets of a 'wall of money' arriving from Japan, in the form of large-scale investment in British financial and physical assets, proved unfounded. The smart money, it appeared, had moved into sterling in anticipation of a third term for Thatcher, and chose the occasion of the actual victory to take profits and shift funds elsewhere. In the old City adage, it was better to travel hopefully than arrive. The strength of the pound and of the London financial markets as the election approached had generated healthy profits for those prepared to gamble on a Conservative victory. When financial markets rise strongly, a period of consolidation usually follows. Indeed, there was vested interest among dealers in perpetuating the story about the Japanese wall of money because the more that it was believed, the greater were the opportunities to make short-term profits out of people who bought sterling assets on the basis of it.

The pound's sharp pre-election climb was not, therefore, sustained. And the Bank of England, having intervened heavily in the markets to hold down sterling, was able to stand back. More significantly, the pound fell back to the extent that Lawson was able to tighten policy by raising interest rates without compromising sterling's ceiling of DM3 against the Deutschmark. The base-rate rise, from 9 to 10 per cent, came on 6 August 1987, less than two months after the election. It was unusual in that the Treasury and the Bank of England traditionally leave August free of interest rate changes and, in particular, increases in interest rates. The previous August increase in rates had been as long ago as 1975. Senior officials and ministers are usually on holiday in August, as are many City traders. Activity in the financial markets is usually well below normal levels. The dangers of basing interest rate changes on movements in 'thin' markets were widely recognized. But in August 1987 none of this appeared to matter. Lawson had been waiting for the opportunity to put policy back on to a low-inflation track and he took his chance when it arose.

The Bank of England's explanation of the move, made in its November 1987 *Quarterly Bulletin*, is particularly interesting:

> By early August it had become apparent that some rise in interest rates was appropriate and the authorities acted to achieve this. Earlier in 1987 the conjunction of massive demand for sterling from abroad and intense pressure for lower interest rates in the domestic markets had created a dilemma for the authorities. On the one hand, much lower interest rates seemed to be not fully warranted by developments in the domestic economy, where demand and broad money were buoyant, asset prices were strong and the pace of wage increase remained above that in our main competitors. On the other hand, pressures in the exchange market indicated that monetary policy was already tight: a sharp appreciation of sterling would have implied a further tightening, and could have damaged industrial confidence, with adverse consequences for the future productive capacity of the economy. Balancing the evidence, and on the basis that the demand for sterling was in part transient, connected with political developments in the United Kingdom, the authorities intervened heavily in the foreign exchange markets and allowed interest rates to fall. At the start of the period under review interest rates were lower than purely domestic factors alone would have indicated. (1987, p. 498)

In other words, it was recognized, apparently by the Treasury as well as the Bank of England ('the authorities' is usually taken to cover both), that holding down the pound had already resulted in interest rate reductions that risked adding to the risks of an inflationary boom in the economy. Lawson, according to officials and advisers, was well aware that the economy needed a cooling-off period, to prevent the re-emergence of inflation. The August interest rate increase from 9 to 10 per cent was merely the Chancellor's first shot. He was prepared to raise them further if evidence that the economy was growing too fast for comfort continued to build. 'He could see that things were starting to overheat,' said one adviser. 'The August move was definitely the first instalment in a conscious attempt to take the froth off the economy.'

The Bank of England's explanation of the August increase in interest rates, and of the earlier reductions, opened up the whole question of the interaction between interest rates and exchange rates in determining how tight, or loose, was monetary policy. A rise in the pound's level had, in the early 1980s, been recognized as a symptom of the excessive tightness of monetary policy, and a signal for the authorities to begin cutting interest rates. But was the rising pound of the spring of 1987 evidence of tight monetary policy? According to the Treasury's model of the economy, a rise in the exchange rate, however caused, denoted a tightening of monetary policy. A stronger pound, by putting pressure on industry in both home and foreign markets, would cause firms to rein back investment, pay and employment. Higher interest rates have much the same effect. Thus, it could be argued that a rising pound was, in its overall effects, much the same as an interest rate rise. But while the latter could be planned by the Treasury and Bank of England, the former was often determined by the whim of the markets. Thus, if monetary policy is deemed to be broadly right but there is a sudden rise in the pound, the authorities are justified in offsetting it by reducing interest rates. The Treasury model suggested that every 4 per cent rise in the pound's average value was broadly equivalent in its impact on the economy to a 1 per cent increase in interest rates. Armed with this knowledge, the currency markets began to expect policy to operate according to the so-called 'one-for-four' rule, under which every 4 per cent rise in the pound would be met by a one percentage point reduction in interest rates.

The theoretical basis for this trade-off could be questioned. The standard monetarist critique of exchange rate targets was that movements in currencies could affect *relative* prices in an economy but did not affect the overall price level, which was determined by the growth in the money supply. Thus, the trade-off may have been appropriate for those sectors of the economy which were exposed to international competition, but large areas of activity were immune from the effects of any rise in the pound and were unequivocal beneficiaries of interest rate reductions.

Thus, while manufacturing industry suffered when the pound rose, and needed the offsetting balm of lower borrowing costs, many service industries did not. And, in the housing market, to take a notorious example, any policy of cutting interest rates, however brought about, could be expected to result in strongly rising property prices. The criticism was not an entirely clear-cut one. Advocates of the trade-off argument suggested that, while the initial impact of a change in the exchange rates was on the so-called traded-goods sector of the economy, the effects would permeate through to less exposed sectors. Any boost to the housing market from lower interest rates could, for example, be nipped in the bud by reductions in pay and employment by industrial companies, which would erode the confidence of potential house-buyers.

The fact remains, however, that the Bank of England's assessment was that interest rates, at 9 per cent in the summer of 1987 prior to the August increase, were too low when set against the economy's buoyancy. Most of the warning signals were plain to see. Bank and building-society lending was growing at an annual rate of 20 per cent. House prices nationally were rising by 15–20 per cent a year, and by more than this in the south of England, and in the south-east in particular. Consumer spending was driving ahead at a rate of no less than 6 per cent in real terms, compared with 2–3 per cent in more normal times. The fall in unemployment that the Government had prayed for was no longer tentative. Indeed, many companies started to report serious skill shortages. Investment, relatively weak since the 1980–81 recession, now started to rise strongly, prompted both by a renewed mood of confidence on the part of businessmen and the highest levels of capacity utilization in industry since 1973. The trade figures were showing a marked deterioration as the strength of demand sucked in imports. The current account of the balance of payments, in surplus by just under £300m in the first quarter of 1987, was in deficit by £1.3bn in the third quarter, and £2.3bn in the fourth.

Whether the August rise in base rates from 9 to 10 per cent would have been sufficient, if maintained, to hold back the boom was open to extreme doubt. Policy had, however, moved in the right direction once the pre-election dilemma had faded. Operating an exchange rate target did not, it appeared, result in any permanent and damaging loss of control over domestic monetary policy. Sterling's froth had been a temporary problem and the March to May sequence of interest rate cuts had caused some sharp intakes of breath at the Bank of England. But whatever damage had been done was being corrected, and it was open to the authorities to take further corrective action.

It was in this spirit that Lawson prepared a speech to deliver at the annual meetings of the International Monetary Fund and World Bank at the end of September 1987. Unlike most of the Chancellor's IMF speeches, which were put together by Lawson and Sir Terence Burns fairly quickly on the plane to America or at the British Embassy in Washington on the night before they were due to be given, this one was carefully thought out. The aim was to provide an important piece of original thinking on the future of worldwide exchange rate management, and to put the international policy initiatives that had spawned the Plaza and Louvre agreements on a more formal basis.

Lawson's proposals were for 'a more permanent regime' of managed floating, under which international cooperation would be even closer and exchange rate targets more explicit. The Plaza and Louvre agreements had been a success in that governments, acting in concert, had given a higher priority to the exchange rate in economic policy and had cooperated closely in the achievement, first of a downward shift in the dollar, and then of exchange rate stability. 'I do not see the past two years simply as a temporary phase,' Lawson said. 'Our objectives should be clear: to maintain the maximum stability of key exchange rates, and to manage any changes that may be necessary in an orderly way' (1987b). The permanent regime he had in mind was one which would retain more flexibility than the old Bretton Woods system, but be more formalized than the Plaza and Louvre arrangements. It was possible, at some future date, that the leading countries would publish the bands in which their currencies were being targeted. And Lawson also had a clear idea about how adjustments should be achieved within his proposed regime:

> For the future, it is important that we continue to keep an adequate degree of flexibility in terms of the width of the bands within which currencies are able to fluctuate. And, if and when the time comes to adjust one of the rates, that adjustment should be made by moving the midpoint within the confines of the existing range. This means that the markets are not given a one-way bet, and the authorities retain tactical flexibility.   (1987b)

The speech was interesting in three respects. It also included a proposal for how the G7 countries, in managing exchange rates, could make sure that they were not taking their eyes off inflation. Lawson proposed a series of indicators, including world commodity prices, to be collectively monitored. James Baker, the US Treasury Secretary, went further in a speech at the same meeting, suggesting that the gold price should be a key element in a system of inflation early-warning signals. The proposal, seized upon in some reports as an American desire to return to the Gold Standard, was never quite that. But the Lawson and Baker contributions underlined the extent to which two of the key G7 players had high ambitions for exchange rate management and international economic cooperation. Others within the G7, notably Édouard Balladur, the French Finance Minister, were also keen to move to more formal, and long-term, arrangements.

The IMF speech also showed that Lawson was happiest when operating on the international stage. Around that time, ministers laboured hard to give the impression that the rest of the world wanted to replicate the Thatcher economic miracle. Britain, it appeared, could offer other countries a do-it-yourself kit which included privatization, taming the unions and the achievement of low inflation. Whether Lawson, in the vanguard of this movement, was so concerned with spreading the word that he diverted his attention away from domestic concerns is open to debate. But it was a clear example of pride coming before the fall.

Lawson's proposals, which built on the Plaza–Louvre framework of managed floating, assumed that all G7 participants were actively engaged in the process of targeting their exchange rates. And yet this basic assumption was not accepted by others in the British Government. The Prime Minister and her advisers were surprised to read of Lawson's ambitious plan as outlined at the IMF. The Government's official position was that there was no target for sterling. After all, Britain remained outside the exchange rate mechanism of the European Monetary System. That autumn, towards the end of the first year of the Chancellor's policy of shadowing the Deutschmark, and after a month in which Britain's official reserves had been swelled by nearly $7bn as the Bank of England intervened to hold down sterling, Thatcher told the *Financial Times* there was 'no specific range' for the pound. 'We are always free,' she said.

As it turned out, September 1987 was the high watermark for the G7 cooperation process, and for managed floating. The Lawson and Baker proposals for formalizing exchange rate management failed to get off the ground. Dramatic events were about to unfold which dealt a body blow to the whole idea of international cooperation on exchange rates.

Black Monday

On 19 October 1987, Margaret Thatcher was in Dallas, being entertained by her son Mark and his Texan wife. Lawson was at the Treasury, putting the finishing touches to the Government's sale of 31.5 per cent of its holding in British Petroleum, intended to raise £6bn, for the Government. At the same time, BP was issuing £1.5bn of new shares to finance its expansion. The BP sale, part of a privatization programme which generated £30bn of proceeds for the Government over the period 1979–91 (excluding sales of council houses, land and other non-financial assets), appeared to be more straightforward than most, despite its massive size. The Government was only a minority shareholder in BP, so the company was not moving from the public to the private sector in the manner of the gas, electricity and water industries. The stock market was already familiar with the company. But that day, 19 October, to be known for ever as Black Monday, world stock markets plunged, wiping £50bn off London share values. Next day, prices dropped by more than £40bn. And, to a greater or lesser extent, this fall was replicated around the world.

There was an eeriness about the events of October 1987 which unnerved many investors. On Friday, 16 October, a freak hurricane had blown across southern England, ripping centuries-old trees from the ground throughout the London commuter belt of Kent, Surrey, Sussex, Hampshire and East Anglia, and causing extensive damage to buildings. One vivid personal memory is of a tree-lined suburban street near my home. Against each house a tree lay at a 45° angle, having crashed through a roof or bedroom window. That Friday, with transport severely disrupted, the Stock Exchange suspended share trading. On Monday, after a weekend of clearing up, dealers returned to their desks to find a different sort of hurricane, a financial one, blowing. It was small wonder that the talk was of cosmic forces at work, exerting retribution for the new spirit of greed at work in the financial markets.

The cause of the stock-market crash was, however, rather more mundane. Share prices had risen strongly during 1987, partly driven by optimistic hopes that the Louvre agreement represented a new age in economic cooperation, from which the fruits of strong, sustained economic growth would flow. This optimism was not shared, however, by bond markets, which are driven by interest rate expectations, in which there was concern about rising inflation and a shortage of global liquidity. Thus, share prices were responding to a prospect that the bond markets were highly sceptical about. Equities, in their optimism, had moved out of line with bonds. On the basis of past relationships, something had to give. And exchange rates, now held together by the Louvre agreement, were not taking the strain.

On Wall Street, where international events are traditionally given a much lower priority than domestic news, the Louvre agreement had taken on a particular importance. This was because it was seen as buying time for American policy-makers. The twin deficits – budget and trade – had to be tackled, no one was in any serious doubt about that. But if, because of a collapsing dollar, they had to be tackled immediately then the only practical way of doing so was by generating a deep recession in the United States. The G7 arrangements offered the Reagan Administration an easier way out of the twin-deficit problem. As long as the White House committed itself to policies designed to eliminate the deficits, then the other countries would cooperate in support of the dollar. America could, to a very large extent, have her cake and eat it.

This was why, when serious strains began to emerge in the Louvre agreement after the September 1987 IMF meeting, world share markets, beginning on Wall Street, began to question the basis of their earlier optimism. The cause of the problem was a public row between James Baker, the US Treasury Secretary, and the German Bundesbank. The Bundesbank, independent of the Bonn Government, shared some of the concern of the bond markets about emerging inflationary pressures in the world economy, and more particularly in Germany. The Bundesbank had participated fully in the Plaza and Louvre currency arrangements but its President, Karl Otto Pöhl, had always made clear that German monetary policy could not be compromised in the interests of wider international ambitions. In Washington, the German team, consisting of Pöhl and Gerhard Stoltenberg, the Finance Minister, dutifully restated their commitment to exchange rate stability. But one of the Bundesbank's first acts after the meeting was to signal to the German money markets that it was raising interest rates in response to inflationary concerns. Baker was furious. With America entering a crucial phase in the run-up to the presidential election (for which he was later to leave the Treasury and handle George Bush's campaign), the last thing he wanted was a round of international interest rate increases. More fundamentally, there were serious doubts about whether the Louvre arrangements, which had shown signs of fragility even as Lawson and Baker were advocating more permanent arrangements, could survive.

The rise in German interest rates, Baker said, was not in the spirit of the international cooperation between the leading industrial countries on exchange rates. And he hinted in mid-October that, rather than following German rates up, the US Administration might have no option but to let the dollar fall. The Louvre agreement was in danger of breaking down completely.

Wall Street, sensing that it was losing its main source of support, responded quickly. In the first half of October, the New York share market fell by 16 per cent, culminating in its sharpest fall on Friday 16 October, the day of Britain's hurricane. On Black Monday, 19 October, Wall Street's fall turned into a worldwide panic. New York ended the week of 19–23 October a further 13 per cent down. London, Tokyo and other markets fell by around 20 per cent.

As the markets crashed, the phone lines buzzed between the finance ministries and central banks of the G7 partners. One dilemma was that of the role of exchange rate management in the crash. The proximate cause of Wall Street's dive had been the apparent collapse of the Louvre accord. But there was also a strong argument which suggested that, by imposing artificial stability on the exchange markets, the G7 had transferred massive instability to the share markets.

Lawson was sceptical about the true impact of a market crash brought on by the actions of 'excitable young men in striped shirts'. In spite of the collapse in share prices, he was determined to press on with the BP sale, reasoning that to cancel it would undermine the markets further. In America, however, the collapse on Wall Street brought back unhappy memories of the 1929 crash. Alan Greenspan, who had succeeded Volcker as Chairman of the Federal Reserve Board, together with Baker, the Treasury Secretary, were keen to follow the classic central-banking prescription of supplying liquidity to the markets to maintain confidence.

The lines were hot between the US Treasury building, a few blocks from the White House in Washington, and Lawson's office in Whitehall. Baker was being leaned on by the big US investment banks, who had agreed to take on a proportion of the BP share offer before the crash, but now stood to make a heavy loss at a time when they could ill afford it. Michael Wilson, Canada's Finance Minister, made similar representations on behalf of Canadian banks. Thatcher, on her American visit, had picked up the sense of panic. Surrounded by wealthy Texans at a celebration dinner in Dallas, America's oil capital, she and they watched fortunes being wiped out in a few hours of hectic trading. It may not have been the collapse of capitalism but it was far from being its finest hour.

Lawson had big doubts. On Tuesday, 20 October, as Mihir Bose recounts in his book *The Crash*, he appeared on BBC radio and described the market crash as 'an absurd over-reaction'. 'My advice to the millions of small investors who have entered the stock market in the past few years would be to keep calm,' he added (1988, p. 32). But if he was determined not to pull the BP sale, what else could the British Government do? The Chancellor had two responses. The first was to join in with a round of international interest rate reductions, in an effort to boost market confidence. The second was to put in place an elaborate scheme, whose parentage was claimed by both the Treasury and the Bank of England, under which the latter would agree to buy back the newly issued BP shares from the markets if they fell below a certain level. The buy-back scheme was a success. The fact that it was there meant, paradoxically, that the shares received natural support and, except in a tiny minority of cases (about 2 per cent of the shares issued), the Bank of England was not called upon to buy them back.

The interest rate cuts were a much more doubtful policy response. Lawson later admitted that he overreacted to the crash and should not have reduced rates as much as he did. Base rates, having been increased to 10 per cent in August, were cut to 9.5 per cent on 26 October, 9 per cent on 5 November and 8.5 per cent on 4 December. 'He was too ready to be swayed by Jim Baker,' said one Whitehall adviser. 'The crash was genuinely bad luck,' said another. 'I am sure that without it Lawson would have been putting interest rates up rather than down.' There remained the question of why interest rates were reduced at all. The rationale was that, by reducing the wealth of individuals, the stock-market crash would cause a slowdown in consumer spending, while business investment would be hit by the crash's knock to business confidence, as well as the new difficulties of raising finance on the stock market. Cutting interest rates was, therefore, a means of offsetting the recessionary effects of the crash. There were, however, doubts about the strength of these wealth effects in Britain, and they were expressed by the Bank of England at the time, and published in its November 1987 *Quarterly Bulletin.*

Critics of the interest rate reductions argued that they were a strange interpretation of the classic central-banking prescription of supplying liquidity to the markets at times of acute financial uncertainty. According to Sir Alan Walters, in his book *Sterling in Danger*:

> One such excuse, according to the *Economist* and many other supporters of the monetary expansion, is that monetary ease was the appropriate response to the 19 October 1987 crash. By this means we would then avoid the mistakes made following the crashes of 1929 and 1931. But the appropriate response to a crash is not inflationary expansion. The problem in October might well have been a run on the banking system or some other form of liquidity run. This calls for the central bank to stand ready to discount paper at penal rates to stem the run, not to flood the market with cheap money. In the event, the Federal Reserve Board of the United States handled the October crash in an exemplary manner which should have been a model for the United Kingdom. In the Economic Report of the President of February 1988 it was shown that, in spite of October's troubles, the Fed actually tightened monetary policy in 1987 – because it feared that the expansionary policies of 1986 would promote inflation. This is exactly what was required in the United Kingdom. There was nothing that prevented such a prudent policy being pursued.   (1990, p. 108)

There was, however, an important factor that stood in the way of what Walters describes as prudent policy. This was that sterling, after its summer lull, had started to rise strongly again, and was pushing up against the Chancellor's Deutschmark ceiling of DM3. The Bank of England was again called upon to intervene heavily to hold down the pound. As a result, Britain's official reserves rose by $9.5bn, or more than 25 per cent, in the October–December period of 1987. The stock-market crash was, therefore, convenient for Lawson in that it allowed him to disguise the true purpose of his interest rate cuts. The first reduction in base rates, on 26 October, was a direct response to the crash and the desire to ensure a successful BP sale. The next two, in

November and December, were largely to prevent the pound from rising above the DM3 ceiling. The idea that Lawson carried on cutting interest rates solely in response to what he had viewed as an absurd market over-reaction, defies logic. Sterling, according to officials, was the dominant factor. The Bank of England, which had been instructed by the Treasury to intervene on an unprecedented scale to hold down the pound and to cut interest rates against its instincts, was getting worried. The dilemma of policy of the pre-election period had returned with a vengeance. But this time there was no knowing when the upward pressure on sterling would stop. There were growing market doubts about the Louvre agreement and the ability of central banks, when pressured, to withstand sharp movements in exchange rates. Sterling was being boosted by a market belief that it had fallen too far in the wake of the plunge in world oil prices in 1986, and that it needed to rise to somewhere above DM3 before it reached its 'correct' level. Lawson's target range for the pound was, it appeared, at too low a level. In addition, the era of floating exchange rates had demonstrated that the foreign exchange markets are drawn to the currencies of economies that are growing faster than the rest. This had been the case for the dollar in the first half of the 1980s. And it was true for sterling at the height of the Lawson boom in 1987–8. The confidence that had emerged in the months before the June 1987 general election survived the crash unscathed. The economy was booming and foreigners wanted to participate in it. Foreign portfolio investment in Britain (investment in stocks and shares) totalled more than £30bn in 1987 and 1988 combined, nearly three times the level of outward portfolio investment flows.

The Deutschmark ceiling was under severe pressure, and the only weapons at the disposal of the authorities were heavy intervention and interest rate reductions. Lawson was too committed to the target to abandon it, and the interest rate cuts continued, in spite of official concern. The Bank of England, having set out its view that the 9 per cent base rate of the previous summer was too low in the light of domestic economic conditions, had to accept, by December, a rate of 8.5 per cent. And this on the fragile argument that the stock-market crash would cause a marked slowdown in the economy. In spite of such worries, the Chancellor made it clear, in evidence to the House of Commons Treasury and Civil Service Committee at the end of 1987, that he was in charge. 'When I think interest rates should go up, they go up,' he said. 'And when I think they should come down, they come down' (1987a).

The 1988 Budget

During the weekend of 9–10 January 1988, Lawson, together with senior Treasury officials, ministers and advisers, were gathered in the government-owned retreat of Chevening in Kent, a seventeenth-century, 115-room, Inigo Jones mansion. Chevening at that time was the Foreign Secretary's official residence. By tradition, it was lent to the Treasury each year for a weekend early in January, the purposes of which were to plan strategy for the spring Budget. This was one of the jollier weekend meetings under Lawson's Chancellorship. Ministers took on top Treasury officials at snooker and parlour games were played.

Unlike in earlier years, there was no sterling crisis or other unpleasantness to distract from the main purpose of the meeting. Lawson outlined his ideas in the library at Chevening. The centrepiece of the Budget, he said, should be an assault on higher rates of income tax. He had spoken during the previous summer's election campaign of the desirability of making radical reductions in the top and higher marginal rates of income tax. There were, in addition, many advantages to doing so at the earliest opportunity in a new parliament. Any objections to the tax cuts on egalitarian grounds, and the inevitable charge that the Conservative Party was rewarding its own, wealthier supporters, would have faded by the time the next election came around. And, if lower tax rates on higher-income earners had strong incentive effects, then there would be time to prove that cutting tax rates, far from reducing the proportion of tax obtained from top earners, could increase it. Professor Patrick Minford of Liverpool University, writing in the March 1988 *Quarterly Bulletin* of the Liverpool Research Group in Macroeconomics, suggested that there was clear evidence based on the 1979 reduction in the top rate of income tax from 83 to 60 per cent that the affected group was both working harder and being paid more for doing so. The supply-side argument, originally expounded by Professor Arthur Laffer in America, was that cuts in tax rates could actually increase revenue. Minford's conclusion was that this had happened in Britain with the 1979 cuts, and that the case was for more of the same. The counter-argument was that the higher tax take from those at the upper end of the income scale reflected growing income inequalities that were not based on any incentive-generated increase in effort. At the same time, many of the perks introduced in the 1970s to circumvent incomes policies had been converted into cash salaries with the abandonment of such policies. Lawson, who when cutting the basic rate of income tax from 30 to 29 per cent in 1986 was sceptical of the idea that such reductions could be self-financing, accepted it in the context of the higher-rate tax reductions.

The clinching argument was that the opportunity to transform the tax system so radically only comes along once in a Chancellor's political lifetime. The public-sector borrowing requirement, or PSBR, which the Government had struggled to control since 1979, had turned into what the Treasury christened a public-sector debt repayment, or PSDR. The budget deficit had become a budget surplus, as the booming economy produced rapid growth in tax revenues and falling unemployment cut the social security budget. The PSDR was £3.2bn in the 1987-8 financial year and, although it was not expected at the time, turned out to be a massive £14.4bn in 1988-9. The Chancellor had more room for manoeuvre on tax cuts than any of his post-war predecessors.

The decision to cut the higher rates of income tax was, therefore, in place at an early stage in the Budget planning process. One option was to combine large cuts in tax rates for higher-income earners with a removal of some of their fiscal privileges, notably the higher-rate tax relief on mortgage interest payments. Another was to establish a more sensible system for National Insurance contributions, by removing the upper earnings limit on such contributions. In this way, the top rate could have been reduced to around 35 per cent. In the end, however, Lawson opted for a more straightforward, although nevertheless highly dramatic move. All the higher rates of income tax above 40 per cent, which ranged up to 60 per cent, were abolished, leaving a single higher rate of 40 per cent. It was not as low as in the United States but it was undeniably low in comparison with the rest of Europe. The intention was to establish Britain as the enterprise centre of the European Community, a country where people could make money and, more importantly, keep it. The long-term effects of the reductions on incentives and reversing the 'brain drain' remain a source of heated debate. The late Professor Chuck Brown of Strathclyde University headed a school of thought which argued that any incentive effects were negligible. A survey he conducted with Cedric Sandford for the Institute for Public Policy Research, based on interviews with accountants and their clients, showed that the incentive effects of the 1988 cuts were negligible and that, in some cases, people had taken advantage of lower tax rates to reduce their work input, and yet still have a higher post-tax income than before.

This sort of question may only be settled in the long-term, and even then the results of any research will be hotly debated. Does the popularity of Britain as a location for inward investment from Japan depend on low tax rates for executives, or does it have more to do with relatively low labour costs, the English language and the ready availability of golf courses? In the weeks after the 1988 Budget, I was told repeatedly at City lunch tables that the higher-rate tax reductions had broken an important barrier. Suddenly, financial market dealers from Paris, Brussels and Frankfurt looked favourably on the idea of working in London. Whatever the shortcomings of London's infrastructure, low taxation was a major attraction for the internationally mobile. Unfortunately, this attraction was never fully tested. As we shall see, the City of London's great expansion did not survive for too long after the 1988 Budget.

With the centrepiece of the Budget in place at an early stage, the question in the Treasury was what other elements would be included. It is the job of Treasury officials to urge caution on their political masters. In the case of the 1988 Budget, the worry was that the October 1987 crash had not killed off the boom. By January and February of 1988 it was becoming clear that the crash, later described by Lawson as an economic non-event, had not tipped the economy into recession. Some indicators showed clearly that the boom that the August 1987 interest rate rise had been intended to damp down was very much in place. Indeed, the accelerating rate of increase of house prices suggested it was growing in intensity. Stories began to appear in the press saying that Sir Terence Burns, the Government's Chief Economic Adviser, was urging a cautious budget. If it was a political imperative to slash the higher rates of tax, then the Chancellor would have to do so. But there was a good case, strongly put, for delaying further reductions in the basic rate of income tax, then 27 per cent, until later in the Parliament.

Lawson appears to have been inclined towards this view initially. He recognized that, while it was good on political grounds to make reductions in the higher rates of income tax early in a Parliament, the opposite was probably true for the basic rate of income tax. The 1986 and 1987 basic rate cuts had left them fresh in the memory of voters in June 1987. There was a case for a similar course of action this time, postponing further reductions until 1990 or 1991. The Chancellor's political advisers told him, however, that a Budget that only reduced taxes for the better-off would look extremely one-sided, in favour of the rich. Other discreet soundings within the Conservative Party, and of Thatcher herself, told him much the same thing. Cut the higher rates of income tax by all means, he was advised, but balance it with a reduction in the basic rate. 'Lawson wanted to get the top rates of tax down above all else, but he was prevailed upon by political and other advisers to cut all rates,' said one Treasury official. Others disagree, arguing that the Chancellor, who still harboured ambitions of a triumphal exit from the Government, wanted to make his March 1988 effort a Budget to end all Budgets, even if it meant taking risks with the economy. 'He wanted that Budget to be a celebration, a showcase for all his talents,' said one Downing Street adviser.

For Treasury officials, one difficulty was that, in spite of strong growth in the money supply and house prices, official economic indicators published in January and February provided mixed evidence on the strength of the economy. In particular, the batch of statistics on economic growth, including industrial production and unemployment, appeared to suggest that the economy was suffering some delayed reaction to the stock-market crash. Most such figures, as it turned out, were subsequently revised higher. But they made a contribution to the policy mistakes of the period, particularly in the key months when the 1988 Budget was being planned. By casting doubt on the buoyancy of the economy, they weakened the Treasury's arguments in favour of a cautious Budget.

Robin Leigh-Pemberton, the Governor of the Bank of England, in his April 1990 Durham University speech, a combination of *mea culpa* and a rap on the knuckles for the Treasury, said:

> Before it became apparent that we had a very serious inflation problem on our hands, it was pretty clear that domestic demand was growing at an unsustainable rate. I say only 'pretty clear' because over the past three or four years there have been significant discrepancies in the official statistics, and material

revisions to them, which has made interpretation difficult. In particular, the output and domestic demand statistics for 1987 and 1988 have been consistently revised upwards, with cumulatively very substantial results. This is one reason why policy has not seemed impressively effective.   (1990, p. 216)

The Treasury and the Bank of England should not, however, be let off too lightly because of the inadequacy of the official data. The Government Statistical Service had been a victim of earlier cuts in public expenditure and had lost both staff and morale. In addition, as part of a deliberate aim of reducing the bureaucratic burden on companies, the coverage and reliability of the network of information-providers in the private sector were not as good as in the past. And, even with unreliable statistics, many independent economists, and not just the monetarists, were of the view that the economy was growing too fast and did not need a Budget stimulus. The Bank of England, in its February 1988 *Quarterly Bulletin*, published a month before the Budget, said:

> The fears that accounted for the response to the events of mid-October have now receded: the latest economic and monetary indicators depict a still-buoyant economy amply provided with credit, giving little sign so far that the pressures from domestic demand will abate soon ... Maintaining the anti-inflationary thrust of policy will continue to require a non-accommodating stance in the period ahead. This can only be reconciled with the preservation of international competitiveness if domestic costs in the tradables sector of the economy are strictly contained. It will also be important for the preservation of both internal and external balance that the anti-inflationary burden continues to be shared between monetary and fiscal policy.   (1988, p. 8)

The final sentence in that assessment was Bank of England code for its recommendation, given privately to the Chancellor, that the Budget be cautious. But one difficulty was that, within Government, dogma got in the way of a rational assessment of the statistics. The debate was over whether the economy was growing too fast in a conventional sense or whether, as a result of the supply-side reforms of the 1980s, it had moved on to a higher growth plane. Ministers naturally favoured the latter explanation. The Confederation of British Industry, which proved accurate in plotting the course of the subsequent recession, maintained in 1988 that the boom was not unsustainable because industry was now more efficient than before. The economy, said the CBI, was not overheating. Again, the Bank of England warned of the dangers. In the same bulletin, it said:

A period of relatively fast output growth is to be welcomed for the contribution it makes to raising living standards, reducing unemployment and stimulating investment. And the United Kingdom is capable of financing moderate current-account deficits for several years; indeed that is probably a necessary, if modest, contribution to the widely sought improvement in the US external deficit. There most, however, be some question about the sustainability of growth of domestic demand in this country at a rate above that currently being achieved by most other major countries.   (1988, p. 7)

One of the clearest indications of the unsustainability of the boom was in the balance of payments statistics. The current account, in deficit at an annualized £2.3bn in the first half of 1987, deteriorated to show an annualized £6.1bn deficit in the second half of that year, and £13.5bn in the first half of 1988, worsening further after that. And yet Treasury ministers seemed determined to ignore the message of the figures. Lawson, in his September 1987 speech to the IMF, had set the tone. He said:

There is no law that dictates that the current accounts of the major industrial countries should always be in balance. We have an integrated world economy and we encourage the free flow of capital and goods. Clearly there are limits to the accumulated external liabilities or assets that can be sustained without creating major anxieties for capital markets. But investment opportunities inevitably differ from country to country and it is natural for this to produce substantial, and often sustained, capital-account flows. These flows necessarily have their counterparts in current-account surpluses and deficits.   (1987b)

Lawson later cited the case of Denmark, which had run current-account deficits since the 1950s, as an example of the long-term sustainability of such a situation. The emergence of Britain's current-account deficit in 1987 and 1988 could therefore be presented as the natural consequence of the long-term capital inflow from overseas that reflected renewed international confidence in the British economy. This fitted the facts reasonably well in 1987, partly because investment managers in Britain repatriated funds in the wake of the October 1987 crash. Overseas direct and portfolio investment in Britain exceeded flows in the opposite direction by £10.5bn. This was not the case in 1988, however, when Britain recorded a net long-term capital outflow of £8.3bn. The current-account deficit of £15.2bn was, therefore, financed by short-term inflows of 'hot' interest-sensitive money, which by its nature is unlikely to be sustainable.

The result was that the Budget decisions were taken by a Chancellor who either did not see, or did not want to see, that the economy was in a boom that needed cooling, and not stoking up further. The political pressure on him to cut the basic rate has to be taken into account, but he was strong enough to resist such pressure if he deemed the action it advocated unwise. Had the Budget not included a reduction in the basic rate, there is no doubt that Lawson would have had a stormy time. As it was his Budget speech was disrupted by a Labour party protest and opinion polls taken after it indicated widespread public disapproval of the higher-rate tax cuts. But the job of Chancellor is all about resisting siren calls for inappropriate policy changes. Perhaps Lawson's real difficulty was that, having set his mind on a 40 per cent top rate of tax, he was determined not to soften this ambition. The basic rate was, therefore cut to 25 per cent, achieving the target proclaimed in the 1987 election campaign at the first opportunity. A new target, of a 20 per cent basic rate, was posted in its place. The total size of the Budget 'giveaway', including the higher-rate tax reductions, was £4bn in the first year and £6bn in a full year. By the standards of post-war demand management, it was a huge fiscal boost to the economy, and this at a time of boom, not slump.

Those close to Lawson at the time think he genuinely believed that the British economy had been so transformed as to be able to cope with and generate much faster growth in demand than in the past. There was always an upbeat tone to his speeches in this period, a fact that made his role in achieving the subsequent and necessary correction in the economy that much harder to achieve.

The 1988 tax cuts, widely regarded as the most ill-timed tax change in the post-war period, are not seen in this light by Lawson and his supporters. Their first point is that, when set against the £40bn expansion of credit during 1988, tax cuts worth £4bn in the first year and £6bn in a full year were a relatively small source of expansion. But this, perhaps intentionally, misses the key point. This is that the tax cuts and the growth of credit were inextricably linked. Their confidence and their after-tax income boosted by the cuts, people were prepared to borrow as never before. And savings, who needed them? In 1988 the personal saving ratio fell to a thirty-year low of 5.4 per cent, dropping to just 2.5 per cent in the final quarter. As one Treasury official put it: 'Lawson maintains that the Budget did not make any difference but that cannot be right. It added to the mood of the time, the feeling that the good times were here for ever.'

The credit argument would carry much more weight if there was any evidence that the Chancellor was aware of the dangers of its growth, and was acting to rein it back. But this was far from the case. Giving evidence to the House of Commons Treasury and Civil Service Committee a fortnight after his Budget, Lawson said:

> I am not concerned in the sense of worries that it has got out of control, or that there are great inflationary forces in the economy. I think that we have it under control, but it is obviously something which has to be watched very carefully. Let me say this: the rapid growth of credit is not a new phenomenon. Pretty well every year for the past ten years or so there has been a fairly constant growth in credit in the economy, and of course, what makes the position much sounder now than it has been for a very long time is that the public sector is no longer making any demands on the nation's savings at all, because we now have a public-sector debt repayment rather than a public-sector borrowing requirement. (1988, p. 34)

This brings us to a second defence of the tax cuts, that the Budget could not have been expansionary because the public sector had a debt repayment of £14.4bn in the 1988–9 financial year. Thus, looked at mechanistically, policy changes that result in a budget deficit are expansionary, those that result in a surplus cannot be. Again, this does not survive close examination. The shift from public-sector borrowing requirement to debt repayment in 1987–8 mainly reflected the effects of the economy on the Government's finances, and one that should have been picked up as another warning signal by the Treasury. A booming economy boosts tax revenues and reduces public expenditure on, for example, unemployment benefits and government support for nationalized industries. Adding to the boom can, in the short-term, enhance such effects, giving the impression of a sustainable shift in the Government's financial position. This was precisely what happened in 1988–9, following the March 1988 Budget. The fact that the shift was largely due to the boom is confirmed by the Treasury's expectation, at the time of the Budget, that the debt repayment would be only £3bn. Put simply, those that argue that the 1988 Budget was not expansionary are saying, in effect, that large-scale tax cuts have no immediate effect on domestic demand.

The third argument, which is related to the above, is that tax cuts should not be analysed in terms of their short-term impact. Rather, they are long-term, supply-side measures, and the timing of their introduction is immaterial. Lawson, in the same Treasury and Civil Service Committee session, said:

> I am concerned that the economy should be on track. I am very concerned that the fiscal position should be sound, and we have now got a sounder fiscal position than we have had for a very long time, and I am concerned to keep it that way, with, as I said, a balanced budget as the norm hereafter. I am also concerned that monetary policy should be adequately tight. I believe that a stable exchange rate within that context is helpful – helpful in countering inflation and helpful to industry. I also believe that it is necessary to take various measures to strengthen the enterprise economy and the enterprise culture, because that is what produces good economic performance; that is what we have seen, and I want to see that continuing. Against those really important matters, the question of what level, within a wide range, the current account of the balance of payments is in a particular year is really a very second-order matter.   (1988, p. 35)

In this case, the Chancellor's actions were a more useful guide to the true position than his words. A year later, at the time the 1989 Budget was being framed, the fiscal position was even 'sounder' than it had been a year earlier. And yet there were no tax cuts in the 1989 Budget. The fact is that, even in a Conservative Government that had ostensibly eschewed the demand management of the post-war period, Chancellors had to take into account the state of the economy at the time when they are introducing tax changes. Lawson did in 1988, but he miscalculated. Whether or not the tax cuts were right as a measure to secure the future of the enterprise culture, they were introduced at the wrong time.

As it was, many people were fooled by the 1988 Budget, and not just in Britain. In America, the *Wall Street Journal* said, 'Britain has returned to the lead in the global swing toward free economics and pro-growth policies based on individual initiative.' *Newsweek* said, 'Lawson's Budget was probably a landmark in Britain's post-war fiscal history – and perhaps that of Europe as well.' *Business Week*'s verdict was that 'Thatcher is taking over from a flagging West Germany the job of keeping the world economy on an even keel as the US slows.' In Germany, *Handelsblatt* said, 'The once sick man of Europe has become the most dynamic economic nation in Europe.' *Die Zeit* concluded that 'in the past the German model was praised in an almost embarrassing manner and compared with Great Britain's bad example. Now it is the other way around.' Even in France the praise was gushing. *Libération* referred to 'the exceptional dynamism of the British economy'. *Le Monde* described 'a gold Budget realizing the impossible dream of every finance minister: a balance of receipts and expenditures, combined with major tax reductions'. The Italian newspaper *Corriere della Sera* wrote: 'An Italian observer would have had to struggle yesterday against a deep feeling of envy while the Chancellor of the Exchequer, Nigel Lawson, presented his Budget to the House of Commons.' *Asahi Shimbun* of Japan said it was 'a Budget too bold for the Japanese Government'.

Fuelling the Housing Boom

There is one aspect of the 1988 Budget over which there is no debate. Treasury officials, Lawson himself and other ministers agree with critics that a major error of the Budget was to give an unnecessary boost to an already booming housing market. One specific tax change, announced by the Chancellor in a 15 March Budget speech that was already rich in content, produced a final, spectacular leap in house prices and housing turnover, before the market collapsed, exhausted. The change appeared innocent enough. The Treasury was always looking for ways of restricting the tax relief on mortgage interest payments, both because of its cost (£8bn a year in lost tax revenue by the early 1990s) and because of its distorting effect on economic decisions. The tax relief encouraged individuals to invest in property rather than, for example, putting their money into the shares of industrial companies where it could provide the basis for productive investment. Under Lawson, who was also in favour of restricting the relief, its real value had declined because of an upper loan limit which had been held at £30,000 since 1983, in spite of rising house prices. Now another, more direct, assault on the relief was proposed. The existing system tied the relief, not to properties but to individuals. Thus, two people jointly purchasing a house worth £60,000 could do so by means of two £30,000 mortgages, each subject to full tax relief. However, and tellingly, a married couple was only entitled to one amount of tax relief. The situation existed, therefore, where a couple living together but not married could obtain twice the tax relief of a similar married couple. Treasury ministers saw that, in advocating a restriction of the relief, they could bring moral as well as economic arguments into play. The system was variously described as a tax on marriage and an inducement for 'living in sin'.

The decision was taken, therefore, to limit the tax relief on mortgage interest to one per household, rather than tying it to individuals. The building societies pressed for the retention of the relief in its existing form, arguing that in areas such as London and the south-east, where property prices were very high, young people could often only gain a foothold on the housing ladder by clubbing together to buy a house or flat, using the available tax relief to the full. Lawson's mind was, however, made up, and Thatcher, a supporter of mortgage tax relief in general terms, could see no objections to the change.

Treasury officials proposed that the new system should come into force from midnight on Budget day, with all mortgages arranged from then on subject to the restriction of only one set of tax relief per household. The Inland Revenue advised, however, that to introduce the change with so little notice would create chaos and protest. Many housing transactions that were already under way would be scrapped because the buyers had made their calculations on the basis of the old tax-relief arrangements. There would be an unseemly rush to finalize mortgage arrangements in the seven hours from the time the measure was announced in the Budget and midnight, and the banks and building societies would be unable to cope. The tax authorities would also face extreme difficulty in adjudicating on the eligibility of mortgages for the old, multiple tax relief. The compromise, on Inland Revenue advice, was that the change be introduced but with effect, not from midnight on Budget day, but from 1 August, more than four months later.

The result, far from providing home-buyers with a quiet time to arrange their affairs, was a free-for-all. Estate agents saw a unique opportunity to sell properties at inflated prices, on the argument that if potential buyers who could benefit from the old system did not act quickly, they stood to lose thousands of pounds in tax relief. Many estate agents, in London in particular, operated a kind of home-buyers dating service, bringing together strangers who shared the common aim of wanting to enter the housing market before the old system of relief disappeared. The risks seemed few. After all, with property prices rising strongly sharers who did not get on with one another could always get out after a couple of years, after making large capital gains. Unfortunately, this was not the case. The summer of 1988, in the south of

England at least, was the housing market's last great thrash. In the third quarter of the year alone, average house prices in the south-east, excluding Greater London, jumped by 15 per cent. For 1988 as a whole, prices rose by 30 per cent compared with 1987. For some types of property, and in some areas within the south-east, annual rises of 50 per cent or more were common. But a painful hangover was to follow.

Lawson, while blaming poor Inland Revenue advice for the decision to delay the introduction of the change, later accepted that the breathing space was a big mistake. Lord Young of Graffham, a Cabinet colleague at the time, said, 'The Chancellor rightly wanted to stop this racket but why the hell he had to wait until August to do it escapes me.' One adviser at the Treasury commented that the manner of the change's introduction was 'a disaster'. A senior Treasury official said, 'The mortgage component of the Budget was disastrous. It was a stupidity we should never have allowed ourselves to commit.'

Such admissions are welcome, if only because they show that people do admit to mistakes. The wider question concerning the 1988 Budget remains, however. If one small tax change could cause so much damage, what about the consequences of introducing much bigger changes, in the form of the higher- and basic-rate income-tax cuts, at the height of the boom? The verdict on the 1988 Budget must be that, intentionally or not, Lawson introduced a tax package that stoked up the boom and, in doing so, added to the inflation problem that he and his successors were forced to tackle through painful measures.

7

SABOTAGING THE SOFT LANDING

The End of the Deutschmark Ceiling

While Nigel Lawson was grappling with the details of his showcase Budget in 1988, he had not forgotten about his Deutschmark target for the pound. Sterling had continued to push higher until mid-December 1987, even after the third of the base rate reductions which followed the October 1987 stock-market crash. At this point, with base rates at 8.5 per cent, and the Bank of England becoming convinced in its view that the economy had survived the crash virtually unscathed, a crunch was looming. Officials at both the Bank of England and the Treasury were concerned that further interest rate reductions would have been dangerous on inflation grounds. Robin Leigh-Pemberton, the Governor of the Bank of England, said later to the Treasury and Civil Service Committee:

> It follows that . . . the reductions in interest rates last autumn were, in fact, over-generous in terms of the monetary conditions at that time because they related to a danger that never materialized. It certainly was the position, both of the Treasury and the Bank, at the beginning of this year – or, indeed, towards the end of last year – that if it were possible to raise interest rates and get a better structure in relation to domestic monetary expansion, we should do so. (1988, p. 21)

The unanswered question was whether the Chancellor, in his commitment to the Deutschmark ceiling of DM3, would have insisted on further interest rate cuts and heavy foreign-exchange-market intervention, in order to maintain it. The question was to remain unanswered for several weeks. It is a characteristic of the foreign exchange markets that they tend to focus upon one issue at a time. In the words of one City economist: 'They can't chew gum and walk at the same time.' In the second half of December 1987, the topic at hand was renewed dollar weakness, following the publication of some poor US trade figures. The Deutschmark strengthened against the dollar, with the pound left on the sidelines, partly because a softening of world oil prices had cast doubts upon the sustainability of its rise. By the end of December, the pound had slipped to DM2.96, four pfennigs below the ceiling. Analysts had deduced, meanwhile, that having started with a fairly wide range for the pound of DM2.80 to DM3, the Treasury was now happiest if sterling was at the top end of that range, around DM2.95 to DM3, because within the context of a stable exchange rate policy a firm pound offered a better defence against inflation.

The position was, therefore, reminiscent of the previous summer, the last time that strong upward pressure on the pound had suddenly abated. This time, it was hoped, foreign exchange dealers had finally got the message about the Chancellor's determination to achieve a stable exchange rate. On 1 February, base rates were tentatively raised from 8.5 to 9 per cent. Cynics said that this was merely to establish a level from which Lawson could deliver the customary post-Budget cut in interest rates. The motive, however, was rather higher than this. Having decided that interest rates had been cut too much during the previous autumn, and mindful of the continuing strength of the economy, the authorities sought, to paraphrase the Governor of the Bank of England, a level of interest rates that was more appropriate in the light of domestic monetary conditions. At this point, therefore, the jury was still out on the question of whether the Deutschmark target could be held. On two occasions, in the spring and autumn of 1987, holding the pound below its DM3 ceiling had necessitated an uncomfortably high level of currency intervention, as well as interest rate reductions. But both times, admittedly with difficulty, the line had held. More importantly, the smokescreen of the October 1987 crash had prevented too many awkward questions being asked about exchange rate targets, particularly by the Prime Minister, still instinctively a free marketeer, in currencies as in other things.

The lessons of exchange rate management are, however, only learned by experience, and two miscalculations were made at this time. The first was the 1 February increase in base rates. This move, while perfectly justified on economic grounds, just as some of the earlier interest rate cuts were unjustified, had the side-effect of conveying a clear message to

the foreign exchange markets. This was that, with the pound then at
DM2.96, the British Government did not want to see it any lower. The
Treasury and the Bank of England had, inadvertently, told the markets
what, in practical terms, was the pound's floor. And if a currency has a
clearly established floor, not only are the risks of holding it greatly
reduced, but dealers feel almost honour bound to assess the robustness
of its ceiling.

The second miscalculation, by the Chancellor if not by the Bank of
England, was the failure to allow for the impact of the 1988 Budget on
the foreign exchange markets. International money men are used to
finance ministers making upbeat assessments of their economy's performance and prospects. Such assessments are often taken with a large pinch
of salt. In the case of Lawson's 1988 Budget speech, however, the
confident words were backed by equally confident actions, in the form
of the most eye-catching tax-reduction package that anyone could remember from a British Chancellor. Britain, according to the snap judgement
of the markets and, as described in Chapter 6, of the international
media, was the place to be. Something was stirring there that would
have been unthinkable even a few years before. With policies such as
this in place, the economy, the stock market and the currency had only
one way to go and that was up. The Budget also reinforced the view
within the international financial community, which had taken the
Prime Minister to its heart, that even in the first year of a new
Parliament, she was unsinkable. Set against the moribund, slow-growing
economies in the rest of Europe, the view was, Thatcher was turning
Britain into an oasis of enterprise. The mood may not have lasted long,
but while it did it was powerful. The result was something akin to the
wall of money, widely expected in June 1987, and now belatedly arriving
in the form of capital inflows from overseas. The fact that these inflows
were of short-term capital did not seem to matter greatly. The long-
term investment would come later.

Even before the Budget, sterling had begun to climb strongly. The
1 February base rate rise to 9 per cent, coming when the pound was at
DM2.96, reinforced the markets in their view that this was the pound's
effective floor. For the remainder of February, sterling pushed higher,
again bumping up against the Deutschmark ceiling of DM3. The Bank
of England realized that the policy dilemma was returning. Its own
foreign exchange dealers, in their contacts with others in the market,

had picked up that a period of heavy buying of the pound was imminent, on a scale that would probably even dwarf the purchases that led to the strong upward pressure of the previous autumn. The Bank, in other words, was fearful of a situation that it could not easily control. Reversing the 1 February interest rate rise would run serious inflation risks by once more reducing interest rates below the level necessary to keep a semblance of control over domestic monetary conditions. The other traditional concern, that unless currency intervention is 'sterilized' by sales of gilts (government securities) it is inflationary, was less pressing, because of the shift from a public-sector borrowing requirement (budget deficit) to a public-sector debt repayment (budget surplus).

The issue came to a head early in March, a fortnight before the Budget. Robin Leigh-Pemberton, the Bank Governor, advised both the Chancellor and the Prime Minister directly that the policy of holding down the exchange rate could not easily be sustained against heavy market pressure. The price of a stable pound, he suggested, could be the highly damaging one of opening the inflation floodgates.

At the beginning of March, foreign money began to pour into sterling assets in anticipation of the Budget. Dealers always like to make their move ahead of events, in line with the old market adage that it is often better to travel hopefully than arrive. Put more crudely, the rule of thumb is: 'Buy on the rumour, sell on the fact.' Lawson, then putting the finishing touches to his Budget was, therefore, faced with the biggest test yet of his stable sterling policy. His initial response was to order the Bank of England to intervene heavily to hold the pound down. The scale of this intervention was enormous. In the first four days of March the Bank committed more than $4bn to the task of holding the pound down. Inside Downing Street, the policy was viewed with dismay; Lord Griffiths, the head of the Number 10 policy unit, submitted a memo to Thatcher recommending, in line with the Bank of England's advice, the abandonment of the Deutschmark target. Griffiths, a Welshman, had come to Downing Street from the City University Business School, where he was Dean. A monetarist, he put forward his views with the zeal of one suited to the pulpit. Indeed, he had made a name for himself by writing books which explored the relationship between Christianity and economics.

The Prime Minister, increasingly irritated by a policy to which she was temperamentally opposed, and which had been kept from her in its early stages, had been waiting for her chance. She had never understood her Chancellor's conversion to the virtues of the European Monetary System, and his spirited advocacy of full British membership. Still less did she comprehend a strategy explicitly designed, as she saw it, to prevent the pound from finding its own level in the foreign exchange markets. There were echoes of Ronald Reagan's earlier attitude to the rising dollar in her approach. If sterling was going up because international investors believed in the dynamism of the British economy, then why stop it? She summoned Lawson and told him to abandon the policy. According to an account in the *Sunday Times*, the meeting was brief. Thatcher opening by saying, 'I haven't got much time. I've only time to explode and get my way' (1988). The Chancellor, one of the few ministers in Thatcher's Cabinet to stand up to her, defended his policy. The upward pressure on the pound, he said, represented the short-term reaction of frothy markets. Far better to keep it stable for now, he suggested, than face a damaging reversal later as currency dealers switched to another game. The monetary consequences of intervention, the Chancellor claimed, could be adequately dealt with, not least because the public-sector borrowing requirement had been eliminated.

Lawson was, however, in a minority in defending his policy. Even in the Treasury, doubts had emerged about the strategy. It was one thing, officials argued, for the pound to be held stable within the context of a properly operating Louvre agreement. It was another for Britain to try to achieve exchange rate stability in a volatile world. The Bank of England's position was clear; so was that of Thatcher's own advisers, including Sir Alan Walters, at that time still offering counsel on occasional visits to Downing Street and by telephone from Washington. The Prime Minister, of course, was used to receiving advice but ignoring it. Many of the changes introduced under her premiership had been against the advice of experts. This time, however, the advice chimed in with her own prejudices and she was determined to have her way. Lawson, recognizing that the writing was on the wall, reluctantly agreed. His concern, however, was to ensure that the abandonment of the DM3 ceiling did not lead to the return of free, and volatile, floating.

Lawson's idea was to allow the markets their fling but then to re-establish stability for the pound. It could be that the upward pressure on the pound would blow itself out. If not, then a new target, at a slightly higher level than before could be put in place. On Monday 7

March, the foreign exchange markets opened with dealers once more preparing to do battle with the Bank of England around the DM3 ceiling. This time, however, to their considerable surprise, they found that they were pushing at an open door. The pound pushed above DM3 and carried on rising, with no effective resistance from the authorities. Dealers feared a trap, but none had been set. Within days, the pound had climbed to DM3.10, the old ceiling in ruins.

Thatcher, having ordered Lawson to draw back from his policy of using currency intervention to restrain the pound, appeared to accept in private that too big a rise for sterling would be damaging to industry. The compromise between them was that she would not welcome or encourage the pound's rise. Unfortunately for the Chancellor, and for their relationship, her belief in unfettered market forces kept breaking out. The agreed line was forgotten during the heated atmosphere of Prime Minister's Question Time. 'There is no way in which one can buck the market,' she told the House of Commons. This was what Sir Geoffrey Howe meant, in his resignation speech two years later, when he said of Thatcher: 'Every step forward risked being subverted by some casual comment or impulsive answer' (1990).

Lawson, during what should have been his hour of triumph in presenting his tax-cutting Budget, was angry and frustrated, much more so than when he had been thwarted on sterling's proposed entry into the European exchange rate mechanism three years earlier. From then until his resignation twenty months later, the atmosphere between them was at best cool, at worst hostile. 'The mood was never good after that,' said one Downing Street adviser. 'After March 1988 I don't think she really trusted him again.' The two would meet to discuss the economy and Treasury business, at least every Wednesday. But the old partnership, Lawson's intellectual gifts tied to Thatcher's political force, was gone.

The Chancellor, having lost the battle to keep the pound below DM3, refused to accept that he had lost the war over managing sterling. Colleagues say that this, and pride, offer the only explanations of why, in the weeks after his 15 March Budget, he again embarked on a policy of cutting interest rates in order to restrain the pound. 'It became an obsession with him,' said one adviser. 'He believed he was right and he was determined to prove it.' Lawson's strategy was twofold. He lost no opportunity to tell the markets that the pound's rise would not continue. With sterling at DM3.08, he told the Treasury and Civil Service

Committee, 'Any further significant rise in the exchange rate, certainly against the Deutschmark would, in my opinion, be unlikely to be sustainable' (1988, p. 40). The markets were therefore faced with the bizarre situation of a Chancellor trying to talk his currency down, while the Prime Minister appeared to be relishing its rise. In this case, they decided that Thatcher had the last word. The pound traded above Lawson's 'unsustainable' level of DM3.08 for fifteen months, reaching a peak of almost DM3.30. It was not until the autumn of 1989 that it fell back below the old DM3 ceiling.

In the spring of 1988, Lawson returned to his pre-Christmas policy of cutting interest rates to prevent the pound from rising too far. It was back to the old 'one-for-four' rule, whereby every 4 per cent rise in the pound's value was offset by a 1 per cent reduction in interest rates. Bank base rates were cut from 9 to 8.5 per cent on 17 March, two days after the Budget, and again to 8 per cent on 11 April. Finally, they came down to 7.5 per cent, their lowest since May 1978, on 18 May. And this was in spite of the Bank of England's publicly stated opposition to the pre-Christmas strategy of cutting interest rates to inappropriately low levels in order to keep the pound down. Lawson, to paraphrase Oscar Wilde, went down the same mistaken route twice: to do so once was unfortunate, to do so twice was unforgivable. But there was no calming voice telling him to stop. Indeed, it is a criticism of Thatcher and her advisers that, while they were not prepared to see large-scale currency intervention to hold down sterling, nothing was done to prevent interest rate reductions intended to achieve the same end. Indeed, throughout her period in office, Thatcher never objected to an interest rate reduction proposed to her by her Chancellors, although there were cases where she delayed or prevented interest rate increases.

How damaging were these interest rate cuts during the March–May period? Lawson later defended them, arguing that they were not maintained for long enough to do any damage. But this ignores a vital point. This was that the cuts came after the big tax-cutting Budget and, most importantly, a Budget that had given every encouragement for a short-term boom in the housing market. It is difficult to conceive of a headier brew than the one that was served up during the spring of 1988. Income tax had been cut dramatically, interest rates were at their lowest for ten years and, in the case of multiple mortgage interest relief, official policy encouraged a 'buy now while stocks last' mentality. It would have taken a saint not to be tempted by such a combination. And the British consumer had shown himself to be anything but saintly during the 1980s.

Walters and the Reversal of Policy

By May 1988, everyone officially concerned with economic policy, including Lawson, was aware that interest rates, at 7.5 per cent, were dangerously low. But the pound had refused to respond, either to the rate cuts, or to the Chancellor's repeated observations that its rise was unsustainable. 'Actual interest rates were reduced over a period during which we now see they clearly should not have been,' said Robin Leigh-Pemberton, the Governor of the Bank of England, in his candid speech at the University of Durham two years later (1990). The economy was in an inflationary boom, the most obvious indicator of which was the breakneck pace of house-price increases. In the south-east, where the property boom had set in well before the 1987 general election, the situation threatened to get completely out of hand. A converted broom cupboard in Knightsbridge, measuring just 11 ft by 5 ft 6 in., sold as a flat for £36,500. But, just as the upturn in inflation was to be dismissed by Lawson as a 'temporary blip', so this frenzied activity in the housing market could be played down as a short-term phenomenon, with no damaging long-run effects. Shortly after his March 1988 Budget, again in evidence to the Treasury and Civil Service Committee, Lawson said, 'House prices are just one relative price which does not tell you anything about inflation. It just tells you what is happening in one particular sector of the economy' (1988, pp. 39–40).

In spite of the lifting of the Deutschmark ceiling in early March, interest rate policy was still largely determined by the behaviour of sterling. Sir Alan Walters, who was to play a central role in the transition from economic boom to bust, and in Lawson's demise as Chancellor, wrote in his *Sterling in Danger*:

> The question remained: Were the authorities *still* operating with an exchange rate band as the target? Although the band had been moved to DM3.10 to DM3.30 or so, the rate was kept in that band until September 1989. But the evidence of incipient inflation became more evident with every passing day. House prices were booming, unemployment was falling as fast as ever and labour shortages were spreading – all the signs of overheating were there for

anyone to see. The need for a substantial increase in interest rates, whatever
the exchange rate consequences, was manifest.   (1990, p. 109)

Walters, the son of a Leicester grocery clerk and born, on his own
admission, in a slum, had been Thatcher's personal economic adviser
from 1981 to 1984, having come to know her through the free-market
Institute of Economic Affairs. The contrasts between Walters and
Lawson were many. Walters, with his cadaverous appearance and shock
of white hair, was the physical opposite of Lawson, with his squat frame
and black mane. Lawson's wealthy middle-class background had allowed
him to progress, first to Westminster School and then to Christ Church,
Oxford. Walters, having failed his eleven-plus, struggled through to
become accepted as an external student at the University of Leicester.
Each had a sizeable, but different, chip on his shoulder. And Walters,
having swum against the tide in espousing monetarism in the 1960s and
early 1970s in Britain, against the overwhelming Keynesian conventional
wisdom of the day, was no backroom academic. He loved publicity, and
over the summer of 1988 he was to get plenty of it. Even Thatcher was
later to admit, of her adviser, that one of his shortcomings was that he
was a vain man.

   A plain speaker, with a gift for cutting through complex arguments,
he was one economist who Thatcher could listen to. He also became,
during this period, a gift for journalists. Here was a man who informally
advised the Prime Minister from his Washington base – where he was
an adviser to the World Bank and Professor of Economics at Johns
Hopkins University in Maryland – and was in and out of Downing
Street on his visits to Britain. But here too was a man who was ready to
criticize, in no uncertain terms, the strategy of the Chancellor of the
day. Walters, in a series of newspaper articles and interviews, wrote in
the summer and autumn of 1988 about Lawson's 'misguided' policies
and about the wasted years in the battle against inflation. The Chancellor's policy, he wrote, was like a Greek tragedy, the denouement of
which was not in doubt. The European exchange rate mechanism, entry
into which was the purpose of Lawson's shadowing of the Deutschmark,
was a 'half-baked' system. He wrote around this time:

The pressure from Europe and the British establishment to conform and join
the ERM has been enormous. But the arguments have never attained even a

minimum level of plausibility. My advice has been for Britain to retain its system of flexible exchange rates and to stay out of the present arrangements of the ERM. So far Mrs Thatcher has concurred ... It would not be in Britain's, or, I believe, Europe's interest to join the present half-baked system. (1990a)

This article, which surfaced in October 1989, provided the trigger for Lawson's resignation. In 1988, his known views were enough to allow even the most casual observer to conclude that there were deep divisions on economic policy between the Prime Minister and the Chancellor.

The pound's rise in the spring of 1988 appeared to be breaking all the rules. It came against a background of a widening current-account deficit and growing evidence that a serious inflation problem lay ahead. More significantly, it occurred in spite of a fall in British interest rates to their lowest level for ten years. The only way that sterling's continued rise could be rationalized was that it went up because it was expected to continue going up. In other words, the prospect of further currency gains outweighed the fact that interest rates were being reduced. Almost by its nature, such a situation could not go on for ever. Sooner or later, a position would be reached where the markets would decide that sterling's climb had gone far enough and that the economic fundamentals of a deteriorating balance of payments position and an overheating economy would exert themselves.

This position was reached within a fortnight of the 18 May base rate cut to 7.5 per cent, which turned out to be the last interest rate reduction Lawson made as Chancellor. In the space of a few days at the end of May and in early June, sterling dropped from DM3.19 to DM3.09. In any circumstances, a currency fall as sharp as this would have been of concern to the Treasury and the Bank of England. Coming at a time when the exchange rate was the key determinant of interest rate policy, it provided a clear sign that the time had come to start raising interest rates again. Significantly, Lawson did not let the pound drop right down to the old DM3 ceiling. The response to overheating pressures in the economy had, indeed, been to move the target range for sterling higher.

In eight months, from October 1987 to May 1988, economic policy had gone completely off track. Interest rates were cut on several occasions, when they should have been raised. Tax cuts added fuel to an already roaring economy. A botched move to limit the tax relief on mortgage interest payments ensured a Klondyke-style boom in the housing market, the inflationary effects of which were ignored. The Bank of England's Leigh-Pemberton, in his Durham speech, said, 'It is clear from the rise in inflation over the past two or three years that something has gone quite badly wrong, and I shall not deny that policy mistakes and forecasting errors played a part' (1990).

The Cabinet watched, some ministers mildly alarmed about what was going on, but powerless to intervene. Most, however, were convinced that Lawson was still working his own brand of magic on the economy. After all, Thatcher herself had heaped praise on her Chancellor. 'Nigel's Budget was a real humdinger,' she told Conservative Party activists at a meeting in Buxton in March. Sir Geoffrey Howe, the Foreign Secretary, said at the same meeting, 'I must say, the young man is doing very well.' Most ministers were, however, kept well away from the action. Throughout the period there was no general Cabinet discussion of economic policy. Policy was fixed as a result of direct negotiation between 10 and 11 Downing Street and the Cabinet's role was merely that of receiving information on policy slightly before the general public got to hear of it.

The falling pound of early June provided the excuse that the Bank of England, and to a lesser extent the Treasury, had been waiting for. In spite of public denials by the Chancellor, there was a growing perception that tough action was needed to rein back the economy. And so, in June 1988, the brakes began to be applied.

The Soft-landing Strategy

The reversal of the earlier interest rate cuts, when it came, was dramatic. Base rates were raised to 8 per cent on 3 June, 8.5 per cent on 6 June, 9 per cent on 22 June and 9.5 per cent on 29 June. It was achieved, importantly for Lawson, without pushing the pound sharply in either direction. Sterling held within a range of DM3.10 to DM 3.15 for the remainder of June. The interest rate increases during the month, while cumulatively quite significant, were of half a percentage point a time. The old Treasury rule on interest rates, 'up in one, down in halves' was not followed. And the overriding impression was that higher interest rates were driven, not by worries about the economy's inflationary boom, but to keep the pound within its new, higher range.

Treasury and Bank of England officials now recognize that, once the inflation danger was fully recognized by mid 1988, the best course would have been to stamp down on it harder by raising interest rates more sharply. Ministers, with the benefit of hindsight, agree. 'Nigel shouldn't have pussy-footed around, putting rates up by half a point at a time,' said one of Lawson's Cabinet colleagues. 'He should have hit us on the head by putting up rates by two or three points at a time.' According to Walters:

> From June 1988 monetary policy was successively tightened by raising interest rates frequently but by only half a percentage point. This was new. Normally in a squeeze the interest rate is put up substantially – usually by two percentage points. Then the market is less certain about the next move of interest rates, whereas using the innovation of Mr Lawson, the market was certain of the direction of the next interest rate movement. (1990, p. 109)

Lawson, however, had reasons for proceeding as he did. The Treasury badly underestimated the strength of the boom, and the potential for an upsurge in inflation. Pride was also a big factor. It is not easy to explain to the electorate, or to political colleagues, why policy has shifted suddenly from cutting interest rates to raising them very sharply. If credit growth was the concern, why had the Chancellor been so slow to see it? Thus it was important, for presentational purposes, to present the reversal of the earlier interest rate cuts as a series of gentle touches on the tiller, mainly in response to the fact that sterling had come down from its post-Budget highs. There was also the need to ensure that the policy response fitted the diagnosis. Lawson said publicly, and appeared to believe, that there were no great inflationary pressures in the economy. If so, why use a sledgehammer to crack a nut?

Meanwhile, Walters was publicly criticizing the Chancellor and, in newspaper articles and interviews, warning that interest rates would have to rise sharply as a result of the earlier economic mismanagement. Base rates, Walters said, would have to go up to at least 12 per cent. Lawson, stung by such criticisms, did not want to give Walters the luxury of being proved right.

Most importantly, officials believed that they had a strategy for gently bringing the economy down to earth, steering a prudent course between high inflation and recession. The strategy, christened the soft landing, was based on the idea that it was possible to skim the froth off the top of the economy, without damaging its productive base and without unduly damaging the 'economic miracle' of high-productivity, low-inflation growth. Even a gentle rise in interest rates, it was thought, would hit over-borrowed consumers hard and force them to curtail their spending. Individuals were, to use the jargon, highly geared. They had borrowed on the expectation that low interest rates would continue (most mortgage and other consumer borrowing in Britain is on variable rates of interest). They were vulnerable, it appeared, both practically and psychologically, to higher interest rates. Certainly, the scale of consumer borrowing was dramatic. Christopher Huhne, in his book *Real World Economics*, described it:

> The key to understanding the Lawson boom is understanding debt. The economy was lifted by a balloon of personal credit which expanded from a mere £90.5bn at the end of 1980 to more than £328bn in 1988. This extraordinary explosion of lending became, after the growth of personal incomes, the greatest single motor behind the buoyant growth of consumers' spending, which in turn was the driving force behind the five years of high economic growth from 1984 to 1989. The credit boom ushered in a society built on values which the Leader of the Opposition criticized as those of 'me and now' ... Most people have contractual savings arrangements which are difficult to vary, such as contributions to their pension fund. They exercise control over the net amount they save by borrowing. Individuals' liabilities – their mortgages, personal bank loans, credit-card debts and so on – rose from 45 per cent of pre-tax incomes at the beginning of the decade to more than 85 per cent in 1988. Never have so many borrowed so much so quickly.
>
> (1990, p. 158)

Companies, as well as individuals, were heavily borrowed. Bank borrowing by industrial and commercial companies rose from £12.1bn in 1987 to £31bn in 1988, partly because in the aftermath of the October 1987 crash it was more difficult to raise finance on the stock market. Even allowing for this, there was a strong rise in company borrowing. Bank of England figures showed a net borrowing requirement for industrial and commercial companies of £23.6bn in 1987, rising to £45bn in 1988 and £49.1bn in 1989, before slipping back to £26.7bn in 1990. However, while it was recognized that companies, and particularly small businesses heavily dependent on bank borrowing, would be affected by higher interest rates, it was thought by officials that these effects would be less severe than on the personal sector. One of the big sources of bank borrowing by companies had been the boom in takeover activity in the second half of the 1980s and, while some large companies were saddled with large debt as a result of such activity, higher interest rates could be expected to lead to a decline in the number of takeovers, as indeed they did.

The soft-landing strategy required, therefore, two elements to work as planned. The first was that consumer spending would be reined back at a relatively low level of interest rates, and certainly very much lower than the 16 and 17 per cent base rates which were required in the early 1980s. Companies, meanwhile, would recognize that the economy was going through a temporary correction and take a longer view, leaving the supply side of the economy more or less intact. The second essential element was that no new factors should emerge to push the economy off course. In particular, sterling had to remain broadly stable, in order to prevent inflationary pressure from emerging through the medium of a falling exchange rate, on one side, and an industrial recession from too strong an exchange rate, as in 1980–81, on the other. On both counts, the strategy failed.

Individuals, their wealth buoyed up by the boom in house prices, proved far less sensitive, initially, to higher interest rates than had been hoped. For the Chancellor, one difficulty was that it was impossible to convey one message to consumers and a different one to company chief executives and chairmen. If the latter were led to believe that interest rates were moving only temporarily higher, and that normal service would be resumed shortly, then so were the former. Companies had embarked on an investment boom, unemployment was falling rapidly, ministers were busy assuring everyone that the economy was in no real difficulties. Why, in such circumstances, should anyone want to cut back? And, as a result of the earlier deregulation of banks and building societies, there was no shortage of funds to borrow. For many people, every time the postman called, a new offer of credit landed on the doormat.

Alan Budd, the Government's Chief Economic Adviser from September 1991, said, 'Everyone came to believe in the Thatcher economic miracle. The personal sector, believing in the future growth of incomes, ran up its debts. So too did companies. And the Government had cut taxes and allowed public spending to increase, also in the belief that growth would continue for ever.'

Financial deregulation had provided the basis for the boom of the second half of the 1980s, and this had been overlaid by inappropriate policy decisions. What was the proper policy response in a booming, financially deregulated economy? A research paper by Adrian Blundell-Wignall, Frank Browne and Paolo Manasse, three economists at the Organization for Economic Cooperation and Development (OECD), suggests that one consequence of financial deregulation is that the 'dosage' of policy has to be increased. In other words, it may take lower interest rates than in a regulated economy to get an economy moving but, by the same token, higher interest rates are needed to slow it down again. According to the paper:

> The impact of policies that operate increasingly through expectations channels is a question of achieving the appropriate policy 'dosage'. Given available information and uncertainty in markets, there will be some level of policy-determined interest rates which will influence expected wealth and private-sector expenditure in the right direction ... But the full impact on private spending will depend on what the authorities' objectives are perceived to be, and how seriously they are expected to pursue them. Are the rate increases expected to be temporary? Are the authorities simply trying to stabilize inflation at a higher rate, or do they intend to reduce inflation from current levels? ... Practical constraints may still be perceived by the authorities if the amplitude and duration of interest rate increases necessary to slow demand are considered to be too large or too long. For example, interest increases are politically unpopular, which may lead to pressure on monetary authorities to respond to inflation threats too slowly (with the likelihood that interest rates will ultimately have to be raised further than would otherwise be necessary). Alternatively, policy-makers themselves may be reluctant to see bankruptcy and financial fragility in circumstances where the private sector is heavily indebted. (1990, pp. 170–72)

The interest rate response in the summer of 1988 thus fell short of what was necessary in a number of respects. The rate increases were certainly viewed as temporary. Indeed, companies and individuals were encouraged to think this by the politicians. There was also a clear reluctance to inflict too much politically unpopular pain on the economy. As for the inflation goal of the authorities, Lawson's reputation in the financial markets increasingly became that of a successful tax reformer who had generated strong economic growth. But, and this was the problem, he was seen as a Chancellor who, despite having described inflation as the judge and jury of monetary policy, was inclined to take risks with it.

Within the Treasury, officials and advisers bemoaned the Chancellor's apparent inability to use tough words to accompany what, in the end, became tough economic policy action. One senior Treasury official remarked, 'We certainly allowed interest rates to fall too low and we did not realize how very strong and buoyant the economy was. But ultimately, we did not act fast enough and I don't think we managed to give the right signal to the world at large. We did not get the message across anywhere near as strongly as we should have done.'

Lawson, in his public speeches, would manage to inject an upbeat element into the framework provided by his officials. It was as if he could not bring himself to believe that, under his stewardship, the economy had been allowed to go dangerously out of control. Interviewed by the *Financial Times* in January 1989, Lawson set out his ambition for a soft landing for the economy:

> Fighting inflation clearly requires monetary policy in particular to be sufficiently tight to secure a steady decline in the growth of nominal national income, sometimes known as money GDP (gross domestic product). But there is no reason whatever why that should imply a recession. There will only be a recession if, within the context of necessary financial discipline, businesses fail to maintain an adequate control of their costs, including labour costs. Given the dramatic improvement there has been in the quality of British management and the healthy climate that government policy has brought about over the past ten years, I do not believe this will happen. The prospect for 1989 is thus one in which the underlying rate of inflation, after continuing to edge up very slightly for a few months more, will resume its downward path, while growth will continue, albeit at a somewhat slower pace overall, but with investment continuing to expand particularly strongly. And, remember, this follows five years of exceptionally strong growth, with inflation on average in low single figures throughout. (1989a)

By then, the trickle of half-point interest rate increases of June 1988 had turned into a flood. Base rates were raised on two occasions in July, to 10 per cent on 5 July and 10.5 per cent on 19 July. They continued to increase in August, rising to 11 per cent on 8 August and 12 per cent on 25 August, with the latter the first full percentage point rise in the sequence. Base rates had reached the level predicted by Walters. The August increases pushed the pound sharply higher – it climbed to just below DM3.25 – and there was a briefly held hope in the money markets that the next interest rate move would be downwards. But it was not to be. The aim of policy in this period was to keep the pound firm within its new, higher range, so there was little question of the authorities using the first bout of sterling strength as an excuse for cutting interest rates. Meanwhile, the economy's continued boom ensured that, on any reasonable assessment, interest rates had to stay high. On 1 November, in his Autumn Statement, Lawson published a new forecast for the balance of payments. The current account, he predicted, would be in deficit by £13bn in 1988 (compared with a Budget forecast of £4bn the previous March) and £11bn in 1989, as economic growth returned to 'a sustainable level'. Even these huge numbers did not go far enough. The actual deficits were £15.2bn in 1988 and £19.1bn in 1989. The sharp deterioration in Britain's external position introduced a subtle change into the relationship between interest rates and the exchange rate. No longer was it the case that interest rates would be raised when the exchange rate weakened sufficiently to allow it. With deficits like these, high interest rates were essential, not just to rein back the domestic economy, but to attract the short-term capital required as a counterpart to the current-account gap.

As if to demonstrate this, balance of payments figures released on 25 November, just over three weeks after the Autumn Statement, showed a current-account deficit of £2.4bn, easily the highest on record. As sterling fell on the foreign exchange markets, the Bank of England, on instructions from the Treasury, signalled a second full percentage point rise in base rates, to 13 per cent. Lawson, having faced criticism for his policy of increasing interest rates half-heartedly, was now attacked from the opposite direction. The new criticism was that the Government, having managed to get the economy firing on all cylinders, appeared to have only one weapon, high interest rates, to control it. 'The Chancellor has put himself in a very strict, tight box in which he has only one policy,' said Edward Heath, the former Conservative Prime Minister, after rates had been increased to 13 per cent. 'In golfing terms, the Chancellor could be described as a one-club man. But if one wishes to take on Sandy Lyle and the rest of the world, one needs a complete bag of clubs' (1989).

The 'one-club golfer' label stuck, despite Treasury protests. Lawson and his officials worked hard to convince journalists, and the public, that in practical terms interest rates were the only short-term and effective instrument of policy. Fiscal policy, they argued, was tight, as shown by the fact that the Government was repaying more than £14bn of public-sector debt in 1988–9 alone. As for direct controls, on credit or incomes, not only were they against the Government's philosophy, but there was no evidence that they worked. Credit controls in particular, it was suggested, had been rendered obsolete by the removal of exchange controls in 1979. It was possible, and perfectly legal, for banks to circumvent restrictions on credit advances in Britain simply by lending to British residents from offshore branches. The argument was never conclusively won. Advocates of controls suggested that hire-purchase restrictions, for example, would still have a marked impact on purchases of cars and consumer durables. Limits on the proportion of a property's value that could be advanced as a mortgage could have prevented some of the worst excesses of the housing boom. Indeed, Robin Leigh-Pemberton suggested in 1991 that such limits could have their merits as a last resort for the authorities.

The increase in base rates to 13 per cent at the end of November 1988, almost double their level of six months earlier, was a dramatic shift in policy by any standards. For Lawson, one crumb of comfort was that Treasury and Bank of England officials concluded that, barring accidents, 13 per cent would be enough. There were other hopeful elements for the Chancellor. The tightening of monetary policy had come early enough in the Parliament to prevent major electoral damage to the Conservatives. And, by the end of 1988, the housing market had started to come off the boil, beginning in the south-east. In early 1989, therefore, official belief in the soft-landing strategy remained strong. The Bank of England, in its February 1989 *Quarterly Bulletin*, said:

> The main effects of the sharp rise in interest rates through the second half of last year and the mortgage rate increases announced in January should become apparent within the next three to six months. A slowdown in consumers' expenditure, possibly quite marked, is likely. The uncertainties reflect among other things the unprecedented extent of the personal sector's move into deficit over the past few years, which has been larger than most observers predicted. It is reasonable to expect that the effect on expenditure of a given change in interest rates will be larger now than in previous years, because households are on average more heavily geared, and because the proportion of floating to fixed-rate debt has risen considerably in recent years . . . Companies are more likely to be influenced by longer-term borrowing costs (which have risen little) and, given their much improved profitability and current utilization of capacity, investment demand should hold up.　　　(1989, pp. 6–7)

The hope, expressed by both Lawson and the Bank of England, was that companies would escape the worst effects of a policy designed to impact mainly on consumer demand. Could this be achieved and, more importantly, could it succeed in bringing down inflation? Inflation had risen strongly during 1988, from 3.3 per cent at the start of the year to 6.8 per cent at the end. But part of this, as Lawson rarely failed to point out, was because of the inclusion of mortgage interest rates in the retail prices index. The paradox, he said, was that a policy designed to reduce inflation – higher interest rates – had the short-term effect of pushing it higher. And, while inflation was expected to rise further in the first half of 1989, the Treasury was confident that this would only be temporary. The emphasis on the distorting effects of mortgage interest rates in the retail prices index, while mathematically correct, was also rather disingenuous. For, while this exaggerated the rise in inflation, there was no doubt that, on any underlying measure, the trend was upwards. The gross domestic product deflator, for example, rose by 7.3 per cent in the 1988–9 financial year, compared with 5.3 per cent in 1987–8 and 3.3 per cent in 1986–7.

Lawson pulled out all the stops to prevent the inflation rate from rising, stooping even to artificial means. In his March 1989 Budget he froze excise duties instead of following the normal convention of increasing them in line with the previous year's inflation rate. The move, which caused consternation among health lobbyists and Treasury officials, was made solely to 'massage' the retail prices index and give the impression that inflation was less of a problem than it was. Despite this, the inflation rate climbed to 8.3 per cent by May, and only edged down slightly, to 7.7 per cent – more than two percentage points above the Treasury's Budget forecast – by the end of 1989.

The problem was that high interest rates, if they were affecting consumer demand, were doing so only very slowly. Activity in the housing market was less frenzied, but house prices were still rising strongly. The average increase in house prices in 1989 was 12 per cent, compared with 23.7 per cent in 1988 and 15.4 per cent in 1987. Even in the south-east, where the impact of higher mortgage rates on over-borrowed home-buyers could be expected to be greatest, prices rose by 12.5 per cent in 1989, after 25.5 per cent in 1988. Rising housing wealth was still buoying up consumer spending, and this was evident both in the official figures and in clear evidence that, in spite of high interest rates, the boom was more or less intact. Consumer spending rose by 3.9 per cent, in real terms, in 1989. This was less than the 7.2 per cent boom of 1988 and the 5.3 per cent expansion of 1987, but it was still, by any standards, very strong growth. Spending on durable goods, which could be expected to be most sensitive to higher interest rates, rose by nearly 6 per cent in 1989, down on the near 13 per cent jump of 1988 but, again, a substantial rise which was reflected in the increase in the current-account deficit to more than £19bn.

Treasury and Bank of England officials could take comfort from the fact that the rise in consumer demand was slowing. At the beginning of 1989 the year-on-year increase was nearly 5 per cent, by the end it was down to less than 3 per cent. The process, however, was a painfully slow one. And, in relative terms, companies were being as badly affected by the high-interest-rate regime as individuals. Manufacturing output, having grown by 7.3 per cent in 1988, slowed to a 4.2 per cent increase in 1989. The rise in manufacturing investment, in real terms, slowed to 5 per cent in 1989, from just under 12 per cent in 1988. The economy, in other words, was growing strongly in 1989 in spite of high interest rates, and there was no evidence that the policy was picking off only the consumer sector and leaving the rest intact. The domestic case for high, perhaps higher, interest rates remained.

The End of the Deutschmark Target

Sir Alan Walters, in his public attacks on economic policy during the summer of 1988, had been a thorn in Lawson's side. He did not, however, have an official role in the making of policy. As a result, the foreign exchange markets viewed his interventions with interest and occasional amusement. While Lawson's reputation was slipping fast, he was still the man in charge. In the autumn of 1988 all this began to change. It was first hinted at, and then formally announced, that Walters would return to Downing Street on 1 May 1989, to resume his early 1980s role as a personal economic adviser to Thatcher, this time in a part-time capacity. One version of the appointment was that it was viewed in Downing Street and the Treasury as the only effective means of silencing Walters. Bernard Ingham, Thatcher's press secretary, had already had a discreet word with Walters, advising him to tone down his comments. Senior Treasury officials made great play of welcoming his return, suggesting that it would stimulate the economic debate within the Government.

Lawson, however, regarded the return of Walters as deeply insulting, even though he believed himself capable of defeating him in any argument. The Chancellor was infuriated and told Thatcher that, given the known position of her personal economic adviser on key issues, his reappointment would be damaging and divisive. 'Lawson was really fed up,' said one Treasury adviser. 'He totally resented Walters.'

In the early months of 1989 there was little hint of the trouble to come. The pound was strong, rising to almost DM3.30 in January and February. The second element of the soft-landing strategy, that of the pound holding up and preventing any unwelcome inflationary shocks, appeared to be working better than the first. All this was to change very quickly, however, following the return of Walters to Downing Street on 1 May. Word started to get around in the City that the debate over the role of sterling in policy had been renewed within the Government and that, as in the early 1980s, Walters was advocating a fall in the exchange rate to prevent a recession in Britain. The true position was that Walters believed that interest rate decisions had to be divorced from the exchange rate to a greater extent than had been the case in the recent past. The distinction, however, was less important than the fact that there were new market uncertainties over the Government's attitude to the exchange rate. Thatcher, in an interview with the BBC World Service, said in response to a question on the timing of Britain's entry into the European exchange rate mechanism that Britain had picked up her 'inflationary tendency' through the policy of shadowing the Deutschmark. Whether it was this or the continuing bad news on inflation and current-account deficit, the fact was that, from May onwards, the pound started to weaken. Official hopes that 13 per cent would represent the ceiling for base rates proved unfounded. The Thatcher–Walters–Lawson disagreement, by spilling over into a loss of foreign confidence in the pound, consigned the soft-landing strategy to the dustbin. A falling pound pushes up import prices and adds to inflation. The result was that, even with high interest rates, inflationary pressures were increasing.

Walters claims that policy was coming unstuck anyway, and that Lawson's policy errors were bound to end in tears. His role, he says, was exaggerated because the press were 'out to get' Thatcher, and he was a convenient tool to use to that end. But Lawson maintains that Walters undermined his policy where it hurt most, in the financial markets. In the summer of 1989 reports began to emerge of City lunches at which Walters had been speaking out against Lawson and his policies, talking openly of the wasted years in the battle against inflation. After one such lunch, with the City discount house Union Discount, at least one person present was telling of the extent that Walters was critical of Lawson. Walters denied the charge, and was supported by the Chairman of Union Discount. But the damage was done. And Walters does not dispute that, in the autumn of 1989, he told an American audience that the pound needed to fall sharply in order to prevent a recession in Britain. According to Lawson, in a BBC interview in 1991, 'She can appoint anyone she likes as adviser but an adviser has to maintain certain proprieties and to be discreet and Alan Walters was indiscreet and unhelpful' (1991).

It was unprecedented. The Chancellor's policies were being undermined, intentionally or not, by the Prime Minister's personal economic adviser, and with her apparent connivance. For the Treasury, the additional irritation was that Walters was rarely open in his criticisms of policy. 'Walters was bloody arrogant,' said one adviser. 'He would come into the Treasury and listen and get the lowdown on what was going on, and then he would slope back to Downing Street and tell Mrs Thatcher.'

Lawson, meanwhile, was driven by a new determination, that of proving he could handle the economy, and hand it over in good shape. 'He was damned if he was going to leave things in a way that people could say he had cut and run,' said a friend. 'By 1989 he was prepared to see it through until the next election if necessary.' As the pound fell, first below DM3.10 in May 1989 and subsequently below DM3 in September, Lawson was forced to raise interest rates on two more occasions. And, as if to underline his own anti-inflation credentials, and his singular lack of political ambition, Lawson appeared to go out of his way to raise rates at politically inopportune times. Base rates were increased from 13 to 14 per cent on 24 May. In Lawson's diary for that afternoon was a speech to a Conservative women's conference. And the Conservative women were already champing at the bit over the high level of mortgage rates. The final move, to 15 per cent on 5 October 1989, came on the eve of the Conservative Party conference, and followed hard on the heels of an increase in official interest rates by the

German Bundesbank. When Lawson told Thatcher that he had no choice but to match the German rate increase, she was incensed. Both she and Walters were angry that the Chancellor had manoeuvred himself into a position where he had to follow the Bundesbank. According to Walters, 'Britain was on the back of a tiger. As the exchange rate fell, or threatened to fall, in the autumn of 1989, so the interest rate was driven up by market expectations. The authorities had the choice of validating expectations or changing them' (1990, pp. 109–10).

In other words, after convincing the markets that the exchange rate did matter, and that the Government would not allow it to fall, there was little choice but to raise interest rates, even if this resulted in a recession. And fear of recession was now deeply felt in Downing Street. Thatcher had survived the 1980–81 recession, although it was touch and go for a while, because of a widespread perception that it was a necessary corrective after years of poor economic performance. But justifying another severe recession, after a decade of Thatcherism, was going to be much more difficult.

Industry's patience snapped. John Banham, the director-general of the Confederation of British Industry, had supported the previous rate rises as necessary in the fight against inflation. But this was a bridge too far. The rate increase, he said, was 'wholly unnecessary' and 'a spectacular own goal'. Home-buyers agreed. The housing market finally responded in the final quarter of 1989 and did so dramatically. Average house prices in the south-east were now *falling* by £2,000 a month.

The rate increase to 15 per cent guaranteed Lawson a miserable party conference week. The *Daily Mail*, a staunchly Conservative middle-market tabloid, ran a fiercely critical leading article on its front page, headlined 'This Bankrupt Chancellor'. The pound was falling, in spite of the interest rate rise. Journalists sensed he was on the run. As he tried to put together a conference speech photographers camped outside his house in Stoney Stanton, Leicestershire, trying for a shot of a man in torment. A tired and dejected Lawson, making his final appearance on the party conference platform in Blackpool on Thursday 12 October, told his audience that the Conservatives never took the soft option on inflation and would never be the party of devaluation. With the critical eyes of Thatcher upon him, it was a brave performance. But the obligatory standing ovation was more out of loyalty and sympathy than admiration or affection.

Lawson's time was nearly up. His resolve to press on was weakened by what he regarded as constant sniping by Walters. The final straw came when Walters's autobiographical article for the *American Economist*, which he had been sending out as a matter of course to journalists requesting interviews or background information, surfaced in the *Financial Times*, which picked up on his critical views of the European exchange rate mechanism. 'The Walters thing just became intolerable for [Lawson],' said a friend. 'But I think he was also getting tired of the whole business of being Chancellor. He had a new set of ministers and was about to start the whole process of making a Budget again. He didn't have the heart for it.'

Lawson resigned on 26 October 1989, after three meetings that day with Thatcher. On each occasion he demanded that she dismiss Walters. Thatcher refused. Within hours, ironically, Walters resigned too. The Chancellor left with a prediction that inflation had passed its peak. Thatcher claims not to understand, to this day, the reason for his departure. But to Lawson it was as clear as daylight. As he said in his resignation speech:

No one, however long he has held the post, lightly gives up the great office of Chancellor of the Exchequer. Certainly, I did not. As the resignation letter that I wrote to my right honourable friend the Prime Minister clearly implies, it was not the outcome I sought. But it is one I accept without rancour – despite what might be described as the hard landing involved. I would only add that the article written by my right honourable friend's former economic adviser was of significance only inasmuch as it represented the tip of a singularly ill-conceived iceberg, with all the destructive potential that icebergs possess. I have long been convinced that the only successful basis for the successful conduct of economic policy is to seek the greatest practicable degree of market freedom within an over-arching framework of financial discipline to bear down on inflation. That being so, a key question is where the exchange rate fits in. Is it to be part of the maximum practicable market freedom, or is it a part – indeed, a central part – of the necessary financial discipline? I recognize that a case can be made for either approach. No case can be made for seeming confusion or for apparent vacillation between these two positions. Moreover, for our system of Cabinet government to work effectively, the Prime Minister of the day must appoint ministers whom he or she trusts and then leave them to carry out the policy. When differences of view do emerge, they should be resolved privately and, whenever appropriate, collectively.   (1989)

8

THE DESCENT FROM
BOOM TO BUST

Major's Inheritance

John Major took over as Chancellor of the Exchequer on the evening of
26 October 1989, in circumstances that could hardly have been more
inauspicious. Interest rates were at their highest level for eight years and
the economy appeared to be staring recession in the face. Yet the pound
was falling, and was given an extra downward push in the market panic
that followed the surprise announcement of Nigel Lawson's resignation.
Major's rise through the ranks of government had been spectacular but
he was still something of an unknown quantity. He had been a competent
Chief Secretary to the Treasury, handling the Treasury's public spending
negotiations with other Whitehall departments in the two years after the
June 1987 election. And, while some, notably former Conservative Party
chairman Norman Tebbit, had marked him out as a future Prime
Minister, this was a minority view.

Major's image was of a grey, accountant-type, or the banker that he
had been before entering Parliament. While charming in private, he was
no great performer either on the conference platform or in Parliament.
The job of Chief Secretary, involving as it did an intimate knowledge of
the details of departmental spending, appeared ideally suited to him.
When in July 1989, Thatcher effectively sacked Sir Geoffrey Howe by
moving him to the job of Leader of the House, with the honorary title
Deputy Prime Minister, her appointment of Major as Foreign Secretary
was an enormous surprise. Not only had he never exhibited any particular interest in foreign affairs but he was also regarded as too junior. The
conclusion was that Thatcher, having had to put up with too much
independence of mind from Howe, wanted someone in the post that she
could order around. Major's short stay at the Foreign Office, where his
determinedly meritocratic style failed to impress a group of civil servants

who have always regarded themselves as the aristocrats of the Whitehall machine, did little to counter this impression. Major maintains now that he was perfectly happy at the Foreign Office, and would like to have stayed much longer. Indeed, when Prime Minister one of his strengths became his handling of foreign affairs. The new Chancellor's reputation, cruel though it was, was of a politician who had advanced mainly because of Thatcher's patronage. Subsequent events proved this judgement wrong, but he was widely regarded as Margaret Thatcher's poodle.

This had important practical consequences in the financial markets. Thatcher's great disagreement with Lawson had been over the latter's targeting of sterling against the Deutschmark and his ambition of taking the pound into the European exchange rate mechanism (ERM). It was reasonable to assume at the time of Major's appointment that both of these sources of irritation would disappear, under a new Chancellor who seemed destined only to obey orders. Entry into the ERM looked to be a much longer-term proposition, perhaps not until after Thatcher eventually stepped down as Prime Minister. And the targeting policy, which was closely associated with Lawson, had surely come to an end. Sterling fell by seven pfennigs, to below DM2.90, in the hours following Lawson's resignation. Major, with Thatcher's approval, instructed the Bank of England to intervene in support of the pound, arguing that such intervention was appropriate in a situation of political uncertainty. The strategy worked for a while. The markets were persuaded that, in spite of Major's inexperience, Lawson's departure made the Thatcher Government a more cohesive whole. The storm appeared to have been weathered. But by mid November sterling was falling sharply again, dropping first below DM2.80 and then, by the end of December, to just above DM2.70.

This time the new Chancellor was urged to raise interest rates to stem the tide of selling pressure on the pound and to underline the Government's commitment to the defeat of inflation. Treasury officials, the Bank of England and Norman Lamont, the Chief Secretary to the Treasury (and Major's new deputy), all advised tough action. The recommendation was virtually unanimous. Rate increases were needed, and quickly, to stop the rot. Officials wanted base rates, then 15 per cent, to be pushed up to 16 or 17 per cent, if only as a temporary measure. Lamont agreed. 'Norman was keen to knock inflation on the

head once and for all,' said one Treasury adviser. Major held out against
the pressure, even though it made for a difficult winter and, as a result
of sterling weakness, made the eventual rise in inflation even worse. 'His
instincts were good on this, even if he did not have the economic
arguments to back them up,' said one official. 'But let's face it, even
if he wanted to raise interest rates Mrs Thatcher would not have let
him.'

Major appeared to be hemmed in. His first important policy act was
to deliver the Autumn Statement of 15 November 1989. In it, he
predicted that 1990 would 'not be an easy year' but, crucially, the
Treasury still saw the economy steering a course towards lower inflation,
without recession. Economic growth was predicted for 1990, albeit at
the low rate of 1.25 per cent. Inflation, running at 7.5 per cent in the
final quarter of 1989, was predicted to fall to 5.75 per cent by the fourth
quarter of 1990. Avoiding recession was an important preoccupation for
Major. He was aware of the political costs of a recession at such a late
stage in the electoral cycle. The Lawson boom had continued well after
the 1987 election but it would be the Major recession that voters would
remember next time. The Lawson legacy was a difficult one – Major
was portrayed in newspaper cartoons as the zoo keeper trying to clean
up the path in the wake of the elephant. The soft-landing strategy, as
first envisaged, had been blown off course. But the hope remained that,
in spite of some obvious turbulence, a hard landing could be avoided.

'I do not in fact anticipate a recession,' Major told the Treasury and
Civil Service Committee on 4 December. 'I think we will have a period
of very slow growth over the next twelve months or so. In terms of
dampening down demand and helping to squeeze inflation out of the
system not only will we have a period of very slow growth, it seems to
me necessary now that we should have a period of very slow growth'
(1989, p. 33). Bill Martin, economist with the stockbroker UBS-Phillips
& Drew and a specialist adviser to the committee, disagreed. He wrote,
'The central question now concerns the scale and duration of the
economy's hard landing. Will it be a short eviscerating collapse followed
by recovery, just in time for the next election? Or is the economy
destined for several years of misery, a fitting retribution for the excesses
of Britain's growth extravaganza in 1987–8, Mr Lawson's big boom'
(1989, p. 83). Martin suggested that Major's best course would be to get
the misery over quickly, if necessary by raising interest rates again.

But if the new Chancellor hoped to avoid recession and yet higher inflation (or, even worse, the mid-1970s combination of recession and inflation that had been christened stagflation), there was little he could do about it. Sterling's fall was dramatic, as the foreign exchange markets came to view it as a currency without friends in Government. Sterling had already weakened under Lawson. Under Major the fall threatened to turn into a rout. Between the spring of 1989 and the end of December it fell by almost 20 per cent against a strong Deutschmark. Major's attitude to its fall appeared equivocal. 'I do not think it would have been accepted by anyone ... indeed I might have been running into some difficulty had I admitted to shadowing the Deutschmark over the period of the last few months,' he told the Treasury and Civil Service Committee (1989, p. 43). The pound's fall had not been as pronounced against other currencies. Even so, the implication was clear. The Deutschmark target, regarded by the markets, and by Lawson, as a prelude to ERM entry, had gone.

Major, to be fair, had been thrust unexpectedly into the job of Chancellor and was finding his feet. In many ways he was the victim of the circumstances he found himself in. He could not raise interest rates, both for fear of triggering a recession that he genuinely thought could be avoided and because of Thatcher's probable veto of such a move. At the same time, reducing rates was out of the question with the pound falling sharply and inflation high. His chosen course of action on interest rates was no action at all. When he took office base rates had been at 15 per cent for three weeks. They remained at this level until October 1990, falling on the anniversary of their rise. For base rates to remain at the same level for a year was a rarity. The only comparable period of relentlessly high interest rates was in the recession of the early 1980s. From November 1979 to November 1980, rates never fell below 16 per cent.

Keeping rates at 15 per cent for a year was not, however, how Major saw things working out in late 1989 and early 1990. As the economy slowed sharply, surely there would be room to bring interest rates down gradually, perhaps as early as the March Budget? The pound was a problem, but then currencies did not fall for ever and, after all, high British interest rates would eventually pull in even the most sceptical international money men. Sterling did turn around for precisely this reason. Having ended 1989 as the world's weakest currency, the pound recovered in January and February. On 22 February the sterling index (its average value against other leading currencies on an index basis, with 1985 as 100) reached 90.3, the level it had been before Lawson announced his resignation. This regaining of the 'Lawson level' was a cause of considerable relief in the Treasury and the Bank of England, because it offered the hope that the long nightmare of a weak currency in spite of very high interest rates was coming to an end. Against the Deutschmark, sterling recovered to trade between DM2.80 and DM2.90. It was not strong, but neither was it obviously weak.

Sterling's rise was helpful but it did not allow Major to cut interest rates, much as he would have liked to. Two problems stood in his way. The first was that the economy's resilience in the face of high interest rates, a feature of 1989, continued in the first half of 1990. Some areas of the economy had clearly responded, in particular the housing market. For the rest, however, the picture was certainly not one of recession, and it was some way from the Treasury's vision of very slow growth. Consumer spending in the first half of 1990 showed a real rise of nearly 3 per cent on the corresponding period of 1989. This was not the sharp slowdown that the Bank of England, in February 1989, had predicted would occur within three to six months. Industry, however, was less fortunate. Manufacturing output showed a rise over the period of just 1 per cent in comparison with a year earlier, although manufacturing investment remained strong, up 8 per cent. Overall private-sector investment was weaker, down 1.5 per cent, but this was mainly due to a decline in house building. For Treasury and Bank of England officials, this was a puzzle. High interest rates had been successful in picking off one area of the economy, housing, but their impact on other sectors, so far at least, was much more muted. There was, however, one slowdown sign that the Government would have preferred not to have. Unemployment, which had been falling continuously since July 1986, began to rise, at first tentatively, in April 1990.

The other serious constraint on interest rates was inflation. Major's November 1989 Autumn Statement predicted that inflation, then around 7.5 per cent, would drop to around 7 per cent by mid-1990, before falling to 5.75 per cent by the fourth quarter. Unfortunately, this forecast failed to allow for the effects of the pound's fall in the remaining weeks of 1989, and the unexpected buoyancy of the economy in the first six months of 1990. Even more damagingly, the Government compounded the problem by actions that added directly to the inflation rate. Lawson, in his final Budget in March 1989, had, as described in Chapter 7, dispensed with the usual convention of indexing excise duties, in a vain attempt to prevent inflation from rising. This meant that Major, unless he did the same thing, faced an automatic increase in inflation as the result of his first, March 1990 Budget. This was another unfortunate legacy of Lawson's chancellorship. Major was caught between two stools. Raising excise duties would add to an already high inflation rate. But freezing them again would not only cost the Government in lost revenue and provide consumers with a bonus that ran counter to the policy aim of achieving a decisive spending slowdown, but it would also store up problems for the 1991 Budget. Before the Budget, the speculation was that excise duties would be increased, but in a way that would exert a minimal impact on the retail prices index. As it turned out, Major announced duty increases of 10 per cent on petrol, cigarettes and spirits, with a slightly smaller increase in duties on other alcoholic drinks. The effect of the Budget was to push the inflation rate up by 0.5 per cent from the 8.1 per cent level prevailing at the time of the Budget.

The centrepiece of Major's first and only Budget was the provision of new tax relief on savings, and the creation of so-called Tax Exempt Special Savings Accounts, or Tessas, in which the interest on savings held for five years or more within building societies would be free of tax. A government that had come into office determined to simplify the tax system and cut back on available reliefs was now happy to add to them. More fundamentally, the Tessa move appeared to be a belated response to the situation that had prevailed during the Lawson boom, when many people forgot the savings habit. For economists, however, a bigger question was whether Major would follow in the footsteps of Sir Geoffrey Howe, his predecessor but one, and introduce a 'hair-shirt' Budget by not raising personal income-tax allowances in line with inflation. The Chancellor was certainly urged to do so, both by his own Treasury officials and by the City. But, as with the earlier decision not to raise interest rates during sterling's pre-Christmas bout of weakness, Major opted for a softer approach. Apart from anything else, he was concerned about the presentational problems of announcing an austerity Budget which would hit those on average incomes so soon after the Lawson tax bonanza for the higher paid. He judged correctly. Had he

taken some of the advice he was offered, and presented a tougher
Budget, his actions would have been blamed for the recession that
followed.

An even bigger problem in terms of the impact of policy on the
inflation rate was caused by the introduction of the Community Charge,
or poll tax. The poll tax, which played an important part in Margaret
Thatcher's downfall, was introduced in April 1990 in England and
Wales, having come into effect a year earlier in Scotland. The tax, a
replacement for domestic rates, had been vigorously opposed by the
Treasury under Nigel Lawson, who recalled later:

> I pointed out, with examples, that a flat-rate poll tax (for that, incidentally,
> was what it was officially called at that time) would be politically unsustainable;
> and that we would be forced to give so many exemptions and concessions that
> we would be in danger of ending up with a surrogate income tax. I pointed
> out, too, that local authorities would seize the opportunity of the transition
> from rates to poll tax to bump up their spending and revenue and blame it all
> on the imposition by the Government of an alien system of taxation. I
> concluded (lest there should be any doubt about where I stood) that the
> proposal for a poll tax would be 'completely unworkable and politically
> catastrophic'.   (1990b)

Lawson was right on all counts. The poll tax produced London's worst
riot in recent memory and provoked a campaign of non-payment. It was
widely regarded as the most unpopular British tax measure of the
twentieth century. It created more losers than winners, and it had been
introduced against the advice of the Treasury. The Government, after
bowing to the mood of the 1987 Conservative Party conference, even
passed up the opportunity of sweetening the bitter pill by phasing in the
tax over four, or in the Department of the Environment's original
proposal, ten years. Substantial concessions were introduced to make it
less of a flat-rate tax (although this was something of a misnomer
because the tax was only levied at a flat rate within the same local
authority area).

Even so, when it was introduced, as Lawson had predicted, the result
was a sharp increase in local taxation. Part of this was, indeed, the fault
of local authorities using the excuse of a change in the system of local
government finance to boost their expenditure. There was, however,
another important factor. This was the so-called gearing problem inherent in the new system. The income of local authorities could be roughly

divided into three segments. The largest, the grant from central government, covered roughly half of the total. The next, the new uniform business rate, accounted for around a quarter. The remainder came from the poll tax. The difficulty was that the first two elements had been fixed the previous summer, when the Treasury was predicting a fall in inflation. Any rise in local authority spending, due to higher inflation or more ambitious plans would, therefore, be added directly to the only variable element in the equation, the poll tax. An increase of 10 per cent in local authority spending would mean a rise of a third in poll tax levels. And this, broadly, is what happened between the summer of 1989 and April 1990. Average poll tax levels were some 30 per cent higher than had been planned. And, unfortunately for the Government, the advisory committee which monitored the composition of the retail prices index had concluded that the poll tax should be included in it. The committee's argument was that because the domestic rates were included in the index, and the poll tax was a replacement for the rates, it too should be included. A significant minority on the committee argued that, as a direct tax, the poll tax had no place in an index of prices. But the majority view held. The result was that a rise of around 30 per cent in poll tax bills in April 1990 (relative to the domestic rates) resulted in an increase of more than 1 per cent in the retail prices index.

Major was, therefore, faced with a significant inflation problem, and one which severely restricted his scope for cutting interest rates. The inflation rate rose to 9.4 per cent in April, from 8.1 per cent in March. And, while some of this increase was artificial, this hardly mattered. Pay settlements, crucially, were responding to the higher published inflation rate. It was, on a somewhat smaller scale, reminiscent of the mistakes of 1979, when action by the Government pushed up the inflation rate and led to higher wage settlements, making the unemployment consequences of the subsequent recession even more serious than they need have been. In the spring of 1990, the Treasury insisted that predictions of 10 per cent inflation or more were unduly alarmist. It was important, not least in the context of the Government's record, that inflation did not go into double figures again. But it was not to be. Without the unhelpful impact of the poll tax and higher excise duties the inflation peak could have been held at around 9 per cent. As it turned out, the rate broke above 10 per cent in August 1990 and reached 10.9 per cent in September, staying at that rate in October, before commencing its fall.

Into the Exchange Rate Mechanism

John Major's sharp and unexpected rise within the Government had been intimately associated with the debate over Britain's entry into the exchange rate mechanism (ERM) of the European Monetary System. In June 1989, Lawson and Sir Geoffrey Howe, the then Foreign Secretary, had confronted Margaret Thatcher on the issue of ERM entry. The confrontation, in Thatcher's study in 10 Downing Street, came on the morning of Sunday 25 June. That day, she and Howe were to fly to Madrid for a European Council meeting of heads of government and foreign ministers, at which Community plans for eventual European monetary union (EMU) were to be the main topic of discussion. Lawson and Howe wanted Thatcher to make a firm commitment to British membership of the ERM, stronger than the standard position that entry would occur 'when the time is ripe'. They had pressed her some days before on the issue, but without success. This time they meant business. According to Howe later, 'The then Chancellor and I, as Foreign Secretary, made it clear that we could not continue in office unless a specific commitment to join the ERM was made' (1990).

Lawson was keen, not just that specific conditions should be set for entry, but that there should be a clear but private agreement that entry would occur within two to three years. The result was that, to the considerable surprise of her European colleagues, Thatcher set out, at the European Council meeting, the precise conditions under which Britain would enter the ERM. The most important of these conditions were that Britain's inflation rate, then just above 8 per cent, should have fallen to the average of the existing ERM members, then around 4.5 per cent; and that the other big countries in the system, notably France and Italy, should have removed their controls on the movement of capital.

There is, to this day, considerable rancour over the authorship of what came to be known as the Madrid conditions. Sir Alan Walters, by that time back in Downing Street, maintains that they were his. 'The Madrid conditions were my conditions,' he said, a claim vigorously denied by Lawson. 'Sir Alan's only contribution was to add some further irrelevant conditions which he well knew were unlikely to be met for many years, if ever,' he said (1990c). The more immediate cause of rancour, for Thatcher, was that two of her most senior ministers had, as she saw it, blackmailed her into reluctantly accepting, and stating publicly, the conditions for ERM entry. Her relations with Lawson were already at a low ebb but, with inflation high and international confidence in the British economy low, she felt that she could not sack him. Howe was less fortunate. Within a month of the pre-Madrid confrontation he was moved to the job of Leader of the House, propelling Major into the post of Foreign Secretary. Three months later, Lawson's resignation and Major's move to the Treasury was, again, closely associated with the differences within the Government over the ERM.

What, however, was Major's own attitude to ERM entry? Treasury officials who had worked with him when he was Chief Secretary could not recall that he had expressed a view on the subject. It was, in addition, a highly sensitive area for a new and inexperienced Chancellor to broach with a Prime Minister of known and very strong views. As the pound fell in November and December 1989, the word went out from the Treasury that Major was, in fact, very keen on ERM entry. As a backbench MP he had, it appeared, made a speech in the House of Commons as far back as 1981 in favour of entry. In January 1990, interviewed by the *Financial Times*, he said:

> We have made it very clear when we shall join the exchange rate mechanism – when the level of inflation is significantly lower, there is capital liberalization in the Community and real progress has been made towards the completion of the single market, freedom of financial services and strengthened competition policy. I am convinced that it would not be in our interests to join before then. Nor would it be in the interest of other ERM members. After the Deutschmark, sterling will be the most widely used and traded currency in the system. So when sterling goes into the ERM it will be a big step, for the other members as well as us, and it is in everyone's interest that the process should go as smoothly as possible. But we will not delay when our conditions are met.   (1990)

The tone was positive but, leaving aside the attitude of the Prime Minister, the Madrid conditions that Major had inherited did not suggest that early entry into the ERM was likely. One main condition, the removal of remaining capital controls by France and Italy, would be met by 1 July 1990. The inflation condition was, however, much more problematical. Inflation, far from converging on to the European average, was moving further away from it. There seemed little possibility, on a strict reading of the conditions, that entry could occur in 1990, and possibly not even in 1991. This created an additional difficulty for the

Chancellor. At a European Council meeting in Strasbourg in December 1989 Thatcher, under pressure from the other EC leaders, had reluctantly agreed to the setting up of two special intergovernmental conferences, one on European monetary union and the other on political union, to begin in Rome in December 1990. The conference on monetary union threatened to create significant strains within the Conservative Party, because its aim would be to secure the necessary amendments to the Treaty of Rome in order to facilitate the eventual move to a single European currency and central bank. Major was aware that Britain was on the fringes of the debate on monetary union, partly because of the failure to enter the ERM, now in the eleventh year of its existence. ERM entry before December 1990 would put Britain in a far better position to influence the debate in the intergovernmental conference.

Within months of succeeding Lawson, Major was strongly convinced of the need for ERM entry. He ordered a review of monetary policy to examine whether, as Labour claimed, there were alternatives to high interest rates as a means of controlling the economy. The review, while not comprehensive – it did not consider limits on mortgage lending – was published in the Budget of 20 March 1990. It concluded that additional controls, such as the bank reserve-asset ratios which were being advocated by the Labour Party, would be ineffective. The implication was that there was no alternative to the course that was being followed, a course that involved interest rates of 15 per cent. The gap in monetary policy was, however, as big as it had been under Lawson's Chancellorship. The broad money-supply targets that had been the backbone of the original medium-term financial strategy had fallen by the wayside four years before. The Deutschmark target had been destroyed by the political squabbles and the poor inflation and balance of payments performance of 1989. Monetary policy was, once more, without an 'anchor', a firm base that the authorities could both use to guide themselves and convince the financial markets that policy was built on sound principles. Without such an anchor, the prospects looked grim. The Government was in trouble, partly because of the economy and high interest rates, but also because of mistakes such as the introduction of the poll tax. The London poll-tax riot of April 1990, beamed by satellite around the world, sparked worries in the international financial markets about the political situation in Britain. The Conservatives were sliding in the opinion polls and Thatcher's personal rating among the electorate was falling even faster. The question was whether, in this situation, the pound could be prevented from dropping sharply, even with 15 per cent interest rates to protect it.

Major embarked on a three-pronged approach. With the help of Douglas Hurd, who had succeeded him as Foreign Secretary, he worked quietly to persuade Thatcher of the need for ERM entry at the earliest possible opportunity. The approach appears to have been much more subtle than that adopted by Lawson and Howe, although it was far from mealy-mouthed. Both Major and Hurd believed themselves to be in strong positions. As one Treasury adviser put it, 'She had lost one Chancellor and Foreign Secretary, so she could hardly afford to do so again.' The debate was over how strictly the Madrid conditions should be applied. Major suggested that the inflation condition had an inbuilt problem. This was that, while it was obviously better if Britain joined the system when inflation was low, achieving low inflation could be difficult if sterling was subject to frequent crises of confidence.

The second prong was a diplomatic offensive, aimed at Britain's European partners. In the spring and summer of 1990 the finance ministries of the other eleven Community countries were visited, either by Major or by one of his senior officials. The message that was conveyed was that first, Britain was serious about entering the ERM at an early stage and secondly, that, in spite of grave reservations about the ultimate goal of a European single currency and central bank, the Government intended to play a full and constructive part in the forthcoming discussions on European monetary union. This was new. Community attitudes to Britain had been coloured by Thatcher's confrontational approach to European affairs. Lawson, while enthusiastic about ERM entry, had tended to view it as an internal matter for the British Government. Many of his fellow European finance ministers regarded him as arrogant, particularly about Britain's economic achievements and their own shortcomings, and there was a certain amount of *schadenfreude* when the British economy ran into difficulties in the late 1980s. Major's approach, both because he took the trouble to travel around Europe explaining his position, and because he had none of his predecessor's arrogance, was refreshingly different. It earned him a significant amount of goodwill.

Finally, there was the necessity of providing the pound with support in the approach to ERM entry. The logic of this approach was that the foreign exchange markets, if convinced that the pound was to enter the mechanism, would not sell it because entry, when it occurred, would provide firm support. With sterling's downside limited by the ERM entry prospect, there would be every incentive for the markets to take advantage of high British interest rates. As long as the carrot of ERM entry was there, the markets could be enticed into holding the pound. The game was not, however, without its risks. It required, not just that the carrot be kept there but that the journey to the final destination of ERM entry be not too long. Any indication that Thatcher had put her foot down again and that the pound would be kept out of the system indefinitely would have sent sterling falling like a stone. Moreover, the more unstable the currency's performance on the exchanges, the greater the ammunition for those who argued that sterling was a naturally volatile currency which had no place in a fixed-exchange-rate framework.

Mindful of the difficulties his predecessor had encountered, Major was cautious in his public statements. In his Budget speech of 20 March 1990, he said that ERM entry was a question of 'when' and not 'if', but appeared to be hemmed in by the Madrid condition on inflation. Privately, however, he was more optimistic about entry prospects, as were his advisers and officials. By May, the message was getting across to the markets. Major gave an interview to the *Wall Street Journal* in which he spoke positively about entry prospects. The *Sunday Times* and the *Financial Times* wrote that the Chancellor had set his sights firmly on autumn entry, in spite of the fact that inflation would still be well above European levels by then. The *Sunday Times* described a 'golden scenario' for the Conservatives in which the ERM would provide the pound with the necessary support to provide for substantial cuts in interest rates, then 15 per cent, before a general election. It was an unusual period. As one who was on the receiving end of Treasury guidance during it, I can testify that had entry not occurred in the autumn of 1990, it would not have been only the markets who would have been disappointed.

The guidance was that the inflation condition would not have to be met precisely. It was important for Britain's inflation to be heading towards the European average. Actually getting there would be preferable but was not essential. I wrote at the time that, having set out the conditions that would determine the date of entry, the Treasury was moving towards a position where the conditions would be modified to suit the Chancellor's desired entry date. Major flirted briefly with the idea of taking the pound into the ERM at the beginning of July, to coincide with France and Italy's deadline for the removal of remaining capital controls. The first of July 1990 was also the official start of the first stage of a process leading to full European monetary union, in the timetable set out by a committee of central bankers which met under the chairmanship of European Commission President, Jacques Delors. ERM entry at the start of July would have fitted the Delors committee timetable – in stage one all EC member countries were to become members of the ERM (with the possible exception of Portugal and Greece) – and it would have underlined Britain's commitment to playing a constructive role in Europe's future. Perhaps for this reason, it was too soon for Thatcher and Major did not push it strongly.

By the summer of 1990, however, Major and his advisers had a clear idea of the timing of ERM entry. There was one instance where, on a car journey to a political engagement, Major asked one of his advisers to write on a piece of paper the best time to take the pound into the ERM. He did the same, and the papers were exchanged. Both had precisely the same timing, the weekend before the Conservative Party conference in October. Indeed, there was some consternation when Major's suit jacket, containing both pieces of paper, was temporarily mislaid, having been hung up by a helpful party official. It was suggested shortly after entry occurred that the original plan was for Thatcher to announce it in her closing address to the party conference on Friday 12 October 1990, but there appears to be little basis for this.

As Major progressed towards his ERM entry goal it was not all plain sailing. The big problem, as before, was with Britain's inflation rate. The March Budget and the poll tax had been self-inflicted wounds. There was unwelcome evidence, as pay settlements moved back into double figures, of the re-emergence of a wage–price spiral. Iraq's invasion of Kuwait, on 2 August, pushed world oil prices sharply higher. And, while all the industrialized countries were similarly affected, it was hard to argue, with Britain's inflation rate above 10 per cent, that the key Madrid condition, even its amended form – that inflation be moving towards the European average – was close to being met. By September 1990, therefore, the markets' belief in the imminence of ERM entry was starting to be tinged with doubt. Sterling began the month strongly, at above DM3, but dropped to DM2.90 by 21 September after a speech by Karl Otto Pöhl, the Bundesbank President, was interpreted by dealers as hinting that Britain was not ready for ERM membership. Bundesbank officials pointed out that Pöhl's remarks were directed at the high-inflation countries of southern Europe but the damage was done. Britain was also a high-inflation country so, dealers asked, what was the difference? When Major arrived in Washington for the annual meetings of the International Monetary Fund and World Bank on 21 September, direct from a gathering of Commonwealth finance ministers in Trinidad, two things were on his mind. The first was an excruciating toothache – he later had an operation on his wisdom teeth during the Conservative leadership battle of November 1990. The second was that the pound, having been buoyed for months by the ERM entry story, was looking very shaky.

The Chancellor's response to the latter, in briefing journalists, was to redefine the Madrid inflation condition once more. The condition, which had started life as a requirement that British and European inflation be roughly the same, had already been amended so that it was enough if inflation rates were merely moving closer together. In its final form, as set out by Major in Washington, all that was needed was that it could be forecast, with reasonable confidence, that convergence between British and European inflation would take place. The new measure was not current inflation rates, nor was it the beginnings of convergence, it was that prospective inflation rates should be converging. This was not as slippery as it appeared to be. Treasury and Bank of England officials were taken by surprise by the extent of the 1990–91 recession but they were confident, in the autumn of 1990, that tight monetary policy had finally got on top of inflation and that there would be a sharp fall during 1991. This is not to say that the policy was without risks. Treasury inflation forecasts had gone badly wrong before. Indeed, in the autumn of 1989 the Treasury predicted 5.75 per cent inflation for the fourth quarter of 1990 but the out-turn was 10 per cent. Major was gambling that this time the Treasury would be right and, as 1991 progressed, it became clear that the gamble had paid off.

The timing of entry was odd in another respect. Thatcher, in her earlier objections to ERM membership, had said that the economy had to be strong enough to cope with it. By September 1990, the gloom was gathering over the economy. I wrote in the *Sunday Times* that the economy had embarked on more than a gentle correction and that a hard landing was under way which would produce a significant fall in gross domestic product in 1991. The message from industry was uniformly bleak. The ERM entry date had been planned without any regard for whether or not the economy would have embarked on a recession by the autumn of 1990. Perhaps for this reason, the Treasury was slow to admit to the economy's true situation, for fear that it would have impeded entry. Throughout the years when, under the strait-jacket provided by Thatcher, ministers had insisted that ERM entry would occur when the time was 'ripe', the vision was of an economy with low inflation and stable growth. As it turned out, entry occurred in conditions of high inflation and recession.

The go-ahead for entry came in a meeting between Major and Thatcher on Wednesday 3 October. Thatcher, however, had one condition. She wanted the decision to take sterling into the ERM to be combined with a cut in interest rates, both because of the intense political pressure to reduce rates and because such a move would soften the objections to entry from the anti-European wing within the Conservative Party. The formal announcement of entry from the Treasury two days later therefore contained several surprises. A relatively high entry rate, of DM2.95, was chosen, around which the pound would operate within the wide ERM bands, 6 per cent either side of the central parity. Thus, sterling had a theoretical range of DM2.7730 to DM3.1270. The announcement came, not as had been expected, after all the important financial markets, including those in New York, had closed for the weekend. Instead, it was at 4 p.m. on a Friday afternoon, just as dealers in Europe were clearing their books. The Treasury came up with a technical explanation to explain the timing of entry – it could occur any time after official currency support operations within the ERM, which were valid during European trading hours, had come to an end. Continental time was one hour ahead of Britain, so a 4 p.m. entry announcement (five in the afternoon throughout the rest of Europe) was within the rules. In fact, the overwhelming reason for the timing of entry was political. The Labour Party had had a generally successful conference in Blackpool. Friday was the final day of the conference. The afternoon announcement of ERM entry ensured, not only that the event would dominate the early evening news, but that it would also squeeze Labour's weekend press coverage. The timing caused friction with Britain's

European partners, Etiquette required consultation, in the forum of the European Community's monetary committee, on the details of entry. Such consultation occurred, but only after Britain had gone public with her entry terms. Membership itself was to begin at the start of trading on Monday 8 October. Some members of the monetary committee were determined to change the entry rate for sterling, if only slightly, to give Britain a rap on the knuckles. Fortunately, Major's diplomatic offensive around the finance ministries of Europe had built up a reserve of goodwill and Britain's entry terms survived.

Another curiosity was the Treasury's ERM announcement itself. Its statement began with the fact that base rates were being reduced from 15 to 14 per cent. This was important, but it was far less momentous than the second part of the statement, which described the decision to join the ERM. Thatcher's economic instincts, in insisting on an interest rate reduction, were good. The economy was in recession, even though she herself would not admit to it, and lower rates were the appropriate response. Tactically, however, combining ERM entry and an interest rate cut was a mistake. The combination, together with the manner of the Treasury's announcement, suggested that entry was for the purposes of short-term political gain. Robin Leigh-Pemberton, the Governor of the Bank of England, was mortified. Interest rate cuts in the context of ERM membership had to be earned, he said in television interviews that weekend. It was a mistake to anticipate favourable market reaction and reduce rates before the currency markets had signalled that it was appropriate to do so. By the Monday, however, he recognized that it was no use crying over spilt milk. Monetary policy had been tough for more than eighteen months, he told Japanese businessmen, and there was increasing official confidence about the economy's slowdown and the prospects for a significant fall in inflation. He said:

> It is this confidence that underpinned the decision of the British Government to announce on Friday a very modest interest rate cut – from 15 to 14 per cent, which remains high and tough; and sterling's entry into the exchange rate mechanism of the European Monetary System. This is a great event in our economic life. It is something I have looked forward to for a very long time.   (1990a)

Leigh-Pemberton, like many long-term advocates of ERM membership and indeed like Major, was prepared to accept Thatcher's interest rate cut as a small price to pay for securing entry. Nigel Lawson was rather less charitable. Aware that Thatcher had insisted on the rate cut, he told the House of Commons soon after entry was announced that the reduction in rates had given the markets precisely the wrong signal. He said:

> I was interested to see the Governor of the Bank of England is reported in the *Financial Times* as saying that he would have been happier had the interest rate cut followed entry into the ERM. This is not a small point because, sadly, the conjunction of the two has led to a degree of cynicism in the financial markets for which we shall have to pay the price. That price will be that the next reduction in interest rates will have to be deferred for longer than would otherwise have been the case.   (1990)

The implication was clear. Thatcher had ruined Lawson's finest hour, his March 1988 Budget, with her interventions on the question of exchange rate management. Now she had done much the same thing for Major and ERM entry. As it turned out, Thatcher was not going to be around for long enough to suffer the consequences. Nor, directly, was Major, who left the Treasury to step into her shoes at 10 Downing Street. It was to Norman Lamont, Britain's third Chancellor in just over a year, that the task of building ERM credibility fell.

The Economy Falls off a Cliff

In the first half of 1990, the main concern of the Treasury and the Bank of England was that the economy was still failing to respond to the high-interest-rate regime that had been in place since late 1988. Although the evidence was mounting of a slowdown, the economy's lack of response to tight monetary policy and the risk that inflation was deeply embedded in the system were the main sources of concern. There were plenty of recession warnings around. Indeed, the final increase in base rates to 15 per cent in October 1989 produced a warning from Sir Alan Walters that the economy was heading into recession. But, as the early months of 1990 passed by, such gloomy assessments appeared unjustified.

The housing market had been hit hard, as had the construction industry as a whole. Housing starts in 1990 were nearly 40 per cent down on their 1988 peak. There were also clear signs of distress among home-buyers, with a sharp rise in mortgage arrears. Sterling's fall, the high level of interest rates and Lawson's resignation had meant that what the economy was going through could never be regarded as a soft landing. But official concern was still mainly directed at inflation rather than recession. The Organization for Economic Cooperation and Development, in a report on the British economy published in August, reflected some of this official thinking. The rise in inflation had yet to be halted, it said, and tough economic policies could be needed for a long time to bring down inflation permanently.

Under the surface, however, the economic strains were increasing. One disturbing indicator of this was the financial position of the company sector. In the first half of 1990 the financial deficit of industrial and commercial companies ran at an annual rate of £28bn. The figure for the whole of 1990 was £26.7bn, compared with £21.3bn in 1989 and a surplus of £0.2bn as recently as 1987. This showed that companies were paying out far more in interest on their borrowings than they were generating in income. Sooner or later, they would have to act to cut back this deficit. If they did so rapidly, by announcing large-scale redundancies and slashing investment, then the economic consequences would be very severe. This helps to explain the Government's determination, in the autumn of 1990, not to admit that the economy was in recession. There were political and market dangers in acknowledging recession, at a time when the task was to rebuild confidence in the Government's handling of the economy, and prepare for membership of the ERM. But there was also a clearly recognized risk that gloomy official statements would spark off even more aggressive cutbacks by the private sector. The recession would be a self-feeding process. Sir Geoffrey Howe, when Chancellor, had adopted a similar tack ten years earlier. Early in 1980, the deepest recession since the war was, in Howe's description, merely 'a significant slowdown in growth' in which there was a danger of 'self-fulfilling pessimism' (1980).

Thatcher, addressing a Welsh Confederation of British Industry dinner at the end of September, was dismissive of recession talk. She said:

> Newspapers talk of world recession; a return to stagflation; and an end to the United Kingdom economic miracle. Every new figure, including the latest CBI survey, is given the most pessimistic interpretation – as heralding the onset of a major economic downturn. We must ask ourselves why, after years

of sustained progress, of the right philosophy, of the right policies, is this self-doubt assailing some of the business community – or perhaps more accurately the press? (1990)

Major was also reluctant to admit to recession. At the September IMF meeting in which he successfully steered expectations towards early entry into the ERM, he insisted that the economy was not in recession. A novice in economics himself, he used a technical argument provided by his officials to explain why he could not say the economy was in recession even if he believed it. This was that, on the widely used American definition of recession, it required two consecutive quarters of falling gross domestic product. Thus, even if the July–September quarter of 1990 had experienced a fall in GDP, it was by no means certain that this would continue in the final quarter of the year.

The speed of decline in the summer and early autumn of 1990, however, was such as to suggest that it was no temporary phenomenon. And the official reluctance to admit to recession appears to have been driven as much by incompetence, and a failure to recognize what was happening, as by the more explicable attempt to put a brave face on things. 'We are not in recession,' Major said in September. 'There is a general slowdown and that is not a surprise. It is not comfortable but it is necessary' (1990b).

The Treasury did not have the excuse that it had not been warned. The Confederation of British Industry's quarterly industrial-trends survey at the end of July was the gloomiest since the early 1980s, and showed a sharp drop in business confidence, orders and expected output, a combination consistent with recession. The CBI's warning, that a recession was likely over the following six months, was too cautious. The recession had already started. In the week of 10–14 September, Major had a succession of meetings with top businessmen, one of which was at a lunch organized by the *Sunday Times*. The message, from the CBI, the Engineering Employers' Federation, British Telecom, British Steel, GKN, Amstrad, Trafalgar House, Grand Metropolitan, Tate & Lyle and other groups, was grim. Since the early summer, business had fallen away sharply. In some cases, particularly construction, the fall was sharper than in the 1980–81 recession, and the picture across the whole of industry was of a disturbingly abrupt decline. Confronted with such evidence, Major was taken aback. This did not fit in with the Treasury's view of things. More importantly, it posed potential problems for his intention of taking the pound into the ERM. Could one take such a momentous step if the economy was in steep recession? Recession, above all, would produce demands for sharp reductions in interest rates, demands that could be incompatible with the policy aim of locking sterling's exchange rate against the Deutschmark, this time formally. The Chancellor therefore turned a blind eye to the gloom, to the bemusement of industry. Thatcher let it be known that she and her ministers did not think much of industry's squeals. Sir Brian Corby, the CBI president, said:

> I don't find it helpful to suggest that the lookout on the boat who points out that there are rocks ahead is whingeing. Nor do I find it obvious that it is necessary to crash the boat on to the rocks in order to find salvation. There has been a marked deterioration in business prospects since the summer. The CBI's latest monthly trends survey provided further clear signs that the economy is moving into recession.   (1990)

Why did the economy, to use one popular description at the time, suddenly fall off a cliff? Alan Budd, then economic adviser at Barclays Bank, likened the economy's performance to that of a cartoon character who runs off the edge of a precipice. The character keeps running in thin air, for a while, before plunging to the ground. In his view, companies kept on going in the first half of 1990, in the expectation that the orders would keep arriving. When it became plain that the downturn in orders was both sharp and sustained, they lost their means of support. A key role in the recession was played, therefore, by business and consumer confidence. As long as confidence was maintained, the dangers of a severe recession were limited. When confidence fell sharply a recession was guaranteed.

Iraq's invasion of Kuwait on 2 August 1990, and the sharp, if temporary, rise in world oil prices that followed it, had a clear impact on business and consumer attitudes. Apart from the direct effects of higher oil prices, the Iraqi move introduced a new uncertainty into the situation. Britain's recession was, however, already firmly in place by the time Saddam Hussein, Iraq's President, gave the order for the invasion of Kuwait. Indeed, the CBI survey predicting the onset of recession was published before events in the Gulf unfolded and the survey sample had been interviewed some two or three weeks in advance of publication.

Gulf uncertainties may have given the economy an additional downward shove, but it was already falling.

The reason it was falling was quite straightforward. It reflected the culmination of the effects of nearly two years of high interest rates. Research undertaken at the Bank of England suggested that the full effects of an interest rate change took around eight quarters to work through. Base rates had been increased to 12 per cent in August 1988 and 13 per cent by November of that year. As importantly, Major's policy of preparing sterling for ERM entry had, by gaining the confidence of the foreign exchange markets, broken the pattern of the pound's decline. In 1989 the impact of high interest rates on companies had been offset by the 12 per cent fall in sterling's average value which occurred during the course of the year. From the spring of 1990 until ERM entry in October, this was no longer the case. The pound was strong against the Deutschmark and other European currencies because of the prospect of entry into the mechanism. It also rose against the dollar because the latter was independently weak. Between April and August, sterling rose by nearly 10 per cent. High interest rates and a rising exchange rate represented a powerful cocktail. At official level there was little realization of how powerful that cocktail was.

It is possible that, by cutting interest rates sooner, the damage wrought by the recession could have been limited. Suggestions around this time that rates should be cut sharply were, however, roundly rejected by the authorities. The *Sunday Times* called for a reduction of two percentage points, to 13 per cent, in August but this was dismissed by the Treasury as tantamount to economic lunacy. Tim Congdon, whose record in predicting the Lawson boom had been better than other economists, now feared deep recession. He wrote:

The danger now is not that insufficient measures have been taken against inflation, but that unless interest rates are cut, the slowdown will become a full recession next year. If so, output will be sliding and unemployment rising as the Conservatives prepare for the next election ... The Government is being too fastidious in its anxiety to have a thoroughly respectable inflation rate when it joins the ERM. If the Government keeps interest rates up for this reason, it will be overlooking the powerful effects its policies have already had on domestic credit. However brave and admirable this may be as a way of controlling inflation, it is the political equivalent of the Charge of the Light Brigade.   (1990)

Major later explained why he had regarded it as impossible to cut interest rates at that time. Reducing rates before ERM entry would have been interpreted in the financial markets as a signal that Britain was not serious about maintaining a firm exchange rate, he told the House of Commons in October. The delay, however, was important. In August and September, at a time of collapsing confidence, falling output and sharply declining demand, the authorities found themselves unable to respond with confidence-restoring reductions in interest rates. And the interest rate cut, when it came in early October, was ill-timed and served only to delay further reductions. During the Lawson boom years, as the Governor of the Bank of England admitted in his Durham speech, interest rates were reduced when they should not have been. By the autumn of 1990, the opposite situation prevailed. Interest rates were maintained when they should have been reduced, and this largely because of a policy ambition, designed well before the onset of recession, of entering sterling into the ERM at the relatively high rate of DM2.95.

The July–September quarter of 1990 was one in which the British economy took a dive, even if Thatcher and her ministers were slow to admit to it. Indeed, Thatcher left office without once accepting, publicly, that the economy was in recession. Gross domestic product fell by 1.4 per cent in the third quarter, an annualized rate of decline of nearly 6 per cent. Private-sector investment fell by 7 per cent, retail sales by nearly 1 per cent, manufacturing output by 1.6 per cent. Unemployment rose by nearly 20,000 a month, accelerating to a 60,000 a month rise in the fourth quarter. New car registrations were 13 per cent down on a year earlier. By September 1990, the broad M4 measure of the money supply was growing at just over 10 per cent a year, half its growth rate compared with a year earlier. The slowdown in bank and building-society lending, from an annual rate of growth of nearly 25 per cent in the third quarter of 1989 to under 13 per cent a year later, was just as dramatic.

The Lawson boom was now but a distant memory, the idea of achieving a soft landing after that boom merely a fantasy. By the autumn of 1990 inflation was in double figures and the economy was in sharp decline. Stagflation had returned. The Thatcher miracle had appeared to offer an alluring combination of low inflation and strong economic growth. Now it appeared to have been nothing more than an elaborate confidence trick. The economy had moved spectacularly from boom to bust. Rarely had pride come before a fall in so dramatic a fashion. The British economy, one moment apparently a model for the world, was now back to a more familiar position, in which the world politely averted its eyes. High interest rates were hitting the new breed of home-owners hard and destroying small businesses. In 1990 44,000 owner-occupiers had their properties repossessed by banks and building societies. The enterprise culture was dying on its feet. Neither the boom nor the bust gave a fair picture of the true position. The economy was never quite as good as it looked when the economic miracle was being proclaimed. Nor was everything lost in the subsequent recession. But the retribution was almost biblical in nature. The Conservative Government, elected on a banner of low inflation and economic prudence, had nurtured an economic boom as irresponsible as anything in the post-war period. Nor were there powerful extenuating circumstances, as in 1974–5 and 1980–81, when world oil crises exacerbated domestic events. The Government had walked into the boom and it had to face what was, in essence, a home-made recession.

There was, perhaps, no way out. The inevitable consequence of the boom years – the real increase in consumer spending over the 1986–9 period averaged more than 5 per cent a year – was that the economy needed a period of correction. The boom had created imbalances that had to be tackled, not least the near £20bn current-account deficit of 1989. It was never very likely that the financial markets would allow the Government the luxury of sorting out such problems at its leisure. Some officials, in both the Treasury and the Bank of England, appear to have recognized this, although they understandably did not spell it out to their political masters. Economic pain and electoral success rarely go hand in hand. The boom had gone on too long after the 1987 election to allow it to be corrected well in time for a 1991, or as it turned out, a 1992 election. The biggest danger, seen from the viewpoint of Bank of England officials and career civil servants in the Treasury, was that the politicians would attempt to postpone the pain, with serious consequences for inflation.

Who could be blamed for the unhappy state in which the British economy found itself in the autumn of 1990? Nigel Lawson was the obvious scapegoat, but he had left office a year earlier. And, in revealing that he had not only proposed ERM entry at a much earlier date but had also presented a plan for an independent, inflation-fighting Bank of

England, he had successfully sown doubts about his culpability. For Thatcher, the problems created by the recession were intensely practical ones. The poll tax and her stance on Europe were the immediate reasons for her downfall. But the idea of a challenge to her leadership by Michael Heseltine would never have come up had it not been for the fact that the Conservatives were trailing Labour by up to twenty points in the opinion polls. And this, in turn, was mainly due to the unpopularity of high interest rates and the reality of the recession. When Thatcher faced the challenge for her leadership at the end of November, the economy offered few saving graces. Recession and high inflation had re-emerged, not as a result of mismanagement by the Opposition, but after eleven and a half years of her premiership. The inflation cat had been let out of the bag, and getting it back in was proving to be extremely painful. To this day, she believes that she was brought down by a combination of disloyalty and others' mismanagement of the economy. Dissatisfaction with the economy's performance, notably in the IMF austerity years and during the 1978–9 winter of industrial relations' discontent, had propelled her into office in May 1979. Now it was dissatisfaction with the economy that cast her out again in 1990. Retribution was severe, and final.

9

THE ECONOMICS OF BURNT FINGERS

John Major, as Chancellor of the Exchequer, had been at the helm of the economy as it made the painful transition from boom to bust. On taking over the job in October 1989 he had coined a useful phrase: 'If it isn't hurting it isn't working.' Now, as he took over as Prime Minister on 28 November 1990, his problem was that it was hurting rather too much. The story of Margaret Thatcher's downfall, and John Major's elevation, has been amply described. Sir Geoffrey Howe's resignation as Deputy Prime Minister in November 1990 followed a row between Thatcher and fellow European leaders at a special summit meeting in Rome. Howe, deciding that Thatcher's anti-European attitudes were hardening to the point where he could no longer continue in the Government, said in his resignation speech, 'The time has come for others to consider their own response to the tragic conflict of loyalties with which I have myself wrestled for perhaps too long' (1990). Michael Heseltine, who had left the Cabinet nearly five years earlier, took up the challenge.

In the first leadership ballot on 20 November, Thatcher won by 204 votes to Heseltine's 152, four short of the required 15 per cent margin of victory over her opponent. Her initial instincts were to continue to the second ballot, a week later, but she was persuaded by Cabinet colleagues that her support was likely to drop significantly, and that many of them could no longer commit themselves to supporting her. Three candidates therefore stood in the second ballot, on 27 November – Major, Douglas Hurd, the Foreign Secretary, and Heseltine. Major won 185 votes, Heseltine 131 and Hurd 56, an outcome that should have resulted in a third ballot. However, both Hurd and Heseltine immediately declared that they would stand aside and the following day it was Major who made the journey to Buckingham Palace to take up the reins of power.

A Winter of Recession

The winter of 1990–91 contained many parallels with the recession winter of 1980–81. Then, there had been serious doubts about Thatcher's ability to survive in office, or at least to be able to do so without abandoning her policies. This time, the uncertainties over her continued rule had re-emerged and had proved to be well-founded. In the early months of 1981, unemployment rose by an average of 100,000 a month. In the February–April period of 1991, unemployment increased by 282,000, only just under 100,000 a month, and this in a period where demographic influences, notably a fall in the number of young people entering the workforce, were supposed to help keep the unemployment total down. In the winter of 1980–81 there were some spectacular business failures, and the loss of some of the traditional big names of British industry. The 1990–91 recession saw plenty of big names fall from grace, notably the retailing successes of the 1980s such as Next, Laura Ashley and Storehouse. Business failures were, however, spread among the layer of small and medium-sized businesses, many of which had been created as part of the entrepreneurial wave of the Thatcher years. Official figures showed a big rise in company insolvencies in the final quarter of 1990, which continued into 1991. Company insolvencies in the first half of 1991 were 65 per cent up on a year earlier. Data from Dun & Bradstreet showed that more than 33,000 businesses failed in the first nine months of 1991. Individual insolvencies rose even more dramatically. In the January–June period of 1991, they were 86 per cent up on a year earlier.

Ten years earlier, the recession winter had been characterized by uncertainty over interest rate policy. Base rates were cut to 14 per cent in November 1980 but, because the sterling M3 measure of the money supply, the basis of the medium-term financial strategy, was still growing strongly, no further reductions came until the following March. The economy entered the winter of 1990–91 with base rates also at 14 per cent, a reduction from 15 per cent having taken effect on 8 October. This time, however, the constraint on further reductions was different, and it was due to Britain's membership of the European exchange rate mechanism (ERM). The cut in interest rates that coincided with entry had, as Nigel Lawson predicted, created enough doubts about the Government's commitment to the new regime to make further reductions difficult to achieve.

Prior to ERM entry, critics of the exchange rate mechanism, particularly Sir Alan Walters, had argued that membership could lead to undesirable pressure for rapid reductions in interest rates, reductions that were inconsistent with the requirements of maintaining tight domestic monetary policy. This 'Walters critique' cited the experience of Spain, a high-interest-rate, high-inflation economy, where entry into the ERM had been followed by a long period in which capital was attracted towards the peseta, creating pressure for big reductions in Spanish interest rates. The Walters critique became, in slightly different form, the 'golden scenario' for the Conservatives, invented by my *Sunday Times* colleague Michael Jones and myself. In this version, the exchange rate protection provided by ERM membership would prop up the pound, allowing a succession of interest rate reductions and a fourth Conservative election victory.

In the event, for the first few months of membership at least, the missing ingredient was one that had been the basis for both versions – a strong pound. Sterling's honeymoon period in the ERM was short-lived. It rose strongly in the first flush of membership, but then fell back. Sterling's average level against the Deutschmark was below DM2.92 in November and under DM2.88 in December, compared with its central rate in the system of DM2.95. Instead of the golden scenario there was, according to Professor Charles Goodhart, a bleak dilemma. Goodhart, former monetary adviser to the Bank of England, said early in 1991:

The dilemma facing the authorities is indeed uncomfortable and bleak. Either we keep monetary policy severely tight just at the moment of entry into a steep recession, or we realign and lose all future credibility both in Europe and with our own markets. As the Irishman is supposed to have said when asked for directions, 'I would not start from here' ... It had indeed been hoped that entry into the ERM would lead us into what had been termed the golden scenario, under which entry could lead to a succession of cuts in interest rates in the months subsequent to such entry ... Why did this not occur? The first reason is that the authorities were, I believe, actually concerned that such falls in interest rates might lead to a premature weakening in the contra-inflationary discipline that they wished to maintain. In order to prevent the possibility of interest rates being forced down quite rapidly, the authorities consciously chose a wider 6 per cent band, partly in order to enable the spot/forward differential* consistent with credibility still to be wide enough to allow UK short rates to remain significantly above the level in Germany. The combination, however, of continuing high interest rates and falling exchange rates suggests that it was not just the wider band that prevented capital inflows and pressures for lower interest rates, but rather the uncertainty and lack of credible commitment to the continued maintenance of the parity that caused the golden scenario to fail.   (1991, pp. 69–71)

There is, indeed, evidence that the Bank of England, in particular, pressed ministers to adopt ERM entry terms that would exert an even tougher anti-inflation discipline on the economy and, by implication, cause an even more severe recession. Some Bank officials wanted a central ERM rate of DM3.10 or DM3.20. The Bank of England, with the backing of Treasury officials, was also adamant that entry into the ERM should be on the wide, 6 per cent, bands, rather than the narrow, 2.25 per cent limits. The case for wide bands could be argued both ways. It would give the Government room for manoeuvre if the pound fell, and there was no guarantee that it would not. With narrow bands, and a relatively short distance for the pound to fall, the Chancellor could have faced unwelcome pressure to raise interest rates at the very time that such a move would heap even more disaster upon the domestic economy. The Bank of England, however, saw things from the opposite point of view. It wanted wide bands to prevent undue pressure for early interest rate cuts. The Bank's November 1990 *Quarterly Bulletin* outlined the position: 'With sterling in the wider band, the United Kingdom can still maintain interest rates higher than in the narrow-band countries, as may be required by domestic considerations' (1990, p. 440).

And this, as was made clear, was the intention:

The stance of monetary policy has not been significantly altered by entry into the ERM: the continuing restraint exercised by interest rates at 14 per cent has been reinforced by the counterinflationary policy stemming from ERM obligations. In the present circumstances, the authorities have continued to indicate that interest rates will not be reduced further until they are sure it would be safe and prudent to do so.   (1990, p. 465)

---

* The pound's expected depreciation over the next twelve months, as implied by the interest rate gap between Britain and Germany and the difference between present (spot) and expected (forward) exchange rates for the pound against the Deutschmark.

John Major's elevation to 10 Downing Street had produced a vacancy for the post of Chancellor of the Exchequer. His successor was Norman Lamont, the third man in the job in just over a year. Lamont, who had been Major's deputy in the post of Chief Secretary to the Treasury had, only eighteen months before, been a junior Treasury minister, below both Lawson and Major. Born in the Shetlands, he had, in the early 1970s, been the youngest MP in the House of Commons, which he had come to from a career in merchant banking. Lamont had not won great favour under Thatcher, holding a succession of junior ministerial posts. His public reputation, such as it was, was that of something of a *bon viveur*. But, like Major, he was in the right place at the right time. When Major announced his candidacy for the leadership of the Conservative Party, Lamont was on hand to run an energetic and successful campaign among MPs, although one consequence of this was that he was viewed with mistrust by Thatcher loyalists. Where, they said, was the great energy and efficiency shown by Lamont and others during Thatcher's own leadership campaign?

Lamont took over as Chancellor at an unusual time in the Treasury calendar. Major had already presented the Autumn Statement on 8 November, one of the two key events in the Treasury's year, the other being the March Budget. The forecast he presented showed that the economy was in recession, as defined in terms of two successive quarters of declining gross domestic product, although Major maintained his reluctance to use what became known as the 'R-word'. He referred to a 'period of weak activity' and a 'modest downturn' in investment. GDP, the Treasury said, would decline by 1.2 per cent in the second half of 1990, but that would be about as far as it went. The forecast was for a 0.1 per cent rise in GDP in the first half of 1991 and a stronger 2.1 per cent increase in the second. Importantly, the forecast failed to fulfil the toughest definition of recession, a decline in GDP in one calendar year compared with its predecessor. The prediction was for 1 per cent growth in 1990, followed by a paltry, but still positive, 0.5 per cent expansion in 1991.

Lamont showed less fastidiousness about the use of the word recession, and he admitted that business conditions were 'rough'. Fresh into the job, however, he maintained that the recession would be mild. He told the Treasury and Civil Service Committee, 'It is very difficult to be absolutely certain about what will be the extent of the downturn, but I think there are reasons why one could believe that it will be relatively short-lived and relatively shallow. I note that a number of forecasts agree with the Government in that respect' (1990, p. 25).

Many disagreed with him. The CBI, receiving gloomy reports about trading conditions from its members, was noticeably more gloomy than the Treasury. So too was the all-party Treasury and Civil Service Committee, which concluded in its report on the Autumn Statement that 'Taking all factors into account, we conclude that the recession is likely to be deeper and longer in duration than the Treasury forecast' (1990, p. xxxvi).

Interest Rates are Becalmed

Lamont's comments came in early December. By November, however, the Bank of England, together with a number of Treasury officials and advisers, had already concluded that the recession was likely to be deeper than the official forecast suggested. Robin Leigh-Pemberton, giving evidence to the Treasury and Civil Service Committee in March 1991, said that the Bank had come to the view in November 1990 that the effects on business and consumer confidence of the impending Gulf war, together with clear evidence of domestic economic weakness, meant that the recession would be longer and deeper than previously expected. Asked why the Treasury's public position was more optimistic than this, he said, 'I do not think I know why they took a different view of the developments. Perhaps I should know but I am afraid I do not' (1991, p. 26).

Was there a conscious attempt to play down the gloom? The Treasury insisted not, and that its published forecast represented its best assessment at the time of the likely outcome. But the economy was at a difficult juncture. Sterling was still bedding down in the ERM and was weak within the system. The gloomier the Treasury's forecast, the greater would have been the domestic pressure for interest rate cuts and the more difficult, arguably, it would have been to achieve them. If the foreign exchange markets sensed that the Government was desperate to reduce interest rates then dealers would mark the pound down in anticipation of rate cuts. There were other reasons why there was a natural bias against excessive gloom in the Treasury forecasts. The Government did not wish to be seen to be talking the economy into a deeper recession than was necessary. The senior officials advising Lamont, notably Permanent Secretary Sir Peter Middleton and Chief

Economic Adviser Sir Terence Burns, had been around for the whole of the Lawson era, and for the shorter Major period at the Treasury. Admitting to a deep recession would, therefore, be tantamount to an admission of the scale of the policy errors of previous years.

The Bank of England's private view in November 1990, that the recession would be deeper and more prolonged than was publicly admitted by the Treasury, did not deflect Bank officials from their opinion that high interest rates needed to be maintained for as long as was politically possible. The Bank saw the inflation danger from strongly rising demand as having disappeared, but still saw serious risks on the costs' side. Ford's manual workers were awarded an inflation-linked pay rise of more than 13 per cent in November. Pay settlements of 10 and 11 per cent became the norm in the early stages of the 1990–91 pay round. By the end of 1990, a combination of high pay settlements and falling output meant that unit wage and salary costs in manufacturing were rising by 12 per cent a year. Within the context of ERM membership, such rates of increase were suicidal. The pound had entered the system at a testing rate of DM2.95. Without a sharp decline in the rate of growth of wages the competitive pressures for an early devaluation of the pound would become intense. According to the Bank:

> The Governor has emphasized that henceforth companies can have no grounds for expecting a lower exchange rate to validate any failure to control costs. The greater stability which ERM membership offers sterling against other European currencies should in itself be welcome to business as it will enable firms to plan and invest with greater certainty. If companies recognize that they are now operating under a changed regime the benefits of lower inflation will accrue sooner, and at a lower cost in terms of lost output, than could otherwise be expected. But if they fail to recognize the constraints under which they now operate the outcome will prove painful for them.   (1990, p. 439)

As the winter of 1990–91 progressed, therefore, two distinct views emerged within the Government. The Bank of England's hard-line view, shared by some Treasury officials, was that the fact that sterling was not strong within the ERM was, if anything, a welcome development. Sterling's downside was limited by membership of the system, while its relative weakness within its bands provided an excuse for keeping interest rates high and ramming home the tough anti-inflation message. Officials, charged as they were with achieving the Government's primary economic objective of controlling inflation, had mani-

festly failed to do so. Reputations had been lost and fingers burnt
during the boom and its aftermath. It was hardly surprising, therefore,
that their policy bias was towards hitting inflation, and hitting it hard,
even if the recession costs were high. Lamont, having come to the job of
Chancellor in unexpected circumstances, was clearly beholden to his
officials, at least in the early weeks. His instincts, however, also appear
to have been on the side of the hard-line approach. He had urged Major
to take a tougher interest rate stance a year earlier. And he later
outraged Labour MPs by declaring that rising unemployment and
business failures were 'a price worth paying' for the defeat of inflation.

For other ministers, and for Conservative MPs, the situation was
rather less comfortable. After delaying so long before entering the
ERM, and doing so when interest rates were high, the Government
appeared to have acquired a pig in a poke. A system that was supposed
to help bring British interest rates down to European levels, appeared to
have the opposite effect – that of keeping interest rates high when, on
domestic grounds, they should have been reduced. As disturbing, it
was a European system that was causing the interest rate problem –
Goodhart's bleak dilemma – and the truce within the Conservative Party
between the pro- and anti-Europeans was fragile enough even without
this additional source of tension.

The winter months were, in financial-market terms, a credibility-
building period. Both Major and Lamont, in New Year interviews,
made it plain that they would not contemplate a devaluation of sterling
within the ERM and this, together with the fact that base rates were
held at 14 per cent, helped the pound recover from a mid-December low
of just above DM2.85. The recession was, however, proving both deep
and long. GDP fell by 0.8 per cent in the final quarter of 1990,
manufacturing output by 3.3 per cent. The recession was taking on a
shape and intensity which drew disturbing parallels with 1980–81.
There was, in addition, a perceived barrier to any sterling rise within the
ERM. This was that, with the recession evidence mounting, dealers
decided that the moment the pound achieved its DM2.95 central rate
against the Deutschmark, interest rates would be cut. There was,
therefore, no incentive for pushing the pound higher than DM2.95. And
the more that the domestic economic situation cried out for interest rate
cuts, the less the foreign exchange markets appeared to be willing to
allow it.

The issue came to a head in February 1991. Sterling had been pushing gently higher from the beginning of the year but was knocked back, first by the markets' belief that interest rates would have to be cut, regardless of the pound's level, and then by the announcement, on 31 January, of a half-point increase in Germany's official interest rates. The Bundesbank, concerned about the inflationary pressures arising from German unification, raised its discount rate to 6.5 per cent and the Lombard rate to 9 per cent. This still left a huge margin between Britain's interest rates and those in Germany but the pound fell, dropping back below DM2.90. The bleak dilemma, originally regarded by the hard-liners as a welcome constraint on interest rate reductions, was now becoming a source of concern. The pound was the weakest currency within the ERM and the rules of the game, as operated by the other members, included the proviso that interest rates were generally not reduced unless justified by a currency's strong position within the system.

To add insult to injury, *The Times* of Wednesday 13 February included a letter from six economists, all of whom, to a greater or lesser extent, saw themselves as guardians of the Government's monetarist conscience. The letter, organized by Professor Patrick Minford of Liverpool University, was signed by Tim Congdon, City economists Bill Martin, Gordon Pepper and Peter Warburton, Sir Alan Walters and Minford himself. It said:

We are deeply concerned about the state of the economy. The principles of good monetary policy imply that interest rates should have been cut significantly by now in response to the clear evidence of recession from monetary and indeed all other indicators. Failure to cut them is increasing the risks of a depression which would get out of control and from which recovery would be long delayed. Many sectors are barely surviving and could be forced to close capacity on a massive scale; and the banking system is fragile, weakened by serious and repeated loan losses. It was just such monetary problems that triggered the Great Depression of the 1930s. As interest rates fall there should also be a sharp depreciation of sterling which is seriously overvalued against the average of our world competitors, especially the North Americans. This would not be inflationary, any more than it was in 1981, after a period of tight money. Inflation is set to fall rapidly in response to the monetary squeeze since 1988.

The exchange rate mechanism obstructs this course. Ideally, we should leave it, in order to adhere to soundly based monetary targets, the best long-term guarantee of a sound currency. Credibility would also be enhanced by such a sustainable monetary discipline, as compared with the present draconian policies that invite dangerous reversal. Yet, even within the ERM, we and others in it have been pressed by the Bundesbank to realign, so that we should not be penalized by their domestic need for high interest rates. Even if others will not realign, it is still open to Britain to do so. Such an outbreak of monetary common sense is desperately overdue. We urge the Prime Minister, the Chancellor and their colleagues in the Tory Party to move rapidly before real disaster strikes the economy.   (1991)

As it turned out, the Liverpool Six did not have to wait long for the first cut in interest rates that they had demanded in their letter, although they were unanimous in dismissing it as too little, too late. And the cut came, not as a result of a devaluation of the pound, but within the existing ERM framework. That morning, the Bank of England signalled to the money markets that base rates should come down from 14 to 13.5 per cent, and the Treasury swore, hand on heart, that the move had nothing to do with the letter from the Six. The timing of the rate cut, officials said, had been determined by, of all things, a cut in Spanish interest rates. With the peseta as the strongest currency in the ERM, and sterling the weakest, a cut in Spain's interest rates had the effect of easing the pressure on the pound, and providing room for a small reduction in British rates. Such was the way things worked in the new environment. The cut was a gamble, in spite of the Spanish move. Had the markets reacted badly, and sold sterling heavily, Lamont would really have been in trouble. As it was, the gamble paid off. The rate cut had broken the foreign exchange market's certainties about the level of the pound that would bring about a base rate cut. The rate reduction had come, after all, at a time when the pound was six pfennigs below its DM2.95 central rate in the ERM.

The 13 February reduction in rates broke the log-jam. By a stroke of good fortune, the Deutschmark then began to weaken against all currencies, including those of the other ERM members. This was because of a series of apparently unrelated events. As the success of the allied forces in the Gulf war became increasingly certain, there was a discernible 'pride effect' for the dollar and the US economy. America was seen as casting off the long shadow of Vietnam and entering a new and confident era. German unification was resulting in a sharp increase in unemployment in the east, and outbreaks of social unrest. The burden on the former West German economy of financing unification now threatened to get out of hand. Meanwhile, the Deutschmark was sensitive to uncertainties about developments in the Soviet Union, and the effects of the collapse of the Soviet economy.

In this environment, interest rates could be cut in the context of a pound rising against the Deutschmark, and in line with standard ERM practice. Base rates were reduced to 13 per cent on 27 February, 12.5 per cent on 22 March and 12 per cent on 12 April. The good fortune of a weak Deutschmark, and the painful winter exercise of building credibility, were beginning to see off the bleak dilemma. It was, however, a long way from a golden scenario. The painful winter of 14 per cent base rates had contributed to a mood of economic gloom and an economy that, even when the conditions were ripe for recovery, would be slow to do so.

Deeper in Debt

The experience of the 1980s can be seen as an exercise in making the British economy sensitive to interest rate changes and, in particular, vulnerable to a prolonged period of high interest rates. Financial deregulation removed previous constraints on the availability of credit. Companies and individuals were encouraged to borrow in the belief that things would continue to get better, in what the economist J. R. Sargent described as a climate of 'exaggerated expectations'. According to Sargent:

> It is hardly surprising that a government which came to power with an avowedly radical programme for the 1980s, challenging the post-war consensus and seeking to transform the economy and its management, should have been eager for signs of success. Nor is it surprising that business leaders, after many years in which a number of measures of the UK's performance stamped it as inferior to its major competitors, should have been ready to abandon pessimism for optimism. Nevertheless, a price is now being paid because the public generally became converted rather prematurely and precipitately in the 1980s to a belief in economic miracles, and literally took the credit before it was clearly due.
> (1991, p. 86)

The economy was doubly vulnerable. The first was the knock to optimistic expectations brought about by the re-emergence of traditional British economic problems – high inflation and a large current-account deficit. The second was the direct effects of high interest rates on overborrowed companies and individuals. Taken separately, either of these factors would have implied a significant downturn in the economy. Taken together, they meant a severe, and lengthy, recession.

The reliance of companies on bank borrowing, and their sensitivity to high interest rates, increased strongly during the 1980s, and particularly sharply in the boom years of 1988 and 1989. There were several factors. Larger companies borrowed heavily to finance overseas acquisitions, investment programmes at home and domestic takeovers. In 1986 and 1987, most of this borrowing was by means of stock-market and other capital-market issues. Over these two years the identified borrowing of industrial and commercial companies totalled £57bn, or an average of 47 per cent of income, of which only £21bn was from the banks. After the October 1987 crash, however, raising capital on the world's stock markets became more difficult but the appetite of companies for finance grew. In 1988 and 1989 together, companies borrowed £113bn, an average of 74 per cent of income, of which the lion's share, £65bn, was from the banks.

The small-business sector, traditionally reliant upon the banks for finance, had expanded rapidly in the 1980s, with the explicit encouragement of the Government. With the onset of the 1990–91 recession, small firms were particularly vulnerable. Many were engaged in occupations in the building and related trades, and were hit hard by the sharp downturn in the housing market that preceded the general recession. Small businesses typically rely on large companies for contracts. As the financial pressure on bigger firms grew, not only were these contracts cut back, but payments for work already carried out became subject to crippling delays. Worst of all, small businesses found themselves to be at the mercy of their banks and suddenly found that a previously friendly relationship had become a cut-throat one. The banks, worried about the bad debts they were incurring on small-business loans because they had over-lent during the boom years, tried to cut their losses. At the very time when they were most vulnerable, many small businesses found they were subject to higher bank charges and demands to repay overdrafts at short notice. When the general level of interest rates began to fall, businessmen found to their dismay that they were not receiving the full benefit. Under the cloak of falling interest rates the banks widened their loan margins – the gap between the interest charged to small business customers and base rate. When this was highlighted, notably in the *Sunday Times*, the Treasury and the Bank of England launched an investigation. This, as well as criticism of the banks from Sir Gordon Borrie, the director-general of Fair Trading, led the banks to produce codes of conduct in respect of small-business lending. The underlying problem remained, however.

Businesses, large and small, were therefore highly vulnerable to high interest rates. As long as the impression was maintained that the economy was undergoing a temporary adjustment, as was the case under Lawson, the interest rate damage was limited but by the same token there was no serious attempt to clamp down on, for example, large pay increases. Thus, any serious attack on inflation had to involve pain for companies. And, once it became clear that high interest rates were not a short-term inconvenience, and that the economy was embarking on something more serious than a gentle correction, the damage was done. Exaggerated expectations of continued strong growth in the economy switched abruptly to realistic assessments of the likelihood of recession. Business confidence plunged, companies announced large-scale redundancies and investment fell sharply. Manufacturing investment in the final quarter of 1990 fell by 13.5 per cent on a year earlier. In the first quarter of 1991 the fall was 19 per cent.

Company indebtedness was one feature of the 1990–91 recession which distinguished it from 1980–81. Then, companies had entered the recession with debts equivalent to around 8 per cent of the capital stock. This time the debt burden was much higher, at around 20 per cent. Another notable feature was that the recession was spread across a much wider range of industries. In retailing, the consumer boom of the 1980s had spawned the most dramatic example of exaggerated expectations. Retailers expanded by buying up available city-centre and out-of-town properties, to the extent that some of the most aggressive chains were christened 'space bandits'. The assumption underlying much of this aggressive expansion was that retail sales would continue to grow strongly, at perhaps 5 or 6 per cent a year indefinitely. When this proved to be far too optimistic much of this investment in retailing capacity became redundant. The financial-services sector was a second dramatic example. Deregulation in the City had created the most powerful image of the Lawson years, the 'yuppy boom'. Stockbroking firms, and individual dealers and analysts, were purchased at prices which, again, reflected exaggerated expectations about future levels of business. The death of the yuppie dream, when these expectations were unfulfilled, was a source of glee to the tabloid newspapers but reflected wider strains within financial services. Insurance companies, banks and building societies bought up chains of estate agents but did so, unfortunately, at the height of the housing boom. Retribution was swift. After the fat years of expansion in the financial-services sector, retrenchment came as a sickening blow. Manufacturing industry had, at least, been through it in the early 1980s. Unemployment reached high up the white-collar ladder. The increase in unemployment in London and the south-east, admittedly from a low base, was larger, in the early stages of the recession at least, than in traditional industrial areas.

Individuals were hit in two ways. The first was the threat or the actuality of unemployment as employers cut back. The second was their own vulnerability, through high debt levels, to interest rates. In the boom years, individuals borrowed as never before. In 1987 total personal-sector borrowing was £39.4bn, rising to £53.9bn in 1988, and remaining high at £48.7bn in 1989 and, even in 1990, £41bn. The ratio of debt to disposable income virtually doubled between the early and late 1980s. Much of this borrowing was for house purchase, and was based on two sets of expectations. The first was that house prices would continue to rise, so that the size of even a large mortgage, relative to the value of the property, would fall quickly. The second was that the burden of mortgage and other debt-service payments would fall because of the growth of incomes. Neither of these expectations was met fully. A significant proportion of borrowers found themselves with a mortgage which was greater than the value of their property. And, the combination of high interest rates, unemployment and, eventually, slower growth in incomes meant that the debt-servicing burden rose rather than fell.

There was, by the summer of 1991, a growing realization among mortgage lenders that the housing market was in a catch-22 situation. Borrowers who did not keep up with their payments had to be disciplined, if necessary by repossessing their homes. But the growing tide of repossessions was, in itself, a barrier to any real recovery in the housing market in that repossessed houses, which were expected to number nearly 100,000 in 1991, had to be sold on an already depressed market.

In the 1980s, financial deregulation and exaggerated expectations came together to create an economy that was acutely vulnerable to high interest rates. The longer that high interest rates were maintained, the greater the damage that would be caused, and the slower the recovery of the economy. The high-interest-rate policy could have been designed to burn the fingers of over-ambitious borrowers. The difficulty was that such borrowers were so common that it was impossible to pick them off without considerable damage to the economy as a whole. J. R. Sargent's view, expressed in the August 1991 *National Institute Review*, was that the accidental interaction of exaggerated expectations and the willingness of deregulated lenders to provide finance was a bigger factor in explaining the boom and subsequent bust than errors in economic policy. This, to my mind, is too charitable a view. Economic policy in the second half of the 1980s, and in particular in 1987 and the first half of 1988, had the effect, intentionally or otherwise, of stoking up the boom. Both the language and the conduct of policy were dramatically expansionary. Companies and individuals may have been foolish to borrow so much, and lenders should have been more cautious in their lending policies, but both sides were given every encouragement by the actions of the Government.

Living with a Home-made Recession

In the eighteen years from 1973, Britain had three major recessions. The first, in 1974-5 (or more correctly 1973-6), came as a shock after the comparatively dull stability that had characterized the post-war period up until then. It was a drawn-out affair, beginning in the final quarter of 1973 when, as a result of a sharp rise in oil prices imposed by the Organization of Petroleum Exporting Countries (OPEC), gross domestic product fell by 0.9 per cent. This was followed by the miners' strike and a three-day week throughout much of British industry, and GDP dropped by 2.1 per cent in the first quarter of 1974. The next two quarters saw a rise in GDP before the fall (1.2 per cent) resumed in the final quarter of 1974. There was a small recovery in the first quarter of 1975, followed by two successive falls, of 1.6 and 0.7 per cent respectively. GDP then rose again for two quarters, its final drop, of 0.8 per cent, coming in the second quarter of 1976. The low point of the recession was in the third quarter of 1975, at which point GDP was 3.5 per cent below its pre-recession level. The recession owed much to policy errors, the mistakes that unleashed the Barber boom in the first place and Denis Healey's short-lived attempt to expand out of the oil crisis. It was, however, made immeasurably worse by the international environment, and the effects of the first OPEC oil shock.

The second recession, 1980–81, was shorter in duration, but far more serious. GDP fell for five successive quarters, the first drop coming in the first quarter of 1980 and the last in the first quarter of 1981. By the first quarter of 1981, the recession low, GDP was 5 per cent below its pre-recession level. Again, there was an interaction of domestic policy errors and international factors. The second OPEC oil crisis of 1979–80 was as serious in its effects as the first one, six years earlier. On top of this, the newly elected Conservative Government, grappling with difficulty with its new monetarist strategy, kept policy tight for too long. In mitigation, ministers could point to both the second oil shock and the inflationary legacy it had inherited from the 1974–9 Labour Government.

The third recession, 1990–91, was in many ways a bigger shock than the first. Even before an economic miracle was being proclaimed in the late 1980s, the Conservative Party's boosters had declared that Nigel Lawson had achieved something, without explicitly trying for it, that had eluded all previous post-war Chancellors. He had, it was said, abolished the business cycle, a boast that Lawson was happy to live with until it proved to be woefully misplaced. Growth may not have been spectacular in the first half of the 1980s – in fact the recovery from the 1980–81 recession was painfully slow. But the economy moved up several gears in the late 1980s. Recessions belonged to the economic dark ages. With the economy's downside apparently having been eliminated, it was little wonder that the climate was one of exaggerated expectations.

The 1990–91 recession, according to the forecasting consensus that prevailed as this book was being completed, was worse than 1973–6 but not as bad as 1980–81. GDP fell for four successive quarters, beginning in the third quarter of 1990. By the second quarter of 1991 it was 3.7 per cent below its pre-recession level. But where were the unhelpful international factors upon which the previous two recessions could, in large part, be blamed? There was the worldwide stock-market crash of October 1987 but the effects of this on Britain's economic policy errors have been exaggerated in the telling. There was, too, Iraq's invasion of Kuwait in August 1990, and the Gulf war of January–April 1991. But, while events in the Gulf may have contributed to the mood of business and consumer uncertainty, it is difficult to argue that it played a major role in Britain's recession. Other oil-consuming countries in Europe, notably Germany, France and Italy, were unaffected. The rise in world oil prices that followed the Iraqi invasion lasted for but a few weeks and was not sustained. The recession, in short, was made in Britain. The Governor of the Bank of England, again, was more open about this than ministers, in a Treasury and Civil Service Committee exchange with Giles Radice, the Labour MP:

> RADICE: Can I just stop you there . . . what you are saying is in that sense it is home grown, our recession?
> LEIGH-PEMBERTON: It is somewhat home grown on account of the events which go back to the late 1980s, about which we have spoken on previous occasions and comments have been made. (1991, p. 26)

In the depths of the 1980–81 recession, the economy's main problem, as perceived by the Government, was inflation. The recession was not planned but when it came it was seen as part of the necessary process of squeezing inflation out of the system. The medicine was harsh, and it had to be. And, as Christopher Johnson recalls in his book *The Economy under Mrs Thatcher*, the Treasury did not talk up the prospects of recovery:

> The Government's immediate preoccupation was to reduce rising inflation rather than to revive flagging growth. Its growth forecasts were extremely gloomy. 'After the recession forecast for 1980,' said Howe in his Budget speech in that year, 'the economy will grow by an average of only 1 per cent a year up to 1983–4.' Ministers made a virtue of necessity, arguing that lower inflation, far from being inimical to higher growth, was a precondition of it.' (1991, p. 7)

In 1990 and 1991, the situation was different. The recession was largely due to errors in policy by a government that had been in power for more than a decade. The inflation problem, while serious, was not on the scale of the early 1980s or, for that matter, the mid 1970s. Apart from being unplanned, whether the recession was necessary or not was a matter of debate. Officials at both the Bank of England and Treasury may have accepted the need for a harsh correction but most ministers were not so sure. This explains both the fact that the Government was slow to admit to the recession and, when it was in progress, was quick to declare that it had come to an end.

Major, in his only Budget as Chancellor, had rejected the idea of a 1981-style austerity package and, as described in Chapter 8, won some political kudos for doing so. Even so, the spirit of 1981 had its echoes in the Budgets of both March 1990 and March 1991, in that they rejected any suggestion of providing a fiscal stimulus to either limit the recession damage or assist the economy's recovery. The 1990 Budget contained a 'fiscal tightening' – a net tax increase – of £430m in the 1990-91 financial year and £955m in a full year (the two figures differ largely because of implementation delays). In 1991, under Lamont, there was also a tightening of policy, of £295m in the 1991-2 year and £1.89bn in a full year.* In both Budgets, policy was characterized as allowing the 'automatic stabilizers' of fiscal policy to work; because tax revenues fall and public spending rises in a recession, there is a tendency for the public-sector borrowing requirement to increase. In the conditions of 1990 and 1991, the effect was to produce a shift from budget surplus to deficit (a public-sector debt repayment was allowed to become a public-sector borrowing requirement). To have attempted to prevent this from happening would have entailed draconian tax increases. Even so, there was a bias towards a tightening of policy, in conditions of approaching recession and actual recession, in both Budgets.

Perhaps more importantly, the detail of both Budgets included changes that were more appropriate to the boom years and, when introduced, served to prolong and deepen the recession. The March 1990 Budget came after a period in which, by general consensus, Britain had a problem of low savings. The view was that this was not merely a cyclical effect associated with the boom years but, rather, that there was a *structural* shortage of savings in the economy. Thus, Major's March 1990 package was a 'Budget for savings', designed to tackle this problem. The central element in it was the creation of building-society Tax Exempt Special Savings Accounts (Tessas), in which the return on deposits held for five years was free of tax. The measure was criticized by some as adding to the raft of tax reliefs, against the Conservatives'

---

* In this case, the huge difference between the two figures is partly explained by a delay in the effect of introducing employers' national insurance contributions on the company car perk, and by retailers initially absorbing the higher VAT announced in the Budget.

stated aim of simplifying the tax system, but it was generally welcomed. The difficulty was that the new accounts became available from the beginning of January 1991, when the macro economic emphasis had shifted completely. In the recession conditions of early 1991, the need was for policies which encouraged consumers to lead the economy towards recovery. Instead, there was a new incentive – apart from the natural one arising from the burnt fingers brought about by the transformation from boom to bust – for people to save. The Budget for savings kicked in at the very time when it was not needed. The personal-saving ratio, saving as a percentage of personal disposable income, fell to a low of 4.8 per cent during 1988. By the winter of 1990–91, it had more than doubled to average over 10 per cent. Whether the new measures encouraged additional saving, as opposed to a shifting around of existing deposits to take advantage of the tax relief, was not clear. However, it is likely that some sort of boost was provided by the March 1990 savings package.

Lamont's March 1991 Budget was much more perverse. The new Chancellor had two ambitions. The first was to try to tackle the pressing political problem of the poll tax. The second was to establish his reputation as a tax reformer. The Government intended to replace the poll tax at the earliest opportunity. The Chancellor's task was to make it more palatable in the years leading to its replacement. The Treasury's solution was to announce an across-the-board reduction in poll tax levels of £140, financed by an increase in the rate of value added tax (VAT) from 15 to 17.5 per cent. Retailers predicted, correctly, a short-term bonanza as shoppers rushed to buy in the twelve days or so before the higher rate of VAT took effect. After that, however, they warned that the effects would be to hold back the consumer upturn upon which the Treasury's economic recovery hopes were based. James May, director-general of the Retail Consortium, said in the *Financial Times*: 'Our immediate reaction is Shock! Horror! at the VAT increase.'

Hitting hard-pressed retailers with an increase in VAT was bad enough, but the Budget also appeared to go out of its way to target two sectors of the economy which were suffering very badly from the effects of recession. In Britain the car industry is heavily dependent upon company car sales and, within the industry, the domestic manufacturers relied heavily on company purchases. In successive Budgets users of company cars had been required to pay increasing amounts of tax on the benefit, as assessed by the Inland Revenue, of this particular perk. Lamont continued this trend but he also announced that, henceforth, companies would have to pay National Insurance contributions on this benefit. The effect was to add around £350 a year to the cost to a company of providing an employee with an average-sized car and fuel. The Society of Motor Manufacturers and Traders described the move as 'indefensible', coming as it did in the middle of the sharpest downturn in the domestic car market since the early 1980s, and on top of the increase in VAT.

The housing market was also suffering more than most parts of the economy in the recession, having enjoyed a notable boom in the second half of the 1980s. The Chancellor's tax-reforming move in this area was aimed at the tax relief on mortgage interest payments, one of the sacred cows of the tax system under Thatcher. Lamont announced that the relief, up to a loan ceiling of £30,000, would continue against the basic rate of income tax. The relief against the higher, 40 per cent, rate of tax was, however, abolished, effectively increasing mortgage payments for around 860,000 mortgage-payers. Peter Drew, chairman of Taylor Woodrow, the construction group, confessed bewilderment at the change at a time when the housing market was so weak.

The Treasury's argument, much as when Lawson had cut income tax at the height of the boom, was that desirable tax changes should be introduced when it was possible to do so, almost irrespective of the position of the economy in the cycle. And, plainly, Lamont's freedom to rein back mortgage interest tax relief had been made possible by the departure of Thatcher. But this argument was by no means followed to the letter. Indeed, a reduction in the main rate of corporation tax from 35 to 34 per cent for the 1990–91 financial year, and 33 per cent for 1991–2, was made with the specific intention of easing the recessionary burden on companies.

The March 1990 Budget, coming at a time when the chief concern was inflation rather than recession, was more defensible than its successor, a year later. Lamont's tax changes in March 1991 were made in the belief that they would not stand in the way of a recovery in consumer spending, itself enhanced by stability or an upturn in the housing market. As 1991 progressed, and it became clear that not only was consumer spending slow to recover but the housing and car markets were particularly weak, the wisdom of attempting surgery on the tax system in the middle of a recession came to be called into question.

The Lasting Damage of the 1990–91 Recession

Lamont, in his Budget speech on 19 March 1991, said: 'Recessions are always painful. But they are an inescapable feature of market economies – and they are temporary' (1991).

This was a far cry from the abolition of the business cycle proclaimed just a few years before. And, to characterize a recession as temporary misses the point. This is because, even if the period of declining output is only four or five quarters, the full effects last for much longer. Indeed, one definition of recession is that it lasts, not until the first pick-up in activity, but to the point where economic growth is back to its long-run sustainable rate of, say, 2.75 per cent a year. Even this may not capture the full effects of the 1990–91 recession; burnt fingers can be painful for a very long time.

The business cycle is good at catching out economists and politicians. In the depths of the 1980–81 recession, too many economists convinced themselves that the economy would never recover. Similarly, the boom of the late 1980s persuaded many normally sensible people that Britain had experienced an economic miracle on the scale of the post-war West German *Wirtschaftswunder*. Thus, any assessment of the long-term effects of the 1990–91 recession, made while it is still fresh in the memory, has to be tentative. Even so, it appears that the experience of 1990–91 is likely to have lasting effects on attitudes and behaviour.

The Thatcher miracle, such as it was, was exemplified by a rapid growth in small businesses and self-employment. Government measures specifically aimed at encouraging the growth of small firms, together with a powerful 'demonstration effect' in the form of notable success stories, appeared to have created the beginnings of an enterprise culture. Directors of relatively small companies became paper millionaires, and in some cases actual millionaires, when their firms were floated on the Stock Exchange's Unlisted Securities Market. It was ridiculous to characterize Britain as the Hong Kong of Europe, as some tried to do. But the mood was one of great optimism. Between 1979 and 1990 self-employment rose from 1.9m to 3.4m. The number of small businesses rose by some 400,000.

Many small businesses and self-employed people survived the recession intact. A significant proportion, however, failed or encountered severe difficulties. In the summer of 1991, when the *Sunday Times* ran a campaign designed to highlight the fact that many small firms were facing higher interest rates and charges from their banks, and in a lot of cases impossibly short deadlines to pay off overdrafts, I was contacted by many hundreds of small businessmen and -women. What struck me most was that many of these people said that, if they could ever escape from the nightmare in which they found themselves, they would never want to set up in business again and, in some cases, would strongly advise their children against it. The upside of the enterprise culture was that it had shown people that they could be their own boss and prosper with it. A new breed of entrepreneurs was created. But the downside was graphically illustrated by the 1990–91 recession. It is bad enough to lose your job. But for many small businessmen and -women there was worse. Their houses had been put up as security against bank loans for the business. When the business failed, not only did they lose their livelihood, but they lost the roof over their heads.

Even if the spirit of enterprise had survived the recession, the availability of finance seemed certain to act as a brake on the growth of the small-business sector. The banks had piled into small-business lending during the 1980s, having burnt their fingers with commercial property loans in the early 1970s, and Third World lending later in that decade and in the early 1980s. Small businesses, in the Thatcher era, appeared to be a safe outlet for funds. But, by 1991, this assumption had been proved incorrect. The banks found that their single biggest source of bad debts was in loans to small businesses. This explained the tough attitude of the banks to their remaining small-business customers. And it also signalled the beginnings of a new, highly cautious attitude to the future provision of small-business finance. Sir John Quinton, the Chairman of Barclays Bank, told his annual general meeting that his bank was no longer looking to increase its lending to small firms.

The question of a generalized 'credit crunch' of the type identified in the United States in 1990 and 1991, was more difficult to answer. By this was meant that economic expansion would run up against a barrier created by the general reluctance of the banks to lend, not just to small businesses, but to all sectors of the economy. For many larger companies, with access to the capital markets, a credit crunch did not appear to apply. The Bank of England regarded the sharp slowdown in bank lending, particularly during 1991 when the growth of the broad M4 measure of the money supply was at its lowest rate for more than twenty years, as a symptom of recession rather than a signal of prolonged slump. In other words, any problems lay mainly in the demand for credit, rather than in its supply. Even so, there were plenty of bigger companies who were constrained from raising finance, either from the banks or from the stock market, by the high levels of debt that they were carrying from having over-expanded during the boom years.

Another long-term change appeared destined to come as a result of the prolonged depression in the housing market, which began almost as soon as the Lawson boom came off the boil, and which looked likely to last well beyond the 1990–91 recession. Mortgage repossessions, which threatened to reach 100,000 in 1991, were a new factor hanging over the market. As building societies and banks became forced sellers of repossessed properties, usually below prevailing market prices, the prospect of a general recovery in house prices was faint. And, for every person who saw his or her property repossessed and auctioned to the highest bidder, there were several more who decided that it was better to rent than buy. The Thatcher dream of a nation of owner-occupiers was under threat.

The housing depression had other significant effects. The first was the general attitude of buyers. In a rising market, people could afford to take a risk. They could buy a property, mortgage themselves up to the hilt and, if they could not keep up with the payments, sell up and still escape with a sizeable capital gain; the simple effect of being the temporary occupant of a property which was increasing in value all the time. The housing depression changed that. People found that, after encountering payment difficulties, either they could not sell at all, or they could only do so by cutting the price so much that they would be left owing significant sums to their bank or building society. In some ways, the change in housing-market attitudes was no bad thing. For years, economists had been describing the obsession of Britons with investment in bricks and mortar as a factor holding back the British economy. Both the Treasury and the Bank of England stressed that they never wanted to see another housing boom on the scale of the late 1980s. There is, however, a difference between not wanting a housing boom and prolonged stagnation in the housing market. If people cannot easily sell their properties, the long-term effect on Britain's already low level of labour mobility will be serious. And, while many people may have decided that the housing depression made renting a much more attractive proposition, there was the problem of finding a property to rent. The

Government had cut back sharply on the council-house building programme – twice as many local authority houses were built in 1979 as in
the next ten years combined – and, despite official encouragement, the
private rented sector had failed to re-emerge to any significant extent.

The legacy of the 1990–91 recession was also likely to show through,
possibly for years, in other areas. Sharply rising unemployment – and
the consensus was that the jobless total would increase to about 3m from
its spring 1990 trough of 1.6m – creates familiar problems of demoraliza-
tion, together with the loss of skills and experience. Those unemployed
for long periods can easily become so disaffected as to effectively opt out
of the labour force. The downturn in unemployment in the 1980s did
not come until five years after the economy's cyclical trough in 1981.

The sharp fall in investment during the recession, admittedly after a
capital-spending boom in the late 1980s, also raised doubts about the
ability of British industry to compete in the medium term, notably in
the post-1992 European single market. The shift from boom to bust in
investment was, as is traditional, more pronounced than for other types
of spending. Commercial vehicle sales in 1991, to give one example,
were running at half their level of two years earlier. It was difficult to
argue that, in spite of the cutbacks, firms would run up against capacity
constraints – most industrialists reported that they were operating well
below capacity. The more telling point concerned the quality and
vintage of the capital stock. The longer an investment slump persists,
the more projects are cancelled that could have given British firms a
competitive advantage.

Attitudes change, sometimes very quickly. The prevailing attitude left
over from the 1990–91 recession was that people and companies, having
had their fingers burnt once, were determined not to make the mistake
again. The British economy, if nothing else, had exhibited a certain
dynamism during the 1980s. At the very least, the cycle of boom to bust
had ensured that recapturing even a part of that dynamism would be
very difficult.

IO

FULL CIRCLE

In October 1990, eighteen years and four months after the Conservative Government of Edward Heath had floated the pound, Margaret Thatcher's Conservative Government pegged it again. Sterling's entry into the European exchange rate mechanism (ERM) did not, of course, represent a return to the old Bretton Woods regime. The October move tied the pound to currencies inside the mechanism, but left it subject to wild swings against others, most notably the dollar and the Japanese yen. During the period of floating exchange rates the British economy had undergone two serious recessions (1973–6 and 1980–81) and begun a third (1990–91). Floating exchange rates had not insulated the British economy from external disciplines. Poor economic performance and political uncertainty were subject to even harsher punishment than under the old regime. In the old days, as in 1967, the markets could be held at bay by a one-off, and relatively small, devaluation. Under floating rates, the pressure was incessant and this, coupled with the tendency of the markets to push currencies further than was necessary on fundamental economic grounds – the tendency to overshoot and undershoot – had the effect of exaggerating cyclical movements in the economy. The key question, therefore, was whether membership of the exchange rate mechanism would have the effect of dampening the cycle; restraining economic booms at one end, but also guarding against serious recessions at the other. Nigel Lawson, of course, said that had his advice to join in 1985 been taken, then the subsequent boom and bust (my words not his) would have been avoided. Christopher Johnson, former chief economic adviser to Lloyds Bank, argued that the mistake was not to join much earlier than this: 'In 1979 the Government mistakenly renounced the options of joining the European Monetary System exchange rate mechanism and making the Bank of England independent . . . During its second term the Government again missed a good opportunity to join the ERM in 1985 and then failed to make use of the fall in oil prices to achieve its aim of zero inflation' (1991, pp. 257–8).

At the end of Britain's first year in the ERM, ministers claimed considerable success for membership. John Major, in his speech to the Conservative Party conference in Blackpool on 11 October 1991, said that membership had confounded the 'selling Britain short' critics, who had said that membership was at the wrong time and at too high a level. Inflation had fallen from 10.9 to 4.1 per cent in the twelve months since entry, and base rates had dropped from 15 to 10.5 per cent. Meanwhile, exports to Europe had grown strongly. There is no doubt that, in many respects, membership went well in the first year. This, incidentally, merely added to the puzzle of why entry had been delayed for so long. But many of the claimed benefits, notably lower inflation and interest rates, were a direct result of the recession and had little to say about the long-term consequences of membership. Indeed, the Government tried to have it both ways, claiming that the recession was a worldwide phenomenon, when it was not, and that the beneficial effects of that recession on inflation were the direct result of ERM entry. History, it appeared, was being rewritten.

Rewriting the History of ERM Entry

One of the themes of *The Rise and Fall of Monetarism* was that politicians, while claiming consistency in policy, had often perpetrated huge changes. The classic example of this was the shift, under the Conservatives in the 1980s, from domestic monetary targets and an abhorrence of exchange rate targets, to a belief in the latter at the expense of the former. In addition, politicians claimed foresight and intent for situations that they had blundered into by accident. Thus, the unplanned 1980–81 recession came to be regarded as a necessary purgative for the economy, and an essential ingredient in the Government's success in bringing down inflation in the first half of the 1980s.

A similar rewriting of history was evident following ERM entry. As described in Chapter 8, the decision to enter in October 1990 was largely political. Thatcher had been brought to the point where she accepted entry, if reluctantly. Meanwhile, the financial markets had come to expect the move into the ERM to occur roughly when it did. Any delay, by removing support from the pound, could have been disastrous. What was not foreseen was that entry would come as the economy was diving into recession. The combination of membership and recession meant that, in some respects, the outcome on inflation and interest rates was better than even the optimists had expected. This was not, however, part of the plan, although the Government made a virtue out of necessity and, in some ways, used the new regime to press home the advantage that the recession had provided in terms of falling inflation.

Was the recession, itself partly a result of the reluctance to cut interest rates before entry and an inability to do so for several months afterwards, the ideal way to adjust to the new regime? By the end of 1991, Britain's inflation rate was close to that of Germany, and the interest rate differential had come down to around 1 per cent. France had taken from 1979 to 1985 to achieve such an outcome. The Government may not have intended to use the sledgehammer of recession to bring about Britain's rapid ERM adjustment but in this case it could be argued that the ends justified the means. The Madrid conditions, in other words, had got things the wrong way round. The time to enter was not when Britain's inflation and interest rates were at European levels, but when they were so high that they could only fall towards those levels. The apparent success of the first year of membership did not, however, kill the debate over whether Britain belonged in the system at all. Monetarist critics of the Government continued to claim that the interest rate reductions achieved within the ERM had not gone far enough and that the economy would suffer from the loss of control over domestic monetary policy. Sir Alan Walters, responding in October 1991 to a laudatory piece on ERM membership in the *Economist*, wrote, 'Real interest rates remain high and Britain is in a deep and persistent recession. Policy continues to be perverse and granted that the ERM matters, it rationalizes and magnifies this perversity ... The ERM is indeed half-baked' (1991).

Non-monetarist ERM opponents, meanwhile, suggested that Britain's relatively high central parity against the Deutschmark of DM2.95, in combination with a weak underlying balance of payments position, would have the effect of placing the economy in a strait-jacket. Unemployment, on this view, would have to be kept high in order to prevent excessive growth in labour costs from undermining Britain's competitive position. The economy would be condemned to an era of slow growth.

When sterling was floated in June 1972, its exchange rate against the Deutschmark was around DM8.3. Its October 1990 ERM entry level of DM2.95 thus represented a depreciation during the period of floating exchange rates of some 65 per cent. The fall had been virtually continuous. In only four years out of the eighteen – 1979, 1980, 1981 and 1988 – did sterling rise against the Deutschmark from one year to the next, and the 1979–81 experience reflected a combination of the pound's petrocurrency response to high oil prices, together with the sharp rise in interest rates at the start of the Thatcher Government's monetarist experiment. The British economy, it appeared, had become addicted to the fix of a depreciating currency, even if the results in terms of economic growth were unimpressive. The question of whether the economy had been weaned off its addiction or would suffer prolonged withdrawal pains is one that will determine the prospect for the remainder of the 1990s. Will the influence of ERM membership be bleak or benign?

Britain in the ERM; Strait-jacket or Golden Age?

Serious consideration of ERM entry within the Government began in 1985. It was at this time too that industrialists began to come out strongly in favour. The Confederation of British Industry's public conversion to membership can be dated from the mid 1980s. Other representative bodies followed. Individual industrialists, bankers, economists and politicians had been pressing for entry for much longer. But the consensus in favour of membership did not begin to take shape until the Treasury, under Lawson, had shifted its position to one of strongly favouring entry. In the second half of the 1980s, as the pressure grew on Thatcher to drop her block on membership, the model that was widely cited was that of France.

In the early 1980s, in an echo of the failed attempt by Britain's Labour Government to expand out of the first world oil crisis, France's Socialist Government under François Mitterrand attempted to move the French economy into a higher gear than the rest of Europe. The ERM commitment, negotiated by Valéry Giscard d'Estaing, Mitterrand's predecessor and political opponent, was of minor importance compared with the pressing need to reduce unemployment in France. The policy provoked the foreign exchange markets into selling the franc, safe in the knowledge that they were unlikely to meet with too much resistance. The French franc was devalued in 1981 and 1982. In the 1979–83 period the pivotal franc–Deutschmark rate changed four times, twice as a result of franc devaluations (in combination with Deutschmark revaluations) and twice as a result of Deutschmark revaluations alone. In the first four years of the ERM's existence the franc lost around 25 per cent of its value against the Deutschmark. France was an errant member of the European Monetary System.

Gradually, however, this began to change. There were two more changes in the franc–Deutschmark parity, in April 1986 and January 1987, resulting in a combined fall of around 10 per cent for the franc. But the emphasis of policy changed. The French Government, still under Mitterrand, followed 'responsible' policies in spite of high and rising unemployment. The ERM commitment, initially regarded as an unwelcome and unnecessary encumbrance, came to be regarded as the central element in economic policy. The *'franc fort'* or strong franc policy came to be taken seriously, not just by the Government but also, increasingly, by pay negotiators. France, having achieved low inflation in the mid-1980s as a result of the fall in world oil prices, did not let it take off again as Britain did. The average inflation rate over the 1985–90 period was 2.8 per cent. After January 1987, successive French finance ministers dismissed any suggestion that the franc should be devalued again. Looked at from the other side of the English Channel France's achievement was an enviable demonstration of the possibilities for Britain inside the ERM. And, while high unemployment represented the dark side of French success in achieving low inflation, Conservative supporters could expect Britain, after a decade of Thatcher supply-side reforms, to do better.

Too late to influence Britain's decision on entering the system, however, the French experience came to be viewed in a different light, not least from within France. Monetary union between East and West Germany in July 1990, followed by unification three months later, resulted in higher German interest rates and inflation. French inflation remained low at around 3 per cent, and in 1991 fell below that of Germany. The worrying thing, not just for France but for other ERM members, was that this did not allow French interest rates to fall below

German levels. Five years of building credibility in the foreign exchange markets was not enough. Dealers still saw that the chances of a French devaluation, however small, were still significantly greater than the zero probability of Germany ever allowing a Deutschmark devaluation. The result, in the autumn and winter of 1991, was a painful one for the French Government. German interest rates, at just below 10 per cent, represented the floor for interest rates in other European Monetary System countries. A wave of industrial unrest spread through France, itself adding to doubts about the Government's ability to resist pressure for a franc devaluation. With unemployment at 10 per cent and rising, and Paris unable to reduce interest rates to boost the economy, the discipline of the ERM was, it appeared, an uncomfortable strait-jacket.

A variation on this theme, in a British context, appeared in the *National Institute Economic Review* of August 1991. John Williamson, a British economist at the Washington-based Institute for International Economics, developed a concept known as the fundamental equilibrium exchange rate. This is defined as the exchange rate which combines internal balance – the highest level of economic activity consistent with low inflation – with external balance, which is the sustainable long-term position for the current account of the balance of payments. According to Williamson the optimal entry rate for sterling into the ERM would have been around DM2.60. It was, therefore, overvalued by more than 10 per cent. An independent assessment by two National Institute economists, using a similar analysis, concluded that the pound was overvalued by between 5 and 10 per cent in 1991. And, taking the analysis into the future, the conclusion was that, in the absence of devaluation, Britain would not merely have to match German inflation performance but undercut it over a period of years in order to claw back competitiveness and maintain a manageable balance of payments position.

According to Williamson in August 1991:

> The decision to enter the ERM at an exchange rate above the fundamental equilibrium exchange rate was singularly unfortunate. It means that the British economy is confronted not just by the task of reducing inflation to the German rate, but of going sufficiently below the German rate for several years to compensate for the initial overvaluation (plus the ground that is still being lost this year and the additional ground that, barring a miracle, will again be lost next year). This is a far more onerous task than that achieved by France over the past decade, since the franc was if anything undervalued when

France first committed itself to stability-oriented policies in 1983. None the less, the price paid by France to achieve virtual price stability was half a decade of growth below the growth rate of productive potential, involving a cumulative growth shortfall of over 5 per cent of gross national product. Presumably Britain faces an even more costly adjustment. In other words, the costs of avoiding realignments is likely to be little growth until the late 1990s.   (1991, pp. 47–48)

The National Institute's own medium-term forecasts suggested that the cost of Britain's ERM commitment would be an average unemployment level of 2.8 million from 1992 until the end of the century. For Williamson, and economists at the National Institute, there was no easy way out of this dilemma. Devaluation would cost dearly in terms of market credibility and could, by feeding market expectations of further devaluations, result in higher, not lower, interest rates. This would be particularly so in a period leading up to European monetary union in which other ERM currencies were maintaining their central parities. The mistake was to enter at too high a rate. The Government had made its bed and, however uncomfortable, had to lie on it.

Other economists saw devaluation, or ideally withdrawal from the ERM, as the way out. The concern expressed in 1991 by Walters and other monetarist economists about Britain's prospects was partly based on the fact that the growth rate of the money supply, and most notably the broad money measure, M4, was insufficient to provide for an upturn in the economy. On two previous occasions – after the First World War and following the 1972–3 Barber boom – monetary growth had shown a similar sharp deceleration. In each case the result had been long periods of economic misery. Lower interest rates were needed to stimulate monetary growth, and if the only way of achieving this was through devaluation, then so it would have to be.

Wynne Godley, the Cambridge economist and determined anti-monetarist, also saw devaluation as a necessary step in improving an otherwise bleak British economic outlook for the 1990s. Godley, who had been warning since the 1970s of Britain's deep underlying balance of payments problem, suggested that joining the ERM at a high exchange rate would have the effect of institutionalizing the economy's competitive problem. The size of the problem was underlined by the fact that, even in the recession year of 1991, Britain was running a current-account deficit of more than £6bn. In a paper, 'Britain's

Economic Problems and Policies in the 1990s', co-written with Ken Coutts, Bob Rowthorn and Gennaro Zezza, he concluded:

> The central issues can be stated quite simply. A necessary condition for achieving sustained growth in the future is that personal consumption over the next few years is held back by a large amount, probably about 8 per cent below trend. But unless there is a very large improvement in investment and net exports to take up the slack, this cut in consumption will merely generate a severe recession with no obvious prospect of recovery in the medium term. The necessary conditions for improving our trading performance are that the real rate of exchange is reduced substantially – probably by 15–20 per cent – below what it is at present, and that investment in manufacturing industry is greatly increased. It is commonly stated that it is impossible to devalue successfully because any depreciation will be rapidly and completely eroded by compensatory increases in money wages. This view implies, though this is not generally recognized, that the only mechanism by which competitiveness can be improved is by raising unemployment to whatever level – presumably well over 3 million – will reduce wage inflation to that of our competitors. This is tantamount to saying there is no solution to the strategic problem we have outlined. The conclusion is the extremely sombre one that there is no alternative, at least in the medium term, to recession and high unemployment. This is not, however, the view we take. There have been effective devaluations in the past.   (1990)

What of the other view of ERM membership, that it would generate long-term benefits for both inflation and economic growth? After all, under the Bretton Woods regime Britain had enjoyed something of a golden age, albeit one that was tarnished in comparison with the record of other countries, as described in Chapter 1. Would not the removal of currency uncertainty and the establishment of a more stable financial environment generate a new mood of confidence among businessmen? The tarnished golden scenario – the short-term interest rate benefits that followed ERM entry – was one thing. But the real prize was to be won or lost over a longer period.

To the extent that this golden-age view was held by the Government, it was not well articulated. Major, in his November 1990 Autumn Statement speech, a month after entry, referred to the ERM only in passing, as an adjunct to the anti-inflationary policy. Lamont, in his March 1991 Budget speech, also stressed the importance of ERM membership in fighting inflation, rather than in stimulating long-term growth. He said:

> The Government's decision to join the exchange rate mechanism last October provides a more secure framework for combating inflation in the future. That is its real significance. Linking sterling to other currencies with a proven track record of low inflation will be an added discipline on monetary policy. (1991)

Admittedly the Government had long stressed the importance of low inflation as a precondition for economic growth. And Lamont, also in his Budget speech, said, 'For the longer term there is every reason to be optimistic about the UK in the 1990s.' But ERM membership was sold as a means of controlling inflation better rather than generating stronger and more balanced economic growth in the medium term. And even on this point there is room for debate over the effects of membership. A fixed-exchange-rate regime acts as a discipline on the traded-goods sector of the economy – companies and individuals producing goods and services which are exported or which compete directly with imports. It has less impact on non-traded goods. There is nothing in the disciplines of the system to bring the price of a hair cut or a hotel room in London into line with Paris or Berlin. A situation could develop where wages and prices are held low in the traded-goods sector but not in non-traded goods, encouraging a shift of labour and investment into the latter. There is also an important caveat to the claim that low inflation stimulates economic growth. If inflation is kept down only by the maintenance of tough policies designed to limit the growth of demand, then it is difficult to see that the optimism of businessmen and consumers, which rose at first after the sharp fall in inflation and nominal interest rates during 1991, can be easily translated into strong economic growth. Much depended on the extent to which the fall in inflation reflected the effects of the recession. If it signalled a permanent change in wage and price-setting behaviour in response to ERM entry then there were grounds for optimism.

An optimistic case can also be made on the basis of foreign investment in Britain. Britain was successful in attracting inward investment from the United States and, in particular, Japan, during the Thatcher years. This was in spite of the fact that for most of the period Britain was outside the ERM and, in many ways, a half-hearted member of the

European Community. Cultural and social factors, such as the English language and the preponderance of golf courses in Britain, played their part in attracting Japanese firms to Britain. The establishment by Nissan and Toyota of car-assembly plants in Britain would, according to some forecasts, have the effect of eliminating Britain's trade deficit in cars during the 1990s. ERM entry, by reducing the currency risk of a British operation in relation to the rest of Europe, could be expected to enhance Britain's attractions as an investment base for non-EC firms. The fact that Japanese car firms could make a success of producing in Britain whereas domestic manufacturers had struggled was hardly a source of national pride. But it suggested that there were structural factors at work which could eat into the underlying balance of payments weakness that was at the heart of most of the gloomier projections of Britain's future in the ERM.

British industry, having been promised a stable, low-inflation regime under Thatcher, and been disappointed, also had high hopes of the new era. British interest rates averaged more than 12 per cent between May 1979 and mid-1991. Even if Germany continues to set interest rate levels within Europe, there are grounds for expecting Britain's rates within the ERM to be significantly lower than 12 per cent. Indeed, the Confederation of British Industry, citing potential gains of £300m a year in currency hedging costs, large savings in transactions costs and the prospect of a European economy in which low inflation and interest rates were normal, pressed for a rapid move from ERM membership, in which currencies could be realigned, to a permanent locking of exchange rates and the eventual goal of a single currency within a European monetary union (EMU). Whether Britain, and in particular some of the disadvantaged regions of the country, will be ready for EMU during the 1990s is another story.

There are, therefore, distinct views on the prospects for the British economy in the new regime. The most likely outcome lies between the extremes of optimism and pessimism. One has to take an extremely gloomy view of the ability of the economy to adjust to new circumstances to forecast a prolonged depression in the 1990s. The range of estimates of what was the 'correct' ERM entry level for the pound was sufficiently wide to suggest that assessments of the Williamson type, suggesting years of weak growth to compensate for pitching the pound into the system too high, must be treated with caution. At the same time, it should be noted that the experience of the original members of the ERM in the 1980s indicated that an improved inflation performance was bought at the expense of high unemployment. Britain, of course, had high unemployment in spite of a more variable inflation performance and so, in this respect, taking the pound into the mechanism may not have involved any great sacrifice.

Barring accidents, one thing seems clear. After exchange rate targets were eschewed for most of the 1970s and 1980s, economic policy is likely to be conducted within the framework of a formal currency link with Europe from now on. The Conservative Party, having taken Britain into the ERM, is plainly committed to it for the long-term. So too, according to the Labour Party's policy statements and the Liberal Democrats' espousal of an early move towards a European single currency, are the main opposition parties. After eighteen years of floating exchange rates and eleven and a half years of isolation from a fully functioning ERM, policy has almost come full circle. We are not quite back to the 1950s and 1960s but we have moved a long way away from the early 1980s.

Burying the 1980s

When John Major took over from Margaret Thatcher as Prime Minister in November 1990 he was faced with a difficult balancing act. It was necessary for the new leadership to distance itself from the mistakes of the old, and the blame for the recession, in order to achieve the boost in Conservative popularity that had been the underlying logic behind the need to replace Thatcher. It was, however, impossible for Major to abandon the legacy of Thatcherism entirely. For one thing, his Cabinet was largely inherited from Thatcher. For another, Conservative Party supporters in the constituencies had been shocked by the coup against Thatcher, and Major would have risked a grass-roots revolt by burying her memory too rapidly. The new Prime Minister spoke optimistically of creating a classless society but the general understanding was that policy would continue in a similar vein as under Thatcher, but with the rough edges removed. Thus, relations with Europe would be more conciliatory and there would be more emphasis on the public services.

The changes sought by Major, while presented in this way, were more far-reaching than this, however. Even before she was deposed,

Thatcher had been forced to remove some of the hard edges from her policies. Major, as Chancellor, made no pretence of persevering with an amended version of the monetarist experiment established in 1979. Having been Chief Secretary to the Treasury from June 1987 until July 1989, and having returned to the Treasury as Chancellor in October 1989, he said in evidence to the Treasury and Civil Service Committee, of monetarism:

> It certainly has not been the theory that the Government have followed during any period I have been in the Treasury. I do not think you can boil down all the causes of inflation to such a simple and straightforward judgement. It is necessary to take a very careful account of the monetary aggregates and . . . keep monetary conditions tight and we take into account a whole series of monetary indicators, including the exchange rate, in doing so.   (1989, p. 42)

Entry into the ERM, less than two months before Thatcher's departure, sealed this policy shift into place. But there were other changes. One of Major's priorities was to abandon the unpopular poll tax, which would surely have been unthinkable had Thatcher, who was closely allied with it, remained in office. Lamont's March 1991 Budget had as its centre-piece a £140 across-the-board reduction in poll-tax bills, paid for by an increase from 15 to 17.5 per cent in the rate of value added tax. Intriguingly, consideration was given to financing the poll-tax reduction by an increase in the basic rate of income tax, although this was rejected on the grounds that it would represent too abrupt a departure from the Thatcher years. Michael Heseltine, who as the newly appointed Secretary of State for the Environment was given the unenviable task of sorting out the Conservatives' local taxation problem, announced plans for a new property-based council tax – which was more like the old system of the rates than the poll tax.

The Thatcher Government had come to power determined to achieve real reductions in public expenditure. When this proved to be impossible there was a shift, from about 1982, to a policy of holding spending constant in real terms. This also proved too ambitious and, so, in 1986 the new policy was one of holding the growth of public spending below that of the rest of the economy, thus reducing its share of gross domestic product. By the end of the Thatcher era, with voter concern growing over the quality of public services and the recession pushing up spending on unemployment benefits, even this more modest target had to be abandoned, although it was stressed that this was only temporary. The definition of what was temporary in this context was, however, fairly flexible. General government expenditure (excluding privatization proceeds) rose as a proportion of GDP, to 40 per cent, in the 1989–90 fiscal year, and further in 1990–91 and 1991–2. Treasury plans indicated a further rise in 1992–3. There were explicit measures to boost public spending. Under Thatcher, child benefit had been criticized as a wasteful way of assisting families with children, because it was received by rich as well as poor households. A better way of helping those in need, it was argued, was to target social security funds at the low-income families who most needed it. The level of child benefit was frozen for three years after the June 1987 general election. Under Major, such arguments were cast aside. Freezing child benefits had been unpopular, and henceforth they would be uprated annually in line with inflation.

Major also made much of his personal commitment to the National Health Service, although this was not enough to prevent the Labour Party from continuing to run well ahead of the Conservatives on this issue. Unlike Thatcher, who took the view that it was every person's right to choose private health care if they wished, and she had done so on several occasions, Major stressed that he had always used the NHS and would continue to do so. It may be that the only change was one of style: under Thatcher the belief held that the Government was cutting public spending in absolute terms, long after that had been abandoned as a policy objective. Major, through adopting a more sympathetic approach, and creating a Citizen's Charter designed to make public servants more responsive to the needs of their clients, may merely have been trying to ensure that the Government gained more credit among voters for the amount it was spending.

The change, however, appears to have gone deeper than this. If the 1980s was the decade of the individual, with tax cuts taking priority over higher public spending, the 1990s promised to be different. Private affluence was popular, but sooner or later it would be outweighed by public squalor. Labour set out a programme under which the top rate of income tax would be increased from 40 to 50 per cent, and the upper earnings limit on National Insurance contributions abolished, to pay for additional spending, notably on state pensions. Lamont, addressing the Conservative Party conference in Blackpool in October 1991, duly restated the Government's commitment to achieving a 20 per cent basic rate of income tax, from 25 per cent, but this appeared to be more of a political slogan than a statement of firm intent. Major, notably, merely promised to hold tax rates down when addressing the same conference.

The other shift, and again the proof of the pudding will be in the eating, appeared to be away from the idea, strongly espoused by Nigel Lawson, that income inequalities provide the spur for enterprise. Greed, to adopt the phrase used in the film *Wall Street*, was good. This was the rationale for the 1979 and 1988 reductions in the higher rates of income tax, but it sat uneasily alongside the kinder, gentler face of Conservatism under Major. Lawson, to give him his due, had wanted to limit the tax reliefs available to the well-off, at the same as he cut their tax rates. But this was not possible until after Thatcher's departure. Lamont's March 1991 removal of the higher-rate tax relief against mortgage interest payments, while greeted as a cruel blow by the house builders, was a step in the direction of greater equality through the tax system. The *Financial Times* leader on the day after the Budget was headlined 'The Slaughter of Sacred Cows'. More controversially, the shift from poll tax to VAT was justified on the grounds that its impact would be greatest on those on higher incomes, because they spent more on the goods and services that were subject to VAT.

The move that perhaps symbolized the post-Thatcher era better than any other was also included in the March 1991 Budget. In the 1980s, the mobile phone had come to be regarded as the trademark of the new breed of self-employed businessman, as well as the tool of the beleaguered yuppy. In his Budget speech, Lamont said:

> I turn now to one of the greatest scourges of modern life: the mobile telephone. I propose to bring the benefit of car phones into income tax and simplify the tax treatment of mobile phones by introducing a standard charge on the private use of such phones provided by an employer. Tax will be paid on £200 for each phone for 1991–2. I hope that as a result of this measure, restaurants will be quieter and roads will be safer.   (1991)

The joke nearly backfired – the tax measure, while small in its overall impact, enraged some of Lamont's own backbench supporters. And, while the mobile-phone tax may only have represented a pinprick in a typical executive's salary, there was an underlying message. Conspicuous wealth and consumption had, in the end, worked to the detriment of the

British economy. Those who did best in the 1980s encouraged, by their actions, spending by others. Behaviour was driven by the belief that money in the 1980s was easy to make and even easier to borrow, and ultimately the benefits of any supply-side improvements in the economy had been outweighed by people's readiness to consume. Greed may or may not have been the stimulus for enterprise in the 1980s but it was the factor that blew the economy off course. The runaway economy of the late 1980s was to give way to a sober and more equitable prospect for the 1990s.

The Legacy of the Bust

The 1990–91 recession, because of its painful effects on both borrowers and, to a lesser extent, lenders would, it seemed, lead to lasting changes in economic behaviour. There is an obvious danger in predicting a return to more prudent, more normal attitudes when the excesses of the late 1980s and the retribution of the early 1990s are still fresh in the memory. Even so, taking into account factors such as the condition of the housing market and the debt overhang from the boom-and-bust years, it seems highly unlikely that the conditions associated with the Lawson boom will be replicated in the foreseeable future. The coming together of deregulated lenders and over-ambitious borrowers in the second half of the 1980s was a once and for all event. Even without the regime change represented by ERM membership it is likely that Britain's emergence from the recession would have been slow and cautious. People and companies have learned, often in the most painful way, that just because funds are readily available it does not mean that it is sensible to borrow them. After years of credit rationing, the response in the 1980s was that of greedy children let loose in a sweet shop, with the open encouragement of the owners and little attempt by the authorities to impose restraint. One of the puzzles of the period was coming across otherwise sensible people who found themselves encumbered with large amounts of credit-card debt, which they were struggling to pay off at penal interest rates of 30 per cent or more.

The 1980s were an easy-money era in more senses than the ready availability of credit. A strongly rising housing market meant that large capital gains could be made by means of nothing more onerous or risky than finding a property and taking out a mortgage on it. The average house price in the south-east, for example, increased by £52,000, from £29,832 to £81,635, between 1980 and 1989. Nationally, average prices rose from £23,514 to £58,917 in the 1980s. Prices doubled in the five years from 1985. The effect was to distribute these capital gains unfairly across the economy. Those who had been owner-occupiers for longest, and whose mortages were smallest in relation to the rising market value of their property, gained most. Sharp regional differences in house prices also emerged.

The 1990–91 recession saw a sharper correction in house prices than its 1980–81 predecessor. In the earlier period, house-price inflation fell to zero at the end of 1981 and real house prices (house prices deflated by the general rate of inflation) dropped by a maximum of 10 per cent. In the summer of 1990, house prices were showing a fall of up to 5 per cent compared with a year earlier, and real house prices were falling by as much as 15 per cent. After the 1980–81 recession house prices recovered fairly quickly; within two years they were rising at an annual rate of 10 per cent and outstripping general inflation. But there were reasons for expecting the recovery from the 1990–91 recession to be much slower than this. One was that the ratio of house prices to incomes, traditionally a housing market yardstick, moved significantly above trend in the late 1980s. The house price/income ratio rose to well over 4 compared with its long-run average of around 3. Restoring the average required either a 33 per cent rise in incomes or a 25 per cent fall in house prices or, as it turned out, a combination of the two. Properties repossessed by banks and building societies would also act as a drag on the market, while borrowers and lenders could be expected to proceed cautiously. The best prospect was of a stagnant market for some time, in spite of lower mortgage rates, followed by a situation in which house prices would rise in line with incomes.

Should this be the case, it would reinforce the view that the growth of demand in the economy will be muted. Some consumer spending, on furniture and other consumer durables, is directly linked to activity in the housing market. In addition, while equity can be extracted even when house prices are stable, it is easier to do so in a rising market. Perhaps most importantly of all, rising house prices make people feel more wealthy and inclined to spend. According to the Bank of England, much of this perceived increase in wealth is illu-sory:

A rise in the price of a house does not benefit its owners unless the household is prepared, either now or at some point in the future, to move to a less valuable property. Following a rise in house prices, the owners of houses can spend more only if they reduce their consumption of housing services or reduce the value of their bequest to the next generation. In this sense, an increase in house prices may create a *false* impression of wealth. Nevertheless, an apparent increase in housing wealth in the late 1980s may have led people to feel that they needed to save less and could safely borrow more.

(1991, p. 261)

In many respects the absence of strongly rising house prices is beneficial to the economy, even if the Government's policy of pumping up the market before letting it down again was hardly the best way to achieve that end. Once the market was down, however, the Government seemed determined not to allow another speculative housing boom. Lamont, in Treasury and Civil Service Committee evidence after his March 1991 Budget, said:

That is why I abolished the higher rate of relief on mortgage interest: that is why two years ago we removed the tax relief for sharers; that is why we removed the tax relief for home improvements as well. We have also taken other measures to try to level up the tax treatment of savings, so housing is not in such a privileged position. Finally, of course, the £30,000 limit [on the size of loan eligible for tax relief on mortgage interest] has been eroded over the years. I think the situation is improving, I would very much hope that the pain and the memory of what happened in the late 1980s would, along with the new measures, contribute to preventing the resumption of house-price inflation. Because if we get into that situation again it means we have to have higher interest rates for industry and commerce in order to cool down the housing market.   (1991, p. 59)

Owner-occupiers are to a very large extent consuming the existing housing stock, rather than the current production of houses. The lower mortgage payments are in relation to income (and the average gearing in 1990 was around 14 per cent), the more income is available to spend on other goods, which have the virtue of being currently produced – generating employment and income elsewhere in the economy. The absence of a speculative market in housing should also have the effect of channelling savings for investment purposes elsewhere in the economy. One long-standing weakness of the British economy has been the disproportionate amount of resources directed into housing. The difficulty, as with so many of the after-effects of the 1990–91 recession, lies in the adjustment to the new situation. Those who bought at the top of the boom were in no position to escape from the situation they found themselves in, overburdened with debt and unable to sell their property other than at a large loss. There is, in addition, the significant problem of breaking the link between housing and other sectors of the economy. Two thirds of households in Britain are owner-occupiers. Until they cease to believe that a rising housing market is a symptom of general prosperity, the income released from housing expenditure is more likely to find its way into savings than into other types of spending.

Some of the other lasting effects of the 1990–91 recession were described in Chapter 9. It may be that, in sum, the recession's legacy has been to make Britain a boring, middle-of-the-road economy, full of risk-averse companies and individuals, at just the time when, with European monetary union beckoning, this is exactly what it needs to be. Certainly, this was the prospect set out by Major in an interview with *The Director* magazine in November 1991. He said:

> I am very conscious of the need to bring the economy out of recession in a way that will leave it in a position where there is sustainable growth. I do not want a sudden boom-and-bust mentality. I want sustainable growth and that means a stable exchange rate, the lowest possible inflation, steady growth so that people have the confidence to invest and create sustainable growth. That is what underpinned my instincts when we joined the ERM and it is what underpins the Government's general approach at the moment.   (1991)

This, of course, was the promise held out at the start of the Thatcher monetarist experiment in 1979, and not achieved. This time, the additional discipline of a formal exchange rate target, as opposed to Lawson's informal target, coupled with responsible policies, would, it was hoped, do the trick. But other European countries have had more experience of steady, non-inflationary growth than Britain has. The Organization for Economic Cooperation and Development, in its 1991 report on Britain, said the economy had been 'inflation-prone since the 1960s'. For a brief period in the 1980s Britain appeared to have found the holy grail of strong growth and low inflation, after decades of relatively low growth and relatively high inflation. The test will be whether, after the dust of recession has settled, Britain can grow as fast as the rest of Europe without running a higher inflation rate. If not, the pessimists will have been proved right.

One aspect of the recession that I have only touched upon briefly so far was its regional impact. There has been a great deal of nonsense talked about the recession somehow reversing Britain's long-standing north–south divide, because it was harsher in its impact on the over-borrowed south. Even if this remains true when all the effects of the recession have come through, it displays a misunderstanding of the nature of the problem. Britain's north–south problem has been the long-term shift of economic activity, particularly to the south-east of England, since about 1860. The recession has not resulted in a significant reversal of that shift. It is not even possible to say that there has been a greater loss of economic capacity in the south compared with the north. The recession itself was partly a result of the overheating pressures caused by an excessive concentration of wealth and economic activity in the south. In an earlier book, *North and South*, I described this effect:

> During the 1980s, the economy has moved from a position where north–south disparities, while unfair, did not act as a constraint on growth, to one where there are potentially very serious consequences arising from the present imbalances. The British economy is vulnerable to problems on both inflation and the balance of payments, and this vulnerability has been enhanced by the uneven regional distribution of economic activity. In addition, as long as there are wide variations in economic performance between north and south, the economy will be obliged to run at below its productive potential. This may not have been immediately apparent during the 1987–8 demand-led boom, but it will reassert itself. The combination of congestion in the south and high unemployment and unused capacity – both public and private – in the north is ultimately a highly inefficient one.   (1989, p. 268)

My earlier conclusion was that the north could enjoy a period in which it closed the gap on the south, although only slightly, partly as a reaction to the fact that the north-to-south shift went beyond trend during the 1980s. The long-term trend in favour of the south, due to factors such as the pull of Europe, the Channel Tunnel and the fact that a concentration of wealth in a geographical area has the effect of creating economic activity in that area, would persist. This is also the view of specialist regional analysts such as Business Strategies Ltd and Cambridge Econometrics, and I see no reason to change my view.

What was undoubtedly true was that the 1990–91 recession hit white-collar workers, and the professions, harder than its predecessors. The

Law Society estimated that solicitors shed 15 per cent of their staff. Between 3,000 and 4,000 qualified accountants, traditionally in short supply, were looking for work at the end of 1991. Architecture was badly hit by the construction slump. Throughout the professions, and in sectors such as advertising and the media, the recession took its toll. The interesting question was the strength of the political backlash that this would create.

Lessons Unlearned

No one comes out of the boom-and-bust story very well. Nigel Lawson, who is usually cast as the villain of the piece, has already prepared his alibis. These are that, had Thatcher acceded to his proposition for taking sterling into the ERM in 1985, most of the subsequent problems would have been avoided. Later, he proposed a fully worked plan for making the Bank of England independent, and responsible for maintaining stable prices. On the conduct of policy during the crucial 1987–8 period he has admitted to three errors: taking the advice of the Inland Revenue and delaying the abolition of multiple tax relief on mortgage-interest payments, responding too vigorously by lowering interest rates in the wake of the October 1987 stock-market crash (but then everyone was advising him to do so and other countries did the same) and allowing the pound to fall too much in the wake of the 1985–6 fall in world oil prices.

Of the three, only the first can be taken at face value. The advice Lawson received on timing the abolition of multiple mortgage interest relief was poor. But for a Chancellor as powerful and dominant as Lawson to hide behind the cloak of the October 1987 stock-market crash really does not do. Most of the interest rate reductions in 1987–8 resulted from the Chancellor's determination to see his Deutschmark target for sterling maintained. Lawson's admission that he should not have allowed the pound to fall so much in 1986 is another way of saying that the pound should have been taken into the ERM, on his advice, in 1985. Of that, more below.

Another possible excuse is that Lawson, as Chancellor, was misled by the Treasury forecasts and by inaccurate official statistics. But Lawson had long stood by Denis Healey's dictum on Treasury forecasts, in which Healey said:

Like long-term weather forecasts they are better than nothing . . . But their origin lies in the extrapolation from a partially known past, through an unknown present, to an unknowable future according to theories about the causal relationships between certain economic variables which are hotly disputed by academic economists, and may in fact change from country to country or from decade to decade.   (1990)

As for the statistics, those that were indicating a booming economy, such as the sharply deteriorating trade balance, strong growth in money and credit, and booming house prices, were conveniently but mistakenly ignored.

Thatcher, having left office convinced that others' mismanagement of the economy had brought about her downfall, can be blamed, in the Lawson version of events, for delaying sterling's entry into the ERM. But had entry occurred in 1985, it would have been at an exchange rate of around DM3.75, the then market level, nearly 30 per cent above its eventual central parity five years later, and just before the sharp downward pressure on the pound that emerged with the 1986 fall in the world oil prices. It is hard not to have some sympathy with the view of Sir Alan Walters that to have gone in at that time and at such a rate would have been extremely damaging, not least to the Conservative Party. He wrote:

In retrospect, the widely reported intransigence of the Prime Minister to entering the ERM was a godsend. If we had entered, then raising interest rates to new highs in late 1985 and throughout 1986 would have jeopardized, even ruined, the Conservative Party's prospects in the election of 1987. After such a very tight monetary squeeze throughout 1986, there would have been a recession – and most likely a deep one – in 1987–8.   (1990, p. 101)

Nevertheless, as with any Prime Minister, Thatcher has to carry the ultimate responsibility for the policies carried out by her Government. The economic miracle, when it was being proclaimed was, after all, the Thatcher miracle. The economy's subsequent fall was the reverse side of that miracle. And part of the blame, probably the greater part of it, for the deterioration in relations between Prime Minister and Chancellor in 1988 and 1989 must be laid at Thatcher's door. The public disagreement between Thatcher and Lawson, with Walters articulating the Prime Minister's objections to the economic policies being pursued by her Chancellor, had an important and damaging impact on financial market confidence in 1988 and 1989, sabotaging hopes of a soft landing for the

economy. This period, when Thatcher was in open disagreement with
Lawson and could barely bring herself to talk to Sir Geoffrey Howe, the
Foreign Secretary, is perhaps the most extraordinary in the whole story.
'When differences of view emerge, as they are bound to do from time to
time, they should be resolved privately and, whenever appropriate,
collectively,' said Lawson on resigning (1989).

What were Thatcher's motives during this time, knowing as she must
have that her incautious words only added to the Government's economic
difficulties. The machiavellian explanation was that she wanted to be rid
of both Lawson and Howe but was fearful of the reaction in the
Conservative Party if she dismissed them. Her second-best solution was,
therefore, to make life as uncomfortable for them as possible until they
eventually lost patience and resigned. This roughly fits the facts but
implies that Thatcher's actions were part of a carefully thought-out
strategy, but it was clear that for much of the time they were not. A better
explanation is that, following the 1987–8 episode of shadowing the
Deutschmark, Thatcher genuinely believed that something akin to ERM
membership had been tried and found wanting. She could not quite
believe it when, following the shadowing experiment, she was still under
extreme pressure to accept sterling's entry into the system. As Lawson
pointed out later, joining the mechanism was the declared policy of the
Government and Thatcher, through her reluctance, was in a minority,
certainly within her own Cabinet and among Conservative MPs. She
therefore fought a rearguard action against entry, albeit a damaging and
unsuccessful one.

In the ten and a half years of Conservative Government from May
1979 to October 1989, there were just two Chancellors of the Exchequer,
Howe and Lawson. After that the turnover of personnel increased
sharply. John Major was in the job for just thirteen months before being
succeeded, on his own promotion to the job of Prime Minister, by
Norman Lamont. Major's achievement was in persuading Thatcher of
the inevitability of ERM membership, and securing entry, where his
predecessors had failed. This was an achievement, although it owed
much to the circumstances of Lawson's departure, and Thatcher's
increased vulnerability. When Walters resigned, on the same day at the
end of October 1989 that Lawson left the Government, he had just
composed a memo to Thatcher predicting that the economy was heading
for recession. Major was the inheritor of a recession-bound economy.

The main criticism of his brief time as Chancellor was that interest rates were held high for too long, partly because he allowed himself to be persuaded that it was necessary for the pound to enter the ERM at a relatively high level. This had the effect of deepening and prolonging the recession. Major, under strong pressure from Thatcher, also committed the folly of cutting interest rates on entering the mechanism, an action which made subsequent interest rate cuts difficult to achieve. This did Lamont, his successor, no favours at all.

Lamont, the first Chancellor under Major, suffered from having been a junior minister, in the Treasury and elsewhere, for too long, and did not easily acquire the stature associated with his new position. He took over with the economy in the middle of the steepest part of the 1990–91 recession dive. He was, however, initially hamstrung on interest rates by sterling's weakness. The rationale for his March 1991 Budget, which was on the tough side of neutral, was that it would increase his room for manoeuvre on interest rates. And, indeed, from February to September 1991 base rates fell from 14 to 10.5 per cent. Other than that, it was difficult to justify many of the details of the Budget, which hit the recession-hit car industry and housing market particularly hard. Indeed, the Budget strategy over the boom-and-bust period was perverse. In 1987 and 1988, when the economy was growing too strongly, taxes were reduced substantially, adding fuel to an already roaring fire. In 1990 and 1991, in conditions of near-recession and recession, there were small net increases in taxation. Lamont also came under criticism for appearing to be too anxious to talk up the economic recovery during 1991, at a time when the economy was still mired in recession. This contrasted with the situation in the early 1980s, when the Treasury was downbeat about recovery prospects and the Government gained kudos for not overplaying its hand.

For the politicians, the message of the boom-to-bust cycle was that pride invariably comes before the fall. There may be a certain quiet satisfaction in seeing one's elected representatives with egg on their faces. But politicians come and go, even leaders as durable as Thatcher and Chancellors as long-serving as Lawson. In the end, it is the economy that suffers. As for the non-elected officials, the Bank of England has been prepared to admit to errors in policy. Robin Leigh-Pemberton, the Bank Governor, in his April 1990 University of Durham speech, conceded that policy mistakes and forecasting errors played a major part in the resurgence of inflation in the late 1980s. Refreshingly, Bank of England officials do not attempt to pretend that they spotted all the dangers at the time, or claim that all their advice was good, but ignored. Where risks were seen by the Bank, officials admit that they were not firm enough in warning of them. As Leigh-Pemberton put it:

> William McChesney Martin, Chairman of the Federal Reserve Board in the 1950s and 1960s, said it was the duty of a central banker to take away the punch-bowl just as the party was hotting up. So it is; and he cannot be expected to be thanked for it. But any criticism of his attempts to clear heads the next day should take the form of a remonstration that he was not firmer the night before. Candidly, I think such criticism is far too rare. (1990, p. 216)

As for the senior Treasury officials associated with the economic policy errors of the period, it is plainly more difficult for them to speak out in a way that would imply criticism of their political masters. In any event, it is a legitimate escape for them to retreat behind the curtain of ministerial responsibility. Treasury forecasters have also used the argument that, while they got things wrong, so did the majority of independent fore-casters, although the Treasury should – with more information at its disposal, not least on the likely course of policy – have a much better chance of getting its predictions right. I detect a remarkable lack of humility, even hurt pride, among Treasury officials, which is disturbing. There has been no internal investigation of what went wrong. Heads have not rolled. The Treasury remains convinced that most of the time it gets policy right. The experience of recent years should have done more to call into question that view.

The important question, rather than attributing blame for what is, after all, water under the bridge, is whether lessons have been learned that will prevent the same thing from happening again. Faced with the same combination of circumstances as in the 1987–91 period, perhaps the politicians, advisers and officials would have responded differently. Hindsight is perhaps the most useful gift of all. But history does not, in general, repeat itself. If ERM membership acts in a similar way to the post-war Bretton Woods framework, and operates as an effective con-straint on Britain's economic policy, then the question of whether lessons have been learned may not need to be answered. This is, however, too optimistic a view of the power of the mechanism. Governments will, for the foreseeable future, still have the power to mismanage the economy.

The root cause of the mistakes of the late 1980s was that, in abandoning monetarism, the Government also adopted a cavalier attitude to the growth of credit, in a way that should have caused more concern in both the Treasury and the Bank of England. There were good reasons for dispensing with the monetary targets of the first half of the 1980s. There was no good reason for ignoring the rapid growth of credit, along with other danger signs. The baby was well and truly thrown out with the bath-water.

Having come full circle to the point where the concern, once more, is over the prospect of a period of very slow growth and rising unemployment, it is unlikely that policy-makers will find it possible to respond adequately. One of the clearest indications of this came during 1991, when growth of money and credit slowed to a snail's pace but the Government was unconcerned. This was the mirror image of the situation in the boom years, but the same arguments for ignoring the message of the monetary data re-emerged. The figures remained distorted, it was said, by the effects of financial liberalization, and they conveyed no useful forward-looking information about the economy. The error in the late 1980s was ignoring the inflationary message of strong credit growth. The danger was that this will be followed by an equally large error on the opposite side, ignoring the recessionary message of very weak credit growth. After all, how do you stimulate an economy when your main instrument for doing so is the level of interest rates, but lenders are reluctant to lend and potential borrowers do not want to borrow?

By the end of 1991, this was the position facing Britain's economy. The recovery had failed to materialize, and the Government's position was looking difficult. Deflating the boom had created a recession that threatened to turn into the longest in the post-war period. The Treasury, accused by Samuel Brittan in the *Financial Times* on 19 December of forecasting a 'fictitious recovery' was increasingly isolated, having erred once more. Brittan had supported the Treasury's recovery forecast. Others, myself included, had not. The debate, indeed, turned from questions on the timing of the upturn, to that of whether the economy had entered a much longer depression, based on a new aversion to debt.

The appropriate parallel to draw is probably with the first half of the 1980s. In spite of the severity of the 1980–81 recession, the priority, after the inflationary excesses of the 1970s and early 1980s, was to stamp out inflation. Policy was cautious, always guarding against a resurgence of inflation. Only after several years of slow growth and rising unemployment did policy-makers convince themselves that inflation was beaten. Barely had they done so, than the resurgence of inflation proved that it had been merely lying dormant. That experience is now engraved on the hearts of the Treasury and the Bank of England. Low inflation may stimulate economic growth. According to the official view, there is no trade-off, particularly in a world where currency depreciation is ruled out, between inflation and unemployment. One must hope that this is right. For, if it turns out that low inflation is only achievable in an environment of slow growth and high unemployment, the political pressures that resulted in boom and bust will reassert themselves. And it would take a brave man to predict that, next time, similar mistakes will be avoided.

11

—— ✦ ——

POSTSCRIPT: PRAGMATISM REGAINED

When I completed the manuscript for the first edition of this book towards the end of 1991 two things could have been expected to happen. The first was that, at some stage, normal cyclical forces would reassert themselves and the economy pull slowly, probably painfully slowly, out of recession. True, as I noted in the previous chapter, 'The debate, indeed, turned from questions on the timing of the upturn, to that of whether the economy had entered a much longer depression, based on a new aversion to debt.' But the majority view of economists and businessmen was that 1992 would see the beginnings of a slow very subdued economic recovery.

The second apparent certainty was that if sterling's membership of the ERM survived a British general election, then it could probably survive anything. After all, a government that had passed up on the opportunity to provide a pre-election boost to the economy, instead choosing to stick to its ERM commitment, would surely not abandon that commitment in the early years of a new Parliament, when the political pressures to generate recovery are typically less intense.

One year on, both of these assumptions had proved to be false. The economy, which showed brief signs of life in the spring of 1992, had sunk back into a condition that went well beyond the experience of previous post-war business cycles. Not only was the recession the longest since the war, but it was also turning into the deepest. 'Depression' – a prolonged period of stagnant economic activity with high unemployment, weak prices and severe strains in the financial system – best characterized the economy's state. As for the ERM commitment, this was swept aside, not by Britain's general election but, instead, by market uncertainties in the run-up to France's 20 September referendum on the Maastricht amendments to the Treaty of Rome (agreed by

European Community leaders at the Dutch town in December 1991).
These amendments, if ratified, would herald European moves towards
closer political and monetary union. It is to these two related issues, the
prolonged recession and the collapse of the Government's ERM strategy,
that I now turn.

Another False Dawn

The British economy was undeniably weak in the early months of 1992.
In the first quarter of the year, gross domestic product fell by 0.4 per
cent, its biggest quarterly drop for a year. The price of sticking to the
ERM strategy was that there was no scope for pre-election interest rate
cuts. The Chancellor, Norman Lamont, had reduced base rates from 14
per cent to 10.5 per cent between February and September 1991, the
latter point coinciding with a rise in business and consumer confidence
that many saw, wrongly, as indicating that economic recovery had
begun. But there were no further rate cuts between September and the
9 April general election. Indeed, when the Bundesbank raised its key
lending rates six days before Christmas 1991, the British authorities
were said to have done well merely to avoid putting UK rates up in
sympathy, particularly with Britain entering a period of pre-election
political uncertainty.

The absence of interest rate reductions over the winter of 1991–2 was
one factor holding back recovery. The Government attempted other
methods of boosting activity. In December, in an attempt to stabilize
the housing market and slow the rise in home repossessions, Lamont
announced a housing rescue package, which included the suspension for
eight months of the 1 per cent stamp duty on house purchases. This,
together with other measures, including a tacit agreement on the part of
the banks and building societies that they would go softer on borrowers
running up mortgage arrears, did not, however, lift a moribund market.
Many home-buyers were caught in the so-called negative equity trap, in
that falling house prices had pushed the market value of their home
below, in some cases well below, the level of the mortgage that they had
taken out to purchase it. Estimates by the Bank of England suggested
that a million or more households were in this position. And, for those
who were not, 1992 saw, far from a stable housing market, an accelerated
decline in property prices.

Another factor apparently preventing economic recovery was uncertainty over the general election itself. The Labour Party, under the leadership of Neil Kinnock, began 1992 in a strong opinion poll position, a situation that held for much of the period until the general election on 9 April. Eve-of-election opinion polls, indeed, pointed to a decisive Labour victory. Labour was committed, in a strategy championed by John Smith, the shadow Chancellor (who was to succeed Kinnock as Labour leader), to a significant redistribution of income through the tax and benefits system. Extra tax was to be raised from those on higher incomes by the removal of the ceiling on employees' National Insurance contributions, and by increased higher tax rates. The effect of removing the employees' NI ceiling – £21,060 for the 1992–3 financial year – would be to increase marginal tax rates on incomes above this level by the 9 per cent amount of the contribution. Further up the income scale, at around £40,000, a new top rate of tax of 50 per cent (up from 40 per cent) was to be introduced. Under Labour, therefore, a £50,000 per year earner could expect to pay £3,600 more in tax and NI contributions than under the existing regime.

Kinnock, aware that this was a potential Achilles' heel for Labour, favoured phasing in the tax and NI changes but Smith argued for a 'Big Bang' approach and won the day. He and other shadow Cabinet members suggested that the better-off had done too well during the Thatcher years, and that this was widely recognized. In addition, any political damage wrought by the proposed tax changes would be limited, and more than offset by the gains that would arise as the public saw what Labour intended to do with the extra money. The additional revenues would be used to finance an increase in state pensions (up £5 a week for single people and £8 for married couples) and in a rise in child benefit to £9.95 a week for all children. Kinnock was right in suspecting that Labour was vulnerable on tax. The Conservatives made it *the* issue of the election campaign and did not stop at the tax increases planned by Labour. Conservative Central Office unveiled what was described as 'Labour's tax bombshell', a claim that a Labour Government would need to raise the basic rate of income tax from 25 to 35 per cent to finance all the party's public expenditure commitments. It was crude but, despite firm denials by Kinnock and Smith, it worked. Labour's planned increases in pensions and benefits were submerged. The Conservative campaign to paint Labour as a high tax party worked.

The campaign was not without its dangers. Most political comment-ators had worked on the assumption that, in the absence of economic recovery, John Major's Government would be defeated at the general election. And, the more bloodthirsty the Conservative warnings on tax, the less people were likely to spend in a way that would generate recovery. Retail sales were particularly weak in March, the month before the election. Major tried to have it several ways, blaming the economy's weakness on a world recession that was not then occurring, and on fear of the tax consequences of a Labour victory, while at the same time claiming that existing policies were already producing a recovery in Britain. 'Vote Conservative on Thursday,' he said at a rally two days before the election, 'and the recovery will continue on Friday'.

In spite of a generally lacklustre campaign and the absence of recovery, the tax issue worked well for the Conservatives. Major secured 42 per cent of the popular vote, against only 35 per cent for Labour, confound-ing the opinion polls (the pollsters later said that, as well as a very late swing in support towards the Government, people were embarrassed to admit they would be voting Conservative because of tax). The Conservatives won a 21-seat House of Commons majority, down from the 100-seat advantage that Major had inherited from Thatcher, but far better than anyone had reason to expect during the campaign. Initially, too, it appeared that Major's confidence in economic recovery was not as misplaced as his earlier predictions during the recession. Many retailers reported that the March lull in sales had been followed by an upturn in activity after the 9 April election. Those who did not were dismissed, mistakenly, as killjoys. Estate agents said there was an increase in interest, if not outright purchases, among potential home-buyers. Sur-veys by the Confederation of British Industry and the British Chambers of Commerce showed a strong rise in business confidence. The level of imports, traditionally a reliable indicator of the state of demand in Britain, showed a significant upturn.

The election result, having come as a genuine surprise to the financial markets, had a dramatic impact. Share prices jumped in anticipation of recovery. The pound, having been weak, although not dangerously so during the election campaign, Labour having endorsed the Government's ERM commitment, also picked up strongly. Its rise towards its ERM central rate of DM2.95, which coincided with an outbreak of industrial unrest in Germany, allowed Lamont to cut base rates from 10.5 to 10 per cent early in May. Briefly, Britain appeared to have entered a virtuous circle, in which a recovering economy, overseen by a stable, right-of-centre administration, could enjoy the benefits of a strong currency and the consequent scope, if the authorities so desired it, for reducing interest rates. With Germany experiencing the worst of its post-unification problems, including untypically high inflation of 4 per cent, labour disputes and rising racial tension, Britain suddenly took on the look of a safe haven within Europe. Could it be, City economists asked, that Britain could break the Bundesbank's stranglehold on the ERM, by reducing interest rates decisively below German levels? Such thoughts were also prevalent in official circles. Mervyn King, director of economics at the Bank of England, wondered about it out loud in a speech in Rome. The theoretical proposition that other ERM member countries could cut interest rates below Germany's and keep them there would, he suggested, be tested empirically over the next twelve months. As it turned out, British interest rates were reduced below those of Germany, but only after sterling's forced exit from the ERM.

A Whirlwind Blows through Europe

The crisis that forced sterling out of the ERM and ensured the abrupt end of the fixed exchange rate strategy over which so much political blood had been spilt began in June 1992. The brief post-election flowering of the economy hardly lasted a month. Like the tenderest of early plants, it proved vulnerable to even a gentle frost. Doubts about the recovery began to emerge even more quickly than during two previous false dawns in 1991, when first the end of the Gulf War and then the autumn rise in business and consumer confidence proved to be unreliable harbingers of recovery. When the giant Canary Wharf project in London's docklands went into administration, effectively bankrupt, it was a sign of the economy's fundamental weakness. Indeed, commercial property was an even more dramatic example of the boom-to-bust cycle than the housing market. The belief that London's rapid expansion as a financial centre would last for decades resulted in a massive, unplanned explosion of office-building in the capital. As the City's star faded, from the time of the October 1987 stock market crash, so London was left with a huge excess capacity of office space, some of it still under construction.

The economy's failure to shake off the recession increased the need for further interest rate reductions to lift the economy. Events elsewhere in Europe, however, were to render such reductions impossible. On 2 June, the Danish people voted on the Maastricht Treaty and, by the narrowest of margins, 50.7 per cent against 49.3 per cent, rejected it. The path to monetary union, which required the agreement of all twelve member states, was suddenly fraught with dangers. And, since the ERM was seen as a precursor of full monetary union, its future was also in doubt. The effect of the Danish referendum was to reinforce the Deutschmark's role as the anchor currency of Europe, although this did not prevent Major saying, in a private conversation with *Sunday Times* journalists a few weeks later, that his ambition was to see sterling replace· the Deutschmark as Europe's anchor. Talk of British interest rates falling below German levels evaporated. Instead, the question was whether Britain could survive the difficult three months to France's Maastricht referendum on 20 September without raising interest rates. Ireland's 'yes' vote to Maastricht, with 69 per cent voting in favour on 18 June, did not remove the doubts. Ratification of Maastricht was required by all twelve member states.

Treasury officials in London had always seen Britain's ERM membership as vulnerable to 'one big event'. Prior to membership, it was thought that such an event was likely to be a British general election. But Labour's support for the Government's ERM strategy allowed sterling to sail through the election campaign unscathed. Now, the big event was the French referendum. The Government's response to the ERM threat was not to prepare a contingency plan to cover the possible collapse of the system, or sterling's departure from it. Instead, Lamont and Major reinforced their commitment to the pound's continuation in the system at the existing central parity of DM2.95. Lamont, in a speech to the European Policy Forum on 10 July, said:

> The ERM is not an optional extra, an add-on to be jettisoned at the first hint of trouble. It is and will remain at the very centre of our macroeconomic strategy. The choice Margaret Thatcher and John Major made in the autumn of 1990 was a momentous one ... We believe that the ERM provides a framework of policy which will enable us to get inflation down and hold it down, which will reduce uncertainty for our exporters, and which will enable us to achieve sustained growth. And it is why we will move to the narrow bands of the ERM in due course at our current central rate of DM2.95.   (1992a)

And, in a passage that was to return to haunt him, he added:

> Many who advocate floating know full well what the consequences would be. They intend a devaluation of the pound. And they would certainly achieve it. For the result of leaving the ERM, combined with large cuts in interest rates, would be a fall in the pound probably unprecedented in the last forty years. It's the cut and run option; cut interest rates and a run on the pound ... Markets would see that, unlike all our major European competitors, Britain lacked the will to pursue the goal of permanently low inflation. And they would be right. We would have given up after less than two years. They would conclude that we were back to our bad old ways; that given the chance we would always delude ourselves by thinking that with a little more inflation we could get a little more growth.   (1992a)

Through the summer, the crisis evolved. The pound, close to its DM2.95 central rate in the aftermath of the 9 April election, began to weaken alarmingly. When, on 2 August, the *Sunday Times* reported Major's view that he wanted sterling to eventually replace the Deutschmark as Europe's anchor currency the reaction was one of bemusement. One City economist said, 'It brought home to us how out of touch Major was. At a time when people were starting to worry about how much interest rates would have to rise to protect the pound, the Prime Minister was fantasizing about it replacing the mark.' Even Treasury officials described Major's view, at the time it was expressed, as 'distinctly unhelpful'. Sterling, at the time the piece appeared, stood at DM2.85. In a few days it was down to DM2.82; within a fortnight it was below DM2.80, perilously close to its absolute floor of DM2.7780. As August progressed, the pound's weakness was beginning to cause serious concern in the Treasury. Sir Terence Burns, the Permanent Secretary to the Treasury, returned from holiday a week early. Lamont also cut short his vacation, having monitored sterling's shaky progress while staying at a villa in Tuscany.

He decided that a repetition of his July commitment to the pound's continuation in the ERM was the appropriate strategy. Journalists, photographers and radio and TV reporters were called to the Treasury at 8 a.m. on the morning of Wednesday 25 August. Expectations were high. An early morning statement from the Chancellor was unusual. Journalists scented a change of policy. But, blinking into the camera flash-lights, Lamont merely reaffirmed the existing policy. He wanted, he said, to remove any 'scintilla of doubt' about the Government's ERM commitment. He would do 'whatever is necessary' to support the pound. That day, the Bank of England spent more than $1bn of the official reserves in support of sterling. At the time concern was expressed at the scale of the Bank support needed. But, compared with what was to follow, it was small beer. The pressure subsided for a few days. Sterling was at the bottom of the ERM but it was not in a critical position. The authorities stood ready, with currency intervention and, as a last resort, higher interest rates, to protect it.

Just over a week later, on Thursday 3 September, Lamont surprised the markets with an audacious plan to raise 10bn Ecus (then £7.25bn) in Deutschmarks and other foreign currencies. The intention was plain; the Government had taken out an insurance policy to get through the seventeen days until France's Maastricht referendum. And, by borrowing in foreign currencies, the Chancellor had ensured that taxpayers' money was riding on the success of his campaign to avoid a devaluation. Any fall in the pound would push up the cost of repaying the foreign currency loan. Thus, it was hoped, the markets would see that there was no possibility of Britain succumbing to devaluation. There was, however, another side to the decision to borrow heavily in foreign currencies, and in action by the Government earlier in the summer, when it had reduced interest rates on certain National Savings products, after the building societies had threatened to increase mortgage rates. Both could be seen as underlying Britain's deep desire, and particularly that of the Prime Minister, not to increase interest rates with the economy deep in recession. The Government wished to have it both ways, to defend the pound in the ERM, but to do so without increasing interest rates. It was this dual aim that, finally, was to scupper sterling.

By coincidence, the weekend of 4–6 September was scheduled for an informal meeting of European finance ministers and central bankers, chaired by Lamont. Such meetings, by tradition, are held outside national capitals. Lamont had chosen the Georgian splendour of Bath for a meeting that was to be dominated by turbulence on the foreign exchange markets, and by strong criticism of the German Bundesbank for its high interest rate strategy. The Bundesbank sets interest rates independently of the Bonn Government. It normally makes no promises or commitments on interest rates at international meetings. But, at the end of the Bath meeting, Lamont claimed a significant concession from the Bundesbank. Helmut Schlesinger, the Bundesbank president, had said there was no need for higher German interest rates 'in present circumstances'. The Chancellor, grateful for small mercies, predicted that this would ease tensions in the ERM, and reaffirmed the joint commitment of all EC countries to avoiding a currency realignment.

Within minutes of Lamont's Saturday evening press conference in Bath proclaiming the breakthrough on German interest rates, Schlesinger was offering a rather different interpretation. Interviewed by Graham Leach, the BBC's Europe correspondent, he said he had not given any new commitment on interest rates. All he had done was to repeat what he had said after a Bundesbank council meeting in July. And he rejected speculation on an early reduction in interest rates. The writing was on the wall. The following week, the Schlesinger line prevailed in the financial markets. Dealers saw through Lamont's attempt to build the Bath declaration into something more significant than it was. The first victim of the crisis was the Finnish markka, not in the ERM but tied to the Deutschmark. The Finnish Government, after running out of foreign currency reserves in a vain attempt to support the currency, announced that it would be allowed to float free. The Swedish krona was next. But Carl Bildt, Sweden's Prime Minister, was made of sterner stuff. He authorized money market interest rates, first of 75 per cent and then of 500 per cent, to protect the krona. Such dramatic action succeeded in holding the line. (The krona eventually succumbed, but not until three months later.) For the weaker ERM currencies there was no such luck.

Black Wednesday

On Saturday 12 September, Sir Nigel Wicks, the Treasury Deputy Permanent Secretary with responsibility for overseas finance, received a call from Jean-Claude Trichet, an official of the French Ministry of Finance who also chairs the European Community monetary committee. The call was to inform Britain that Italy intended a 7 per cent devaluation of the lira, to be announced the following day, in return for which the Bundesbank was prepared to ease official interest rates slightly. Wicks maintained later that no suggestion was made to him that sterling should join the lira in the downward move against the Deutschmark. The following morning, 13 September, in the eerie quiet of a Whitehall Sunday, Lamont chaired a meeting at the Treasury. Others present included Eddie George, the Deputy Governor of the Bank of England, and Sir Terence Burns, Treasury Permanent Secretary. Burns had prepared a list of options, in ascending order of pain. The simplest, and at the time the one which appeared to be the least painful, was to attempt to tough it out until the following weekend and the French referendum. A much more painful option, at least in terms of political credibility, was for the pound to join the lira. Sterling, while under pressure in the preceding week, had not faced selling on the scale of that experienced by Italy. A devaluation of the pound would look like the Government had abandoned the centrepiece of its economic strategy at the first sound of gunfire. More to the point, John Major, in a speech three days earlier, had underlined his commitment to sterling's existing central parity of DM2.95 in the most forthright terms. Addressing the annual dinner of the Scottish Confederation of British Industry in Glasgow, he had said:

> All my adult life I have seen British governments driven off their pursuit of low inflation by market problems or political pressures . . . The soft option, the devaluer's option, the inflationary option, would be a betrayal of our future.   (1992)

When the Italian devaluation was announced, Lamont again rejected any suggestion that Britain should follow a similar course. Italy's move, and the accompanying reduction in German interest rates, 'demonstrated the benefits of continuing close co-operation among Community countries'. And, for Britain: 'The Government has repeatedly made clear that there is no question of any change in the central parity of the pound against the mark and that we will take whatever action is necessary to secure that.' On the evening of Sunday 13 September, speculation began to build up about the size of the still-to-be-announced German interest rate reduction. Suggestions were made that the cut in rates could be as large as two percentage points. Downing Street officials suggested to Parliamentary lobby journalists that the German move would bring forward the next reduction in British interest rates. Giuliano Amato, the Italian Prime Minister, keen to sell the lira's devaluation to a sceptical public, said that the reduction in German interest rates would be 'significant'.

But when, on the morning of Monday 14 September, the announcement from Frankfurt came, the reaction was one of huge disappointment.

The Bundesbank reduced its key Lombard rate by just a quarter of a point, and other money market rates by half a point. Sterling was back under pressure and, it was by now clear, would be unlikely to get through to the end of the week without either a big rise in interest rates or massive support from the Bank of England or, probably, both.

At just after six on the evening of Tuesday 15 September, Lamont was chairing a meeting in his Treasury office. Those present included Robin Leigh-Pemberton, the Governor of the Bank of England, Eddie George, Deputy Governor, Sir Terence Burns, Treasury Permanent Secretary, and other Treasury officials. George, for the Bank, gave a gloomy assessment of the view from the City. Sterling was stuck at the bottom of its ERM band in spite of the previous day's small cut in German interest rates and covert intervention by the Bank of England. The markets, it appeared, aimed to challenge Britain's ERM commitment before the week was out. Not only was sterling falling against the Deutschmark but it was weak against the dollar, in sharp contrast to its position a week earlier, when it had briefly climbed above the $2 level.

As Lamont listened to his advisers, the telephone rang. A journalist from the *Financial Times* had just contacted the Treasury press office to ask about a report on one of the newswires. The report, if true, was dynamite. Helmut Schlesinger, the Bundesbank President, was quoted as saying that the previous Sunday's devaluation of the lira was not enough and that a wider realignment was needed to hold together the ERM. This could only mean one thing: devaluation of the pound. Leigh-Pemberton immediately got on the phone to Schlesinger. The Bundesbank President, forty years with the German central bank but only its chief for a year, was surprised by the call. He had indeed given a newspaper interview to two journalists, from the *Wall Street Journal* and *Handelsblatt*, a German newspaper. *Handelsblatt*, knowing that it had a hot property, had issued a press release. But Schlesinger insisted that it had been agreed that the interview would be cleared prior to publication. On Leigh-Pemberton's insistence he agreed to issue a retraction.

The mood of the Treasury meeting was black. The Bundesbank, not for the first time, was the target of intense British anger. Later, Downing Street was to detail five instances where the Bundesbank, intentionally or otherwise, had hampered Britain's defence of sterling. The Bundesbank's conduct during the sterling crisis was contrasted with its helpful attitude, a week later, during the successful defence of the French franc. According to one official present at the Tuesday meeting, Schlesinger's words had come from 'a clumsiness borne out of a desire to repair its reputation after the previous day's rate cut.' The task of keeping sterling above its DM2.7780 floor was hard enough even without the Bundesbank President's reported comments. The meeting broke up. Lamont left for a previously arranged dinner with the American Ambassador, having reported the situation to Major. The Bank of England team returned to Threadneedle Street, awaiting the Bundesbank's denial. A retraction appeared, saying that the comments attributed to Schlesinger were 'unauthorized'. But, crucially, the denial did not appear until ten in the evening, in spite of further frantic phone calls between the Bank of England and the Bundesbank. During this time, Bundesbank officials were hastily negotiating with the *Handelsblatt* journalist, who at one stage threatened to release the tape of his interview.

The damage was done. The pound had continued to come under heavy selling pressure in the New York markets, outside European trading hours, and beyond the obligation of other European central banks to support it. Late on Tuesday, the possibilities of defeat, of succumbing to pressure from the markets, with all that would entail in terms of lost credibility, began to stare the Treasury and Bank of England in the face. One senior Treasury official said: 'By the time I went to bed on Tuesday night I was pretty gloomy. There was now the first serious doubt about whether we would get through.' Emergency measures were going to be needed, and there was no guarantee that they would work. The Bank of England's advice to the Treasury had been that, by avoiding heavy intervention or a rise in interest rates, the markets could be persuaded that it was possible to hold the line. One official said, 'It's like trying to keep a marble from rolling about on a tray. Once it starts to move, even a little bit, there's nothing you can do to keep it still.'

Early on Wednesday morning, 16 September, the marble had started to roll alarmingly. Overnight in the Far East, the pound had continued to be sold heavily. The Bank of England weighed in with the first part of the strategy agreed the previous evening: heavy, overt intervention, on a scale never seen before in London. The Bank bought sterling at its ERM floor of DM2.7780, selling massive quantities of foreign currency to do so. The operation was enormous. Officials refused to disclose how much support the pound required but market estimates suggested that £10–15bn, half of Britain's official reserves, was needed. An outflow on this scale was unprecedented, confirmation that, in a description Lamont was to use later, a financial 'whirlwind' was taking place. Disturbingly, however, it made no difference. In the Treasury and Bank of England, officials waited in vain for the pound to respond. 'It was huge but it did not make any difference,' said one official. 'We sat and watched sterling on the screens but it did not budge.'

George, at the Bank of England, in constant touch with Burns at the Treasury, told him of the disturbing failure of the intervention strategy. But Burns did not need to be told. Watching developments on the Reuters screen in his own office, he was well aware that a disaster was unfolding. Lamont was experiencing what Lord Callaghan, his predecessor at the time of the 1967 devaluation, described as the most uncomfortable experience a Chancellor could go through: watching the reserves disappear but unable to do anything about it.

Lamont contacted Major to tell him that it was necessary to put the second phase of the operation into play: a rise in interest rates. The Bank of England, which normally signals interest rate changes in its early morning or lunchtime dealing rounds, announced at 11 a.m. that it was reintroducing the old Minimum Lending Rate (MLR), suspended in 1981 but brought out of retirement in a previous currency crisis in 1985, when sterling tumbled to within a whisker of one-to-one parity with the dollar. The Bank signalled a rise in MLR from 10 to 12 per cent. This was highly significant. It was the first interest rate rise during Britain's twenty-three month membership of the ERM. But it was also, in the minds of many investors, a clear indication that the game was up. The British economy could not stand a two-point interest rate rise. Dealers knew that the Government would have to bring rates down again quickly, even if this meant sacrificing sterling. The Chancellor issued a statement saying that the rate rise showed the Government prepared 'to take whatever measures are necessary' to maintain sterling's ERM parity. This time, for the authorities, the response was even more disappointing. 'If anything the pound went down,' said one Bank of England official. 'We had always recognized that the markets might regard a rate rise as counter-productive because of the damage that it would do to the economy. Our worst fears were realized.'

Leigh-Pemberton, the Bank Governor, after a high-speed dash from the City to Whitehall, told the Chancellor that the defence of the pound was failing. Sales of sterling were increasing in intensity, in spite of the huge intervention and the rise in base rates. Lamont, with Leigh-Pemberton, George, Burns and other officials, went to a hastily arranged pre-lunch meeting at Admiralty House, Major's temporary headquarters during rebuilding work at 10 Downing Street. There, Lamont told an inner Cabinet of the Government's most senior ministers – Major, Douglas Hurd (Foreign Secretary), Michael Heseltine (President of the Board of Trade) and Kenneth Clarke (Home Secretary) – that the Bank of England had concluded that it could no longer support sterling in the ERM. The reaction was one of shock followed, it is said, by a calm appraisal of the options. In a few short hours the Government's economic strategy had been blown off course. Could nothing be done to strengthen support for sterling, they asked? Surely, with the French vote only days away, it was possible to hold the line until the weekend?

Lamont, however, who stood to lose more politically from the sinking of sterling than anyone else in the room, with the possible exception of Major, shook his head. Everything that could be tried had been tried. Further heavy intervention would be throwing good money after bad. The decision was taken there and then to suspend sterling's membership of the ERM. But there was still the matter of getting to the end of the day, and the close of the European markets, before announcing that Britain was pulling out. To have done so sooner would have thrown the system into complete chaos. Lamont proposed a temporary interest rate increase to 15 per cent, again using the Minimum Lending Rate weapon, to buy the few hours until the markets closed. When the unprecedented second interest rate announcement came early in the afternoon, everyone knew that the Government had effectively thrown in the towel. If interest rates of 12 per cent were suicidal, 15 per cent rates were in the realms of fantasy. Analysts suggested that, were such interest rates held, the banking system would have collapsed in a month, under the weight of corporate failures and personal bankruptcies.

After the second interest rate announcement, Major called Helmut Kohl, the Chancellor of Germany, to tell him of Britain's intentions. Other European leaders and finance ministries were contacted. The Bank of England, in a conference call with the Bundesbank and other European central banks, passed on the message. There was a chance that, with the gun of British withdrawal at their heads, the rest of Europe would take action. Could there be, as was rumoured in the City on the afternoon of Black Wednesday, a second cut in German interest rates in a week?

It was not to be. Shortly after 5.30 p.m. the same team of ministers and officials re-assembled at Admiralty House. Sir Norman Fowler, the Conservative Party Chairman, who was to be given the job of explaining the policy collapse on TV and radio (Major disappeared from view for two days), was also called in. Two hours later, with Sir Nigel Wicks, the senior Treasury official responsible for overseas finance, already on his way to Brussels for an emergency meeting of European Community monetary officials, Lamont stood in the Treasury courtyard to announce the policy shift. With the pound falling like a stone on the New York exchanges – at DM2.74 it was already four pfennigs below its formal floor – membership of the ERM, over which so much political blood had been spilt, was at an end. Lamont also called for the entire system to be suspended but this was rejected by the other European countries. Italy, however, was also forced to suspend ERM membership and Spain subsequently devalued the peseta. The second of the day's interest rate rises, which had served its temporary purpose while frightening the life out of home-owners and businessmen, was scrapped. Next morning, base rates were back to their original level of 10 per cent.

It had taken Britain eleven painful years to get into the ERM, and just eleven hours to drop out of it. And, as the dust settled on the biggest policy climbdown by any British Government since the 1967 devaluation, the recriminations, and the search for a new policy, began.

Going for Growth

The first key question following Britain's forced departure from the ERM concerned the political survival of Major and Lamont. Major had been Chancellor at the time of ERM entry just under two years before. The rate of entry, and its timing, had been his choices. And, less than a week before Black Wednesday he had, in his speech to the Scottish CBI, reaffirmed in the strongest possible terms his commitment to a policy that was at the centre of the Government's economic strategy. His words in Glasgow, when he had said that to abandon the ERM would be a betrayal of the country's future, were thrown back at him.

Lamont, while privately more sceptical of the virtues of ERM membership than Major, had also publicly put his reputation on the line,
notably in his European Policy Forum speech in July, and in repeated
assurances that there would be no devaluation or realignment of the
pound. There were strong precedents for resignation, at least on the
Chancellor's part. Lord Callaghan left the Treasury for the Home Office
a fortnight after the 1967 devaluation. But both Major and Lamont
made clear that they did not regard the ignominious collapse of their
ERM strategy as a resignation matter. Ministers and officials stressed
that no government could have withstood the pressures that propelled
the pound out of the ERM. They also stressed the unhelpful role of
Germany in Britain's hour of need, citing not only Bundesbank President
Schlesinger's 15 September interview but other occasions, when, it was
said, the Bundesbank had undermined the pound.

Sterling's departure from the ERM was, in any case, different in
character from, for example, Callaghan's 1967 devaluation, which was
widely regarded as a national defeat. In 1967, the devaluation had been
accompanied by an austerity package, including higher interest rates, to
ensure confidence in the currency at its new lower level. September
1992 was closer in style to the decision twenty years earlier by Edward
Heath's Conservative Government to leave the European currency
'snake', the ERM's predecessor. Then, as in 1992, leaving a fixed
exchange rate system had permitted a greater freedom to cut interest
rates, to 'go for growth'. Sterling's departure from the ERM, in spite of
the amount of political capital riding on the pound's continuance in the
system, was relatively easy to sell because so many businessmen and
Conservative MPs had been calling for precisely this course of action.
Lamont, in particular, appeared to relish his new-found freedom, telling
journalists attending the annual Washington meetings of the International Monetary Fund and World Bank a few days later that his wife
had heard him singing in the bath, something he had not done for years.

The Government was, however, still in huge trouble. Major, having
lost the centrepiece of his economic strategy, now faced a serious
challenge on his European policy, which revolved around the speedy
ratification of the Maastricht Treaty. A series of government mishaps
and U-turns followed, including near-defeats over a British Coal decision
to close thirty-one pits with the loss of 30,000 jobs and over Maastricht
itself. Ministers deduced, correctly, that many of these problems eman-

ated directly or indirectly from the continued recession. Within a week of Black Wednesday, interest rates were cut from 10 to 9 per cent, a move unusual in that it broke the recent Treasury and Bank of England tradition of reducing rates only in half-point moves. Four weeks later, in the midst of the Government's crisis over pit closures, rates were cut again, to 8 per cent. On 12 November, in his Autumn Statement, Lamont announced a further reduction, to 7 per cent. Since 16 September, when Britain had apparently faced a barren future of high interest rates and an unchanged exchange rate, monetary policy had been eased dramatically. Sterling fell to the low DM2.40s, nearly 20 per cent down on the old ERM central parity. Sterling's average value, compared with its position immediately before leaving the ERM, was 15 per cent down. Devaluation had been combined with substantial interest rate cuts.

Lamont, in his traditional Mansion House speech in the City of London on 29 October – it was actually delivered at the Guildhall – articulated the new strategy. Leaving the ERM, he said:

> marked a watershed. Though the aims of government policy remain the same, we are now in an entirely different policy environment. We are outside the ERM and are likely to remain so for some time. And with a floating pound we have had more flexibility to reduce interest rates without prejudice to our goal of permanently low inflation.

Just as it was possible for monetary policy to be too loose, so the opposite was true, and over-tight policy had been forced on Britain by the constraints of ERM membership. He concluded:

> Leaving the ERM was a setback, but it *has* given us the opportunity to rebalance our policy to take account of the risks to the world economy. This does not mean that the Government has gone soft on inflation. But the dramatic progress we have made in getting inflation down does allow me now to give greater weight to securing an early resumption of growth.   (1992b)

In normal times, a government would have been prepared to sit back and wait for the impact of lower base rates and sterling's fall to come through. The autumn of 1992 was, however, far from normal. The Major Government was fighting for its political life. Early in September, when Britain was still in the ERM and interest cuts appeared to be a distant prospect, the idea of specific measures to assist the housing and construction industries was put up in the Treasury. Ministers and officials were growing increasingly gloomy about the chances of recovery and feared a self-feeding depression, in which rising unemployment held back consumer spending, which in turn led to more redundancies, and so on. The housing market, which Treasury economists saw as closely linked to the outlook for consumer spending, had embarked on a renewed decline following the failure of Lamont's December 1991 housing rescue package, which included an eight-month suspension of stamp duty on housing transactions of £250,000 or below. Construction industry representatives, in meetings with Treasury ministers, warned that their businesses, experiencing the most severe and prolonged downturn in the post-war period, would not survive without an early increase in orders.

Internal Treasury discussion of a recovery package for the economy was suspended when sterling was swept from the ERM on 16 September. Officials argued that, with the chancellor free to cut base rates and sterling having been substantially devalued, additional fiscal help was no longer needed. But surveys showed that Black Wednesday, and the Government's subsequent difficulties, had produced a sharp fall in business and consumer confidence. To the Treasury's surprise, and against initial Treasury resistance, Major insisted on a recovery package. 'A strategy for growth is what we need; a strategy for growth is what we'll have,' he told ITN on 20 October.

On Major's insistence, the package was to include a relaxation of Treasury rules on private-sector involvement in public-sector projects. The Prime Minister, who had championed the cause of such involvement when Chief Secretary to the Treasury three years earlier, had been frustrated by the lack of progress. The old rules on private finance for public projects had been drawn up in such a way as to exclude virtually any proposal. The private sector had to prove that its proposal represented value for money in comparison with a similar, state-financed project. But, since governments can always raise finance on finer terms than the private sector (because governments are thought never to default), virtually no projects could qualify. This catch-22 was removed, with strict comparability between private-financed and theoretical public sector projects no longer required. The Chancellor, in unveiling the package in his Autumn Statement on 12 November, also promised a Green Paper on road-pricing, opening the way, albeit in the long term, for private construction and management of road networks.

Other sectors were given assistance, including the provision of £750m of extra funding for housing associations to buy up around 20,000 repossessed properties for rental purposes, although one commentator warned that, with repossessions and mortgage arrears at record levels, this would have 'about as much effect in reducing the housing overhang as picking a snowflake off an iceberg'. Car tax was Lamont's pet project. Having hit the motor industry hard in his 1991 Budget, exacerbating the effects of the recession, he had attempted to compensate by reducing car tax (a purchase tax, charged in addition to VAT, on new cars) from 10 to 5 per cent in his 1992 Budget. The Chancellor had intended to abolish it in the March 1993 Budget but, with the political pressure on him to act, brought the abolition forward albeit with a promise to claw back the cost with higher motoring taxes. Once this decision was taken, the way was open for another tax change, the provision of temporarily more generous capital allowances for industry, which the Confederation of British Industry had been pressing for.

These and other measures said as much about the state of the Conservative Party as about the state of the economy. The package, worth £4bn over three years, was small (Nigel Lawson's 1988 tax cuts had been worth as much in the first year). But the aim was clear, to give the impression of a government that was caring and acting, until the hoped-for impact of sterling's effective devaluation and interest rate cuts started to feed through. On this, the jury was still out. Although in normal circumstances such a sharp easing of monetary policy could be expected to produce a significant boost, the economy's circumstances at the end of 1992 were far from normal. High levels of personal debt, rising unemployment and falling house prices seemed destined to hold down consumer spending. The recession fatigue afflicting businesses, and the bitter experience of too many false dawns, suggested that any response would be muted. The Treasury's own forecast suggested a delay in recovery until 1993, with only a weak 1 per cent growth rate then. There was also the fear that Britain's initial post-ERM experience had been just a little too good to be true. Surely interest rates could not be reduced indefinitely without totally undermining international investors' confidence in Britain? This was particularly uncertain against a backdrop of a public sector borrowing requirement officially predicted to reach £37bn in 1992–3 and £44bn in 1993–4, the latter broadly equivalent, as a percentage of GDP, to levels reached in the IMF crisis years of the mid-1970s.

Round in Circles

I called the final chapter to the first edition of this book 'Full Circle', in that after nearly two decades of floating exchange rates Britain had returned, apparently for good, to a fixed exchange rate regime. It is now plain that this conclusion was premature. In some ways we can still be said to have gone full circle, notably in the return to more actively interventionist economic policies evident in the 1992 Autumn Statement (it was also an Autumn mini-Budget, a practice that had apparently been abandoned in 1979). But in very many respects UK economic policy has been going around in circles, in search of a holy grail that probably does not exist. Successive governments have tried new recipes for managing the economy, and for lifting the economy's long-run growth rate. The ERM, as Major said less than a week before Britain left it, was supposed to be the policy regime that ended the tradition under which governments, faced with harsh policy decisions, inevitably chose the easy option, the inflationary option. But in the end the ERM was no different from its predecessors. Perhaps, like monetarism in the early 1980s, it had served its purpose, that of knocking the inflationary stuffing out of the economy, at least for a while. Few would argue with the contention that, on economic grounds, Britain's membership of the ERM had entered a cul-de-sac, from which years of depression offered barely an escape. It remains to be seen whether the prospect outside the system is much better. Growth strategies, as in the Heath–Barber boom of the early 1970s, have a nasty habit of ending in tears. Pragmatism in policy is fine, as long as the operators of the policy know what they are doing. In the late 1980s pragmatic policies ended in disaster.

Finally, each time a policy is tried, and fails, something is lost. The ERM débâcle cost Britain dearly in credibility terms. Ultimately, as a result of the episode, investors will demand a higher risk premium for holding sterling. And, as the full extent of the bust that followed the Lawson boom is revealed, it becomes abundantly clear that claims of a renaissance for the British economy in the 1980s were grossly overstated. The issue of Britain's relative economic decline has yet to be tackled.

APPENDIX: TABLES

1. UK Economic Performance, 1950–92

	GDP (% change)	Inflation (%)	Unemployment (% rate)	Current account (% of GDP)
1950	3.6	2.9	1.6	2.3
1951	1.9	9.0	1.3	− 2.5
1952	0.8	9.4	2.2	1.0
1953	3.9	3.1	1.8	0.9
1954	4.2	1.7	1.5	0.7
1955	3.6	4.6	1.2	− 0.8
1956	1.4	5.0	1.3	. 1.0
1957	1.7	3.6	1.6	1.1
1958	− 0.2	3.2	2.2	1.5
1959	4.0	0.6	2.3	0.7
1960	5.6	1.1	1.7	− 0.9
1961	2.7	3.3	1.6	0.1
1962	1.4	4.2	2.1	0.5
1963	4.0	2.0	2.6	0.4
1964	5.6	3.2	1.7	− 1.1
1965	2.9	4.8	1.4*	− 0.2
1966	1.9	3.9	1.5	0.3
1967	2.2	2.4	2.3	− 0.7
1968	4.4	4.8	2.4	− 0.6
1969	2.5	5.4	2.4	1.0
1970	2.0	6.3	2.5	1.6
1971	1.7	9.4	2.5	1.9
1972	2.8	7.3	2.9	0.3
1973	7.4	9.1	2.1	− 1.3
1974	− 1.5	16.0	2.0	− 3.8
1975	− 0.8	24.2	3.0	− 1.4
1976	2.6	16.5	4.1	− 0.6
1977	2.6	15.9	4.4	0
1978	2.9	8.2	4.4	0.7
1979	2.8	13.4	4.1	− 0.2

1. UK Economic Performance, 1950–92 – *continued*

	GDP (% change)	Inflation (%)	Unemployment (% rate)	Current account (% of GDP)
1980	– 2.0	18.0	4.8	1.2
1981	– 1.2	11.9	8.0	2.6
1982	1.7	8.6	9.5	1.7
1983	3.8	4.5	10.5	1.2
1984	1.8	5.0	10.7	0.6
1985	3.8	6.0	10.9	0.8
1986	3.6	3.4	11.2	0
1987	4.4	4.2	10.2	– 1.0
1988	4.7	4.9	8.2	– 3.2
1989	2.1	7.8	6.3	– 3.7
1990*	0.5	9.5	5.8	– 2.5
1991	– 2.5	5.9	8.1	– 1.1
1992	– 0.8	3.7	9.7	– 2.1

* Start of new series; 1992 estimates are provisional.
Sources: Economic Trends Annual Supplement 1991, Central Statistical Office; *Financial Statement and Budget Report 1991*, HM Treasury; *British Labour Statistics.*

2. Recessions Compared

	GDP, average estimate at factor cost, index numbers (1985 = 100)	Percentage change on quarter	Percentage change on year
1973–6			
1973 Q4	84.5	− 0.9	4.1
1974 QI	82.1	− 2.8	− 3.5
Q2	83.9	2.2	− 1.4
Q3	85.0	1.3	− 0.4
Q4	83.9	− 1.3	− 0.7
1975 QI	84.1	0.2	2.4
Q2	82.8	− 1.5	− 1.3
Q3	82.2	− 0.7	− 3.3
Q4	83.2	1.2	− 0.8
1976 QI	85.0	2.2	1.1
Q2	84.3	− 0.8	1.8
Q3	84.9	0.7	3.3
Q4	85.8	1.1	3.1
1980–81			
1979 Q3	92.8	− 1.2	2.7
Q4	93.3	0.5	2.2
1980 QI	92.4	− 1.0	2.3
Q2	91.3	− 1.2	− 2.8
Q3	90.2	− 1.2	− 2.8
Q4	88.9	− 1.4	− 4.7
1981 QI	88.7	− 0.2	− 4.0
Q2	89.4	0.8	− 2.1
Q3	90.1	0.8	− 0.1
Q4	90.4	0.3	1.7
1990–92			
1990 QI	117.2	0.6	1.6
Q2	117.6	0.3	1.8
Q3	116.2	− 1.2	0.1
Q4	115.3	− 0.8	− 1.0

2. Recessions Compared – *continued*

		GDP, average estimate at factor cost, index numbers (*1985 = 100*)	Percentage change on quarter	Percentage change on year
1991	Q1	114.4	− 0.8	− 2.4
	Q2	113.5	− 0.8	− 3.5
	Q3	113.6	0.1	− 2.2
	Q4	113.4	− 0.2	− 1.6
1992	Q1	112.9	− 0.4	− 1.3
	Q2	112.7	− 0.2	− 0.7
	Q3	112.8	0.1	− 0.7

Source: Central Statistical Office.

3. House Prices

	Average UK house price* (£)	Percentage change
1980	23,514	16.7
1981	24,503	3.6
1982	24,577	0.3
1983	27,192	10.6
1984	29,648	9.0
1985	31,876	7.5
1986	36,869	15.7
1987	42,546	15.4
1988	52,632	23.7
1989	58,971	12.0
1990	64,657	9.6
1991	66,459	2.8
1992	64,453	− 3.0

* At mortgage completion stage.
Source: Building Societies Association.

4. Broad Money and Inflation

	M4 annual growth (%)	*Retail price inflation*
1979	14.1	13.4
1980	17.2	18.0
1981	20.9	11.9
1982	12.0	8.6
1983	13.2	4.5
1984	14.2	5.0
1985	13.1	6.0
1986	15.8	3.4
1987	15.8	4.2
1988	17.2	4.9
1989	18.9	7.8
1990	12.1	9.5
1991	6.2	5.9
1992	5.1	3.7

Sources: Central Statistical Office, Bank of England.

5. Bank and Building Society Lending

	Amount outstanding (£ bn)	*Percentage change*
1981	119.4	n/a
1982	145.2	21.6
1983	169.2	16.6
1984	199.6	17.9
1985	233.5	17.0
1986	280.4	20.1
1987	333.6	19.0
1988	416.4	24.8
1989	504.7	21.2
1990	574.8	13.9
1991	604.8	5.2
1992	622.8	3.0

Source: Bank of England.

6. Output and Sales

	Manufacturing output (percentage change)	Retail sales volume (percentage change)
1979	− 0.1	4.2
1980	− 8.7	− 0.1
1981	− 6.0	0.2
1982	0.2	1.8
1983	2.8	4.9
1984	3.9	3.7
1985	2.6	4.6
1986	1.3	5.3
1987	5.2	5.2
1988	7.0	6.4
1989	4.3	1.8
1990	− 0.6	0.4
1991	− 6.6	− 1.9
1992	− 0.7	0.8

Source: Central Statistical Office.

7. Bankruptcies and Company Failures

	Bankruptcies	Company liquidations
1979	3,500	4,537
1980	4,038	6,890
1981	5,151	8,596
1982	5,700	12,067
1983	7,032	13,406
1984	8,229	13,721
1985	6,778	14,898
1986	7,155	14,405
1987	7,427	11,439
1988	8,507	9,427
1989	9,365	10,456
1990	13,987	15,051
1991	22,988	21,666
1992 *	35,940	24,825

* First nine months, at annual rate.
Source: Department of Trade and Industry.

BIBLIOGRAPHY

Bank of England (1981), 'Exchange Control Abolition and Capital Flows', *Bank of England Quarterly Bulletin*, September 1981.

Bank of England (1987), *Bank of England Quarterly Bulletin*, November 1987.

Bank of England (1988), *Bank of England Quarterly Bulletin*, February 1988.

Bank of England (1989), *Bank of England Quarterly Bulletin*, February 1989.

Bank of England (1990), *Bank of England Quarterly Bulletin*, November 1990.

Bank of England (1991), 'The Role and Scope of Mortgage Limits', *Bank of England Quarterly Bulletin*, May 1991.

Bannock, Graham, Baxter, R. E., and Rees, Ray (1972), *A Dictionary of Economics*, Penguin Books.

Beckerman, Wilfred, ed. (1979), *Slow Growth in Britain*, Oxford University Press.

Blackaby, Frank, ed. (1978), *British Economic Policy, 1960–74*, Cambridge University Press.

Blaug, Mark (1968), *Economic Theory in Retrospect*, Heinemann.

Blundell-Wignall, Adrian, Browne, Frank, and Manasse, Paolo (1990), 'Monetary Policy in Liberalized Financial Markets', *OECD Economic Studies*, Autumn 1990, pp. 145–78.

Bose, Mihir (1988), *The Crash*, Bloomsbury.

Brittan, Samuel (1971), *Steering the Economy*, Penguin Books.

Britton, A. J. C. (1991), *Macroeconomic Policy in Britain, 1974–87*, Cambridge University Press.

Brown, Chuck, and Sandford, Cedric (1991), 'Taxes and Incentives: the Effects of the 1988 Cuts', Institute for Public Policy Research.

Callaghan, James (1988), *Time and Chance*, Fontana/Collins.

Congdon, Tim (1986), in *The Times*, 9 January 1986.

Congdon, Tim (1989), 'Monetarism Lost, and How It Must be Regained', Centre for Policy Studies.

Congdon, Tim (1990), 'Resuscitate – While There's Still Time', *The Times*, 17 August 1990.

Congdon, Tim, and Warburton, Peter (1986a), L. Messel's quarterly macroeconomic forecast, October 1986.

Conservative Party (1977), *The Right Approach to the Economy*.

Corby, Brian (1990), Speech on the recession, quoted in the *Sunday Times*, 30 September 1990.

Coutts, Ken, Godley, Wynne, Rowthorn, Bob, and Zezza, Gennaro (1990), 'Britain's Economic Problems and Policies in the 1990s', Institute for Public Policy Research.

Dow, J. C. R. (1964), *The Management of the British Economy 1945–60*, Cambridge University Press.

Dow, J. C. R., and Saville, I. D. (1988), *A Critique of Monetary Policy, Theory and British Experience*, Oxford University Press.

Financial Times, Editorial on the Autumn Statement, 7 November 1986.

Friedman, Milton (1953), 'The Case for Flexible Exchange Rates', in *Essays in Positive Economics*, Chicago University Press.

Goodhart, Charles (1991), 'The Conduct of Monetary Policy', in *The State of the Economy 1991*, Institute of Economic Affairs.

Hamilton, Adrian (1986), *The Financial Revolution*, Penguin Books.

Healey, Denis (1990), *The Time of My Life*, Penguin Books.

Heath, Edward (1988), Speech to the House of Commons following the November 1988 Queen's Speech, *Hansard*, 29 November 1988.

H M Treasury (1980), *Financial Statement and Budget Report*, March 1980.

Howe, Geoffrey (1980), The Chancellor's Budget speech, March 1980.

Howe, Geoffrey, Resignation speech to the House of Commons, *Hansard*, 13 November 1990, Cols. 461–5.

Huhne, Christopher (1990), *Real World Economics*, Macmillan.

Johnson, Christopher (1991), *The Economy under Mrs Thatcher 1979–90*, Penguin Books.

Johnston, R. J., Pattie, C. J., and Allsopp, J. G. (1988), *A Nation Dividing?*, Longman.

Keegan, William (1989), *Mr Lawson's Gamble*, Hodder & Stoughton.

Keynes, John Maynard (1936), *The General Theory of Employment, Interest and Money*, Macmillan.

Lamont, Norman (1991), The Chancellor's Budget speech, 19 March 1991.

Lamont, Norman (1992a), The Chancellor's Speech to the European Policy Forum, 10 July 1992.

Lamont, Norman (1992b), The Chancellor's Mansion House Speech, 29 October 1992.

Lawson, Nigel (1981), 'Thatcherism in Practice: a Progress Report', speech to the Zurich Society of Economics, 14 January 1981.

Lawson, Nigel (1984), The Chancellor's Mansion House speech, 18 October 1984.

Lawson, Nigel (1984a), 'The British Experiment', the 5th Mais Lecture, 18 June 1984.

Lawson, Nigel (1984b), 'What are We Going to Do When the Oil Runs Out?', speech at Cambridge, 9 April 1984.

Lawson, Nigel (1985), The Chancellor's Mansion House speech, 17 October 1985.

Lawson, Nigel (1985a), on US economic policy and the dollar's strength, *The Times*, 20 April 1985.

Lawson, Nigel (1986), The Chancellor's Budget Speech, 18 March 1986.

Lawson, Nigel (1986a), Speech to the Conservative Party conference, 9 October 1986.

Lawson, Nigel (1987), Speech to the Finance Houses Association, 17 June 1987.

Lawson, Nigel (1987a), New Year interview in the *Financial Times*, 5 January 1987.

Lawson, Nigel (1987b), The Chancellor of the Exchequer's speech to the International Monetary Fund, 30 September 1987.

Lawson, Nigel (1989), Speech to the House of Commons on resigning, *Hansard*, 31 October 1989, col. 208–210.

Lawson, Nigel (1989a), New Year interview with the *Financial Times*, 3 January 1989.

Lawson, Nigel (1990), Speech in the House of Commons following sterling's entry into the ERM, *Hansard*, 23 October 1990, cols. 214–16.

Lawson, Nigel (1990a), Interview in *IMF Annual Meeting News*, September 1990.

Lawson, Nigel (1990b), The Stamp Memorial Lecture, November 1990.

Lawson, Nigel (1990c), Letter to *The Times*, 7 December 1990.

Lawson, Nigel (1991), Interview with BBC TV's 'On the Record', 7 July 1991.

Leigh-Pemberton, Robin (1986), 'Financial Change and Broad Money', speech at Loughborough University, 22 October 1986.

Leigh-Pemberton, Robin (1990), 'Monetary Policy in the Second Half of the 1980s', University of Durham International Celebrity Lecture, *Bank of England Quarterly Bulletin*, May 1990.

Leigh-Pemberton, Robin (1990a), 'Some Remarks on Exchange Rate Regimes', *Bank of England Quarterly Bulletin*, November 1990.

Llewellyn, David, and Holmes, Mark (1991), 'Competition or Credit Controls?', Institute of Economic Affairs.

Loehnis, Anthony (1990), 'The International Monetary System in the 1990s', in *Changing Exchange Rate Systems* (Lloyds Bank Annual Review), ed. C. Johnson, Pinter Publishers.

Macmillan, Harold (1972), *Pointing the Way 1959–60*, Macmillan.

Major, John (1990), New Year interview with the *Financial Times*, 2 January 1990.

Major, John (1990a), The Chancellor's Budget speech, 20 March 1990.

Major, John (1990b), Press conference at the IMF Annual Meeting, quoted in the *Sunday Times*, 23 September 1990.

Major, John (1991), Interview in *The Director*, November 1991.

Major, John (1992), The Prime Minister's Speech to the Scottish CBI, 10 September 1992.

Meade, James (1955), 'The Case for Variable Exchange Rates', *Three Banks Review*, September 1955.

Middleton, Peter (1988), 'Economic Policy Formulation in the Treasury in the Post-war Period', National Institute of Economic and Social Research Jubilee Lecture, 28 November 1988.

Minford, Patrick (1987), in Liverpool Research Group in Macro-economics, *Quarterly Bulletin*, March 1988.

Morris, Derek, ed. (1985), *The Economic System in the UK*, 3rd edn, Oxford University Press.

National Institute of Economic and Social Research (1989), 'The Consequences of Full EMS Membership', *National Institute Economic Review*, August 1989.

Organization for Economic Cooperation and Development (1990), 'The United Kingdom'.

Organization for Economic Cooperation and Development (1991), 'The United Kingdom'.

Reagan, Ronald (1985), on the dollar's strength, *The Times*, 23 February 1985.

Richardson, Gordon (1979), The Governor's Henry Thornton Lecture, June 1979.

Sargent, J. R. (1991), 'Deregulation, Debt and the Downturn in the UK Economy', *National Institute Economic Review*, August 1991.

Smith, David (1987), *The Rise and Fall of Monetarism*, Penguin Books.

Smith, David (1989), *North and South*, Penguin Books.

Smith, David (1990), 'The Blip that Soared', *Sunday Times*, 13 May 1990.

Sunday Times, 'Neighbours, the Row that Split the Street', 20 March 1988.

Sunday Times, 'Major Aims to Make Sterling the Best in Europe', 2 August 1992.

Swann, Dennis (1988), *The Economics of the Common Market*, 6th edn, Penguin Books.

Thatcher, Margaret (1990), Speech to the Welsh Confederation of British Industry, quoted in the *Sunday Times*, 30 September 1990.

The Times (1991), Letter from the 'Liverpool Six', 13 February 1991.

Treasury and Civil Service Committee (1987), Session 1986–87, 'The 1987 Budget', HMSO.

Treasury and Civil Service Committee (1987a), Session 1987–88, 'The 1987 Autumn Statement', HMSO.

Treasury and Civil Service Committee (1988), Session 1987–88, 'The 1988 Budget', HMSO.

Treasury and Civil Service Committee (1989), Session 1989–90, 'The 1989 Autumn Statement', HMSO.

Treasury and Civil Service Committee (1990), Session 1990–91, 'The 1990 Autumn Statement', HMSO.

Treasury and Civil Service Committee (1991), Session 1990–91, 'The 1991 Budget', HMSO.

Walters, Alan (1986), *Britain's Economic Renaissance*, Oxford University Press.

Walters, Alan (1990), *Sterling in Danger*, Fontana/Collins.

Walters, Alan (1990a), 'A Life Philosophy', *The American Economist*.

Walters, Alan (1991), Letter to the *Economist*, 12–18 October 1991.

Williamson, John (1991), 'FEERs and the ERM', *National Institute Economic Review*, August 1991.

Young, Lord (1990), *The Enterprise Years*, Headline.

INDEX